Exploring Society

Edited by
Robert G. Burgess
Senior Lecturer in Sociology
University of Warwick

Published in conjunction
with the
British Sociological Association

London and New York

LONGMAN GROUP UK LIMITED
Longman House, Burnt Mill, Harlow, Essex CM20 2JE, England
and Associated Companies throughout the World.

Published in the United States of America
by Longman Inc., New York

First published 1986

ISBN 0 582 35489 7

Set in 10/12pt Plantin Roman, Linotron 202

*Produced by Longman Group (F.E.) Limited.
Printed in Hong Kong.*

British Library Cataloguing in Publication Data

Exploring society.– New ed.
 1. Sociology
 I. Burgess, Robert G.
 301   HM51

  ISBN 0-582-35489-7

Library of Congress Cataloging-in-Publication Data
Main entry under title:

Exploring society.

  Bibliography: p.
  Includes indexes.
  Summary: Surveys various aspects of sociology,
including gender and the family, social inequality,
racism, welfare, and crime, from the viewpoint of
sociological research and how it influences the
perspective of sociologists.
  1. Sociology. 2. Sociology — Research.
[1. Sociology — Research] 1. Burgess, Robert G.
HM66.E96 1986   301   85-18125
ISBN 0-582-35489-7

Contents

Preface

Many students first encounter sociology through basic textbooks that provide summaries of its aims and scope. While these texts provide accounts of the theoretical and technical procedures involved in sociology, they often omit detailed discussions of sociological research. This collection of essays, therefore, sets out to give a 'taste' of sociology to the beginning student by focusing on sociological research. The contributors examine sociological work by looking at the basic questions that sociologists address, and the impact that different sociological perspectives have upon research. In these terms, attention is devoted to the way in which sociological perspectives influence the choice of topic, selection of research problems and the collection, analysis and reporting of data. It is, therefore, hoped that this approach will encourage readers to consider the kinds of questions, theories and methods that are used by sociologists to explore different dimensions of contemporary society.

Several of these essays have been discussed with sixth form pupils and teachers in order to raise issues that are relevant for the beginning student. At the end of each chapter there are suggestions for more advanced further reading, resources for students to obtain further information and questions that can be used either in class discussion or during periods of reflection by individual students. There is also a glossary which provides a brief guide to some of the main sociological terms used in the essays.

An earlier version of this book was produced as a direct edition by the British Sociological Association who also took responsibility for the marketing and distribution principally among its members. This volume contained the essays by Colin Bell, Janet Finch, Robert Moore, Helen Roberts, Margaret Stacey and myself. Although the first version was based on a relatively limited circulation of a thousand copies it was widely reviewed and well received. Accordingly, this expanded edition was planned with the support of Brian Willan at Longman and Mike Milotte from the British Sociological Association. The original essays have been subject to some minor revisions and references have been added and updated, while new material has been commissioned from Janet Bujra, David Morgan, Bob Roshier and Sylvia Walby.

The first version of this book owed much to the stimulus of the contributors; especially Janet Finch and Helen Roberts and I also profited from detailed comments by Marie Stowell and Margaret Threadgold who made suggestions about the kind of book that would be appropriate for sixth formers and beginning students. I have also been fortunate to have the help of Hilary Burgess who has discussed and evaluated the shape and substance of both versions of this book. Finally, I am indebted to Hilary Bayliss who has provided expert secretarial support and to the members of the Executive Committee of the British Sociological Association who over the years have shown an interest in this project. Needless to say, while I have plundered some of their ideas, they are in no way responsible for any of the deficiencies of this book.

Since the first version appeared I have worked on a number of other publishing projects concerned with the presentation of sociological material to beginning students. This experience has reinforced my view that we need to convey the feel of the research enterprise to students through a range of essays. It is on this basis that I considered a revised collection of essays was desirable.

Robert Burgess
University of Warwick

Notes on contributors

Colin Bell was Professor of Sociology at the University of Aston in Birmingham until 1984. He has been Professor of Sociology at the University of New South Wales and was from 1968–75 a member of the Department of Sociology at the University of Essex. He is the author or editor of *Middle Class Families* (1968), with Howard Newby, *Community Studies* (1971), *The Sociology of Community* (1974), and *Doing Sociological Research* (1977), and with in addition David Rose and Peter Saunders, *Property, Paternalism and Power* (1978), with Margaret Stacey, Anne Murcott and Eric Batstone, *Power, Persistence and Change: a second study of Banbury* (1975), and with Sol Encel, *Inside the Whale* (1978). His most recent publications are *Fathers, Childbirth and Work* (1982), with Lorna McKee, *Social Researching* (1984) edited with Helen Roberts and a number of papers on the impact of unemployment. He is now Social Scientist in the University of Leicester Medical School.

Janet Bujra teaches sociology at the University of Wales in Aberystwyth where she lives with her young son and daughter. She did her undergraduate and postgraduate work at the University of London, and has since taught in Cairo and at the University of Dar es Salaam in Tanzania. She has carried out research in Kenya, Tanzania and Gambia on problems of labour migration, class formation and gender. She has been a consultant to the Open University Third World Studies course for which she has written texts, and is co-editor with Pat Caplan of *Women United Women Divided* (1978).

Robert Burgess is Senior Lecturer in Sociology and Chairperson of the Department of Sociology at the University of Warwick. He originally trained as a teacher and taught in schools before doing sociological research. His main teaching and research interests are in social research methodology; especially ethnography and the sociology of education. He has conducted research on a variety of educational topics and is currently doing a study of a community college. He is the author of *Experiencing Comprehensive Education:*

A Study of Bishop McGregor School (1983), *In the Field: An Introduction to Field Research* (1984), *Education, Schools and Schooling* (1985) and *Sociology, Education and Schools: An Introduction to the Sociology of Education* (1986). He has also edited *Teaching Research Methodology to Postgraduates: A Survey of Courses in the UK* (1979), *Field Research: A Sourcebook and Field Manual* (1982), *The Research Process in Educational Settings: Ten Case Studies* (1984), *Field Methods in the Study of Education* (1985), *Strategies of Educational Research: Qualitative Methods* (1985), *Issues in Educational Research: Qualitative Methods* (1985), and *Key Variables in Social Investigation* (1986).

Janet Finch is a Senior Lecturer in the Department of Social Administration at Lancaster University. She has undertaken sociological research at the Universities of Cambridge and Bradford, where she gained a PhD. She has also taught in secondary schools and in a college of education, and currently specialises in teaching on education as social policy, as well as the sociology of welfare. Her current research spans both sociology and social policy, concentrating on women, the family and welfare. She is author of *Married to the Job* (1983), *Education as Social Policy* (1984), *Research and Policy* (1986) and joint editor of *Practice and Progress: British Sociology 1950–1980* (1981), *A Labour of Love: Women, Work and Caring* (1983) and *A Degree of Choice* (1986).

Robert Moore left school and served for ten years in the Royal Navy. In 1961 he became a student at the University of Hull and then a research worker at Birmingham University – this research resulted in the publication of *Race, Community and Conflict* (1967) with John Rex. After lecturing at Durham University he moved to the University of Aberdeen, where he is now Professor of Sociology. He is the author of *Pit-Men, Preachers and Politics* (1974), *Racism and Black Resistance in Britain* (1975), and *Slamming the Door* (1975), with Tina Wallace, and *The Social Impact of Oil: the Case of Peterhead* (1982). In addition to research and writing Robert Moore has been engaged in work for pressure groups and the churches in campaigning for the rights of immigrants and migrant workers in Britain and Europe.

David Morgan is Senior Lecturer in Sociology at the University of Manchester. His main interests are to do with gender and the family, although he has carried out research on Anglican bishops, shop-floor culture and the Bloomsbury Group. Main publications include *Social Theory and the Family* (1975) and *The Family, Politics and Social Theory* (1985). He is also a co-editor of two collections of papers arising out of a BSA conference on 'Gender and Society' which are entitled *Gender, Class and Work* (1983) and *The Public and the Private* (1983). He is currently interested in the sociology of men and masculinity.

Helen Roberts is Senior Researcher at Bradford and Ilkley Community College. She is a feminist sociologist with an interest ·in qualitative methodology. She is author of *The Patient Patients* (1985) and (with Ann Oakley and Ann McPherson) *Miscarriage* (1984). She is editor of *Doing Feminist Research* (1981), *Women, Health and Reproduction* (1981) and (with Colin Bell) *Social Researching* (1984).

Bob Roshier is a Lecturer in Sociology at the University of Durham. He has previously carried out research at the Centre for Urban Studies, University College, London and taught at Newcastle upon Tyne Polytechnic and the University of the West Indies, Trinidad and Tobago. His teaching and research interests are in the sociology of law, crime, deviance and the mass media and penal policy. He is author (with Harvey Teff) of *Law and Society in England* (1980).

Margaret Stacey was born in London in 1922. She graduated from the London School of Economics in 1943 with sociology as her main subject. After she escaped from a war factory, she worked for the Oxford Extra-Mural and Social Training Delegacies until 1951. She married in 1945 and reared five children in Wales. Appointed to a Lectureship at the University College of Swansea in the early '60s she later became a Senior Lecturer and Director of the Medical Sociology Research Unit there. Her first research on Banbury (1948–51) was published as *Tradition and Change* (1960), followed by the collective second study *Power, Persistence and Change* (1975) with Eric Batstone, Colin Bell and Anne Murcott. She has also written *Methods of Social Research* (1969) and edited *Comparability in Social Research* (1969), *Hospitals, Children* *and their Families* (1970), *The Sociology of the National Health Service* (1976), and *Beyond Separation* (1979) with David Hall. In 1974 she was appointed Professor of Sociology at the University of Warwick where she works mainly on the sociology of health and healing. Her chapter in this book recounts her recruitment to and continuing work in this area. A life-long feminist, she has become increasingly active and outspoken in the last decade. Her work with Marion Price, *Women, Power and Politics* (1981) was awarded the Fawcett prize for the period 1978–82.

Sylvia Walby is a Lecturer in Sociology at Lancaster University, where she has focused on the development of Women's Studies, both as Director of the Women's Studies Minor and as Director of the Women's Studies Research Centre. She is joint author of the Lancaster Regionalism Group's book *Localities, Class and Gender*, and a forthcoming book from the Lancaster Sociology Department, *Contemporary British Society*, and sole author of the forthcoming *Patriarchy at Work*. She is a member of the ESRC Social Stratification Seminar.

Chapter 1

Sociologists at work: an introduction

Robert G. Burgess

To ask individuals about their work is one of the most interesting questions that a sociologist can pose, as the answers can provide much information about the activities in which people are involved. The question 'What do you do?' can also be asked of sociologists as it can help us to discover what constitutes doing sociological work. In common with other social scientists, many sociologists would claim that 'society' is the main subject of their work. In addition, they might also say that sociology involves posing critical questions about social situations with a view to challenging assumptions that are commonly held about social life.

On this basis, sociology is a discipline that is devoted to examining a set of issues that are also part of the subject matter of anthropology, psychology, politics and economics. However, sociology is different from other social science subjects as it uses a distinct range of theories and methods in the course of posing questions about the social world. But what kinds of questions do sociologists ask about the society in which they live? One place where sociological questions are highly visible is on examination question papers. Among the questions that sociology students are often invited to address are:

What are the relationships between education and the economy?
Do modern industrial societies have the least inequality between
  the sexes?
What is the effect of technology upon workers' attitudes?

To what extent has each society its own type of family organisation?
Is crime inevitable?
What factors affect the patterns of social mobility?
Is Britain a secular society?
Is there a ruling class in contemporary Britain?
Is the class system obsolete?
What do strikes tell us about industrial conflict?

While this is a random selection of questions, it does indicate how varied sociological problems can be. Furthermore, it suggests that there are many fields of study within sociology where specialists have worked on these issues as well as many other problems.

We need, therefore, to consider: what does sociology involve? what do sociologists study? what kinds of questions are asked? what concepts are used? what methods of investigation are employed? what kinds of explanations are provided? what is emphasised and what is neglected? All these questions may be asked at a number of levels in relation to different areas of sociology. The contributors to this book discuss the activities of sociology and sociologists and the kinds of analyses that have been provided in a number of areas of social life. In some instances they provide examples drawn from their own work, while in other essays they provide a discussion of the work of their colleagues in a field of study. No matter which approach has been used the objective has been to illustrate the way in which problems, theories and methods are related to each other in the study of sociology.

The view that is taken of sociology throughout this volume is that it is a critical exercise where commonsense knowledge, fact and evidence is critically examined from a particular perspective. It is this kind of position that was well summarised by Tom Burns who considered that one of the hallmarks of sociological work was to unmask stereotypes of the world. He writes as follows:

Sociology defines itself as a critical activity. The purpose of sociology is to achieve an understanding of social behaviour and social institutions which is different from that current among the people through whose conduct the institutions exist; an understanding that is not merely different but new and better.

The practice of sociology is criticism. It exists to criticise claims
about the value of achievement and to question assumptions about
the meaning of conduct. It is the business of sociologists to
conduct a critical debate with the public about its equipment of
social institutions.

Burns, 1967, pp. 366–7.

While description is one element of sociological analysis, it is not
enough. Sociologists need to examine their evidence from a
particular perspective but we might ask: how is this done? In order
to address this question we need to turn briefly to a consideration
of theory and method and to an examination of the conduct of
sociological research. Often discussions of theory and method can
appear abstract and arid. Accordingly, this collection takes to heart
Wright Mills's (1970) view that it is better to have an account of
the way sociologists go about their work than a series of set
procedures. The focus is therefore upon the ways in which problems are posed and examined by sociologists working in different
areas of study.

All too often artificial distinctions are drawn between theory,
methods and research. Yet in reality sociologists need to be able
to use theoretical frameworks and techniques of investigation in
relation to a research problem. Frequently, a distinction is drawn
between the sociologist who works in a library on theoretical problems and researchers who are engaged in the study of schools,
factories and families among many other subjects. But this distinction can be too sharply drawn. It is essential for the theorist to test and
examine the theories that are developed, just as it is essential for
the researcher to think about the kinds of questions that are posed.
Divisions into theory and research therefore do not do justice to
either activity as it does not portray the fullness of sociological
work nor the way in which theory and research are intimately
intertwined with each other. Indeed, as we shall see in the essays
that follow, the authors are concerned about the ways in which
sociologists apply, develop and test conceptual schemes in various
areas of social life as well as collecting basic data about society. It
is this kind of activity that distinguishes research by sociologists
from those activities by researchers who merely provide a catalogue
of information about social life. However, there is a danger that

sociological research can be seen as little more than a search for a theory, while in reality sociologists are engaged in a constant interplay between theory and data. Indeed, there are a number of different ways in which sociological theory and research can be brought together. The sociologist is not able to follow a set of rules; a point that is clearly revealed in a number of accounts associated with doing research, for there is a considerable gap between the idealized versions of how to do research that appear in text books and the accounts of research practice that have recently appeared.[1]

At this point, we need to turn to the conduct of research by examining a classic example of British empirical research that illustrates the interplay between theory and social investigation. Here, we turn to the *Affluent Worker* project that was conducted by John Goldthorpe, David Lockwood, Frank Bechhofer and Jennifer Platt. This project gave rise to three major studies (Goldthorpe and Lockwood *et al.* 1968a, 1968b, 1969) together with a range of articles (for a complete list see Platt, 1984). This project has been widely discussed and reviewed by British sociologists as it brings together theoretical speculation and first hand empirical data. However, the starting point of this project cannot simply be related to sociological theory but also needs to be seen in relation to a series of issues within and beyond sociology and the social sciences. During the 1950s Britain had witnessed a number of rapid social developments but sociological writing appeared to have little to contribute to an understanding of these changes or to an explanation of the successive election victories by the Conservative party. As Jennifer Platt (1984) explains the *Affluent Worker* studies brought together some of these concerns as well as issues relating to 'embourgeoisement'; a term that was briefly defined as the process by which individuals became similar to the middle class. In addition, the project team also examined issues relating to 'class' which was defined so that it included different life styles. As a consequence data collection was wide ranging. However, Platt also indicates how the project continued during a period in which there was a Labour election victory in 1964 and when many changes occurred in sociology. These changes resulted in some of the most significant problems that had initially been posed by the project team being redefined. Among the many influences on this project, Platt argues that John Goldthorpe's contact with French sociology highlighted the importance of examining alienation and class consciousness in relation to their work. As a result the material that was eventually published was different from that which the researchers had originally intended. Clearly, 'embourgeoisement' was still a major theme but the discussion went beyond this issue to a number of other themes including the position of the new working class. The early theoretical formulations within this project were therefore revised as a result of contemporary events in British society as well as developing trends within sociology in Britain, Europe and North America.

However, empirical work in sociology is not only concerned with testing theory but also with modifying and developing it. Sociologists may also generate research material where they question what is regarded as 'evident' or 'obvious'. For example, it may appear that sociologists who spend their time doing research in school classrooms have very little to observe. At first glance, it might seem that teachers are teaching, while pupils sit at their desks listening, reading and writing. Yet in such locations it is important for sociologists to consider the different patterns of interaction that occur, the conflicts, the ritual exercises, the strategies, negotiations and bargains that take place between pupils and between teachers and pupils. In such settings, sociologists use their personal experience as well as their theoretical training to help understand how situations operate and to see the way in which their theories need to be modified in the light of research data (a theme that is discussed in greater detail in this volume by Margaret Stacey in relation to her studies of health and illness).

By analysing the work which sociologists do, we can begin to see how different perspectives, different theories and different methods result in different kinds of interpretations. In turn, we can also begin to see the ways in which different sociological accounts can be provided within the same area of investigation. In this respect, sociologists do not only provide theoretical accounts but can also assist people in a variety of social situations by giving interpretations of different dimensions of society. Indeed, Stacey holds the view that:

> sociology should be for use, that the understanding of social relations and social structure which it has to offer can help members of a society in seeking solutions to problems which face them.

However, she continues:

> This is not to imply that all sociological work should be
> problem-orientated. Theory must be developed, and many will
> necessarily concentrate on this aspect. Others may be more
> concerned with the analytical description of observed social
> relations, some focussing on areas indicated by theoretical
> developments and others on problems identified by members of
> the society. Growth and development only occurs in the subject
> where these two approaches constantly inform each other.
>
> Stacey with Homans, 1978, p. 296.

The sociologist may, therefore, address questions relating to general theoretical issues and to matters concerning policy and practice within particular areas of study. However, the contribution that is made will, in part, depend on the relationships that occur between problems, theories and methods in sociological work. It is, therefore, essential to consider these relationships when reviewing research and especially when comparisons are made between several pieces of sociological research.

The contributors to this book discuss the links between problems, theories and methods in different areas of social life. In turn, attention is focused upon the key questions that are addressed by sociologists, the theoretical and methodological perspectives used and some of the data that are obtained. The contributors, therefore, examine some of the ways in which sociologists work. In some cases, several contributors have dealt with a similar range of concepts and methods that are used in different areas of sociology. In addition, they have also reviewed some of the key issues relating to their particular fields of study. Among the main themes considered are:

1 Marking Frontiers and Settling Territory

Sociologists need to establish particular fields of study and to settle the territories that they define. In all the contributions, attempts are made to define an area of study and to colonise the territory by addressing a number of central questions using sociological concepts. The contributions by Margaret Stacey and Janet Finch in particular offer definitions of their fields of study. Meanwhile, other contributors are involved in distinguishing *sociological* questions from the kinds of questions that are posed by other social scientists. This is clearly illustrated by Janet Bujra in relation to studies of development and by Bob Roshier in his reflections on the study of crime and deviance over the last two hundred years.

2 Theoretical Perspectives

All of the contributors have shown how one or more theories have influenced their thinking and the kinds of questions that they address. Some of the contributors have utilised similar theories and concepts:

a) Class, gender and race are discussed in the contributions by Colin Bell, Sylvia Walby, Robert Moore and Margaret Stacey to reveal different dimensions of social inequality and social stratification in contemporary society.

b) The division of labour in the family and in health care is considered by both David Morgan and Margaret Stacey, while the contributions by Sylvia Walby and Janet Bujra also discuss the way in which sociologists have examined the division of labour in other areas of study.

c) The distinction between paid and unpaid labour is examined in different social contexts in the contributions by Colin Bell, Margaret Stacey, Janet Finch and Janet Bujra.

3 Research Methodology

The conduct of social research is considered by several of the contributors. Special attention is given to the problems involved in using particular methods of social investigation. Some contributors have used particular styles of investigation and discuss their approach to sociological study:

a) Research as a social process is examined by Helen Roberts and Robert Burgess, both of whom consider the ways in which research problems arise and are handled in research projects.

b) Different methods of data collection are used in the projects discussed by Helen Roberts (survey methods and interviewing) and Robert Burgess (field methods: participant observation, interviews and documentary evidence).

c) Case studies of individuals and situations are used to examine the social factors that operate in social settings as shown in the analyses provided by David Morgan, Janet Bujra, Janet Finch, Helen Roberts and Robert Burgess.

Within the individual chapters, special attention has been given to the issues and questions that are posed by sociologists. In Chapter 2 David Morgan begins by looking at the way in which sociologists can raise questions relating to gender based on their research experiences. In turn, his chapter also examines ways in which gender and inequality have been examined in studies of the family. In addition, David Morgan also highlights issues concerned with feminist theory, with the use of case studies and the formulation of questions in sociological work; all of which are discussed in several other chapters. In Chapter 3, Colin Bell examines the concept 'work' and the relationship between this concept and the processes of industrialisation and deindustrialisation. Alongside these processes he also discusses non-work and unemployment which allows him to examine a range of categories and concepts that sociologists use in this area of study. Many of the issues involved relate to different dimensions of stratification; a theme that is also discussed by Sylvia Walby and Robert Moore in Chapters 4 and 5 respectively.

Sylvia Walby reviews some of the key questions that have been posed in sociological research relating to social inequality. In particular, she illustrates how some of the questions that are used in contemporary studies relate to positions outlined in the classical writings of Marx and Weber. In turn, she also demonstrates how the sociological enterprise is never static but raises new questions in relation to changing social circumstances. Her chapter also highlights how studies of social inequality can no longer merely be concerned with social class but also need to take account of gender and race. In this sense, her material complements the following chapter by Robert Moore, who, while focusing on the sociology of immigration and racism, examines the changing sociological perspectives involved in the study of 'race relations', and also the relevance of stratification by social class and by gender. This chapter also has links with the discussions by Colin Bell and Janet Bujra, as Robert Moore looks at the international dimensions of migration and job movement through an analysis of the labour process and unemployment. Finally, he provides a brief historical perspective on the sociological study of race relations by discussing the concepts that sociologists now use in studying race and immigration compared with those that were used some twenty years ago.

In Chapter 6 Janet Bujra takes us beyond Britain to look at some of the issues that have been raised in earlier chapters. Her main task is to illustrate how distinctly sociological questions can be asked about development. However, she also raises questions about women and the family, women and work, and gender and class by drawing on cross-cultural case study material. In turn, she also examines the way in which sociologists raise questions about the sexual division of labour; an issue that is also taken up by Margaret Stacey. In Chapter 7 Margaret Stacey looks at the questions sociologists have asked about medicine, health, illness and healing. In particular, she points to the ways in which sociologists working in this area have suggested that the institutions of health and healing not only reflect but reproduce social stratification by class and by gender in contemporary society. She also shows how data about the treatment of illness challenges conventional sociological theories and concepts concerned with the division of labour and paid and unpaid work. In this sense, Margaret Stacey indicates how sociologists can begin to challenge analyses of those aspects of social life that are regarded as 'natural' or 'normal'.

Some of these themes are followed up in Chapter 8 by Janet Finch, who, in the process of discussing the sociology of welfare, begins to examine the distinctions that can be made between sociological and commonsense explanations about the social world, on the gender order in society and the use of unpaid labour. She focuses on the particular questions that sociologists might pose about social welfare, drawing on illustrations from her own research on the frail elderly. As Bob Roshier indicates in Chapter 9 this approach has much in common with studies of crime and deviance where discussions occur about the relationship between sociology and other social sciences and where debates arise about the contribution that sociology can make to the study of social problems. In his chapter, Bob Roshier provides a systematic review of the changing shape and substance of studies of crime and deviance. In common with other contributors he also highlights particular debates that occur between researchers working within different theoretical perspectives and the implications this has for their research strategy.

In the last two chapters, Helen Roberts and Robert Burgess discuss the style and strategy of empirical research by reference to their own research projects. In Chapter 10, Helen Roberts looks at the educational and career aspirations and achievements of a sample of 16-year-old boys and girls in the Bradford Metropolitan District. Her research takes up questions on the relationship between school and work, on gender divisions in society, and the ways in which sociologists go about their work. She turns her attention to the processes involved in collecting data using questionnaires and interviews, the problems involved in this style of data collection, and the ways in which these problems can be overcome. Some of these themes are followed up in the final chapter by Robert Burgess who looks at the social processes involved in the conduct of social research with particular reference to a study that he conducted in a co-educational Roman Catholic comprehensive school. His contribution not only focuses upon his research experience in the school but also examines the social factors involved in the selection of research problems, research strategies, and the collection and analysis of data. On the basis of considering the processes involved in sociological research, he outlines some questions that can be used to evaluate sociological research projects.

A number of approaches to sociology are, therefore, presented in the following chapters. Together they demonstrate how sociologists question the assumptions that are made about society in their attempts to provide some understanding of social life.

Note

1 See, for example, the accounts of research practice that are provided in Bell and Newby (1977), Roberts (1981a), Burgess (1984a), Bell and Roberts (1984).

Suggestions for further reading

Abrams, P. and Brown, R. K. (1984) (eds.), *U.K. Society: Work,*

Urbanism and Inequality, (2nd edn.) (London, Weidenfeld and Nicolson), provides a critical assessment of statistical data on trends in British society relating to cities, education, work, women, elites and social welfare.

Bell, C. and Roberts, H. (1984) (eds.), *Social Researching: Politics, Problems, Practice*, contains a series of essays on recent empirical projects in Britain. This collection includes the reflections of Platt (1984) on the *Affluent Worker* project.

Burns, T. (1967), 'Sociological explanation', *British Journal of Sociology*, vol. 18, no. 4, pp. 353–69, reprinted in D. Emmet and A. MacIntyre (1970) (eds.), *Sociological Theory and Philosophical Analysis*, (London: Macmillan), pp. 55–75. An inaugural lecture in which the author discussed the distinctive features of sociology by examining the way in which sociologists have conducted empirical studies.

Cuff, E. C. and Payne, G. C. F (1979) (eds.), *Sociological Perspectives*, (London: Allen and Unwin). An unusual basic text which introduces a variety of theoretical perspectives in sociology and discusses the implications that these perspectives have for empirical studies.

Eldridge, J. (1980), *Recent British Sociology*, (London: Macmillan). A review of the discipline. There are discussions of work in the major areas of sociology together with an analysis of recent trends in theory and method. This book contains a good bibliography.

Lee, D. and Newby, H. (1983), *The Problem of Sociology*, (London: Hutchinson); provides a clear discussion of theory and research in sociology.

Resources

A basic resource that is available in most public libraries is the *International Encyclopaedia of the Social Sciences* (Sills, 1968). This contains articles on specialised fields of the social sciences and is well worth consulting. A weekly magazine that contains articles on sociology and other social sciences is *New Society*.

A series of resource books on various *Issues in Sociology* are published by Macmillan. See, for example, Graham (1985) on health and welfare and Burgess (1985) on education.

Questions for discussion

(Editor's note: These questions relate not only to some of the issues that are raised in this chapter and the further reading that has been suggested, but also to issues in subsequent chapters in this book. You may, therefore, want to keep these questions in mind and come back to them when you have read more widely.)

1 What do you think constitutes 'the sociological perspective'?
2 Examine the relationship between theory and research in any *one* sociological study that is discussed in:

   C. Bell and H. Newby (eds.), *Doing Sociological Research*, (Allen and Unwin).

   H. Roberts (ed.), *Doing Feminist Research*, (Routledge and Kegan Paul).

   R. G. Burgess (ed.), *The Research Process in Educational Settings: Ten Case Studies*, (Falmer Press).

   C. Bell and H. Roberts (eds.), *Social Researching*, (Routledge and Kegan Paul).

3 What do you consider are the main characteristics of sociological work?

Chapter 2

Gender and the family

David H. J. Morgan

Introduction

My first research project was a study of the changing social and educational backgrounds of Anglican bishops over the period 1860–1960. Reflecting some years later on my reading of their biographies and autobiographies, I was intrigued by a figure who lurked in the background of many of these lives: the bishop's wife. While the importance of the bishops' family life was often acknowledged and the wife frequently described as a 'helpmate', it was clear that the wife remained backstage in her private, domestic sphere while her husband was out front on the public stage. I later learned of the continued and often unacknowledged significance of the unpaid labour and support of wives in the lives and work of men from many different walks of life (Finch, 1983).

After completing that project, I took part in a very different kind of research; a participant observation study of an electrical components factory. I found myself in an assembly department composed almost entirely, with the exception of the managerial and technical staff, of women. The work was, for the most part routine, perhaps monotonous. In contrast, the conversation that often accompanied this routine work was wide ranging, sometimes hilarious, at other times thoughtful and fatalistic, and covering media personalities such as Shirley Bassey or the stars of 'Coronation Street', the way the work was organised and the relative merits of different tasks, the budget and its likely effect on working-class families and the

Royal Family. But more often than not, conversation would return to family life: births, deaths and marriages; sick or disabled elderly relatives; children. In many of these conversations there seemed to be a clear continuity between the homes and families of the workers and their social relationships at the work-bench or during the tea breaks. With the men, in contrast, it was difficult to grasp any such continuity. Their discussion focused on the work, their career aspirations, their leisure and sporting interests.

I would not, with hindsight, like to make too much of this contrast. The women, as I have indicated, were certainly interested in the work and the ways in which their earnings might be affected. The fact that men did not talk about home and family might reflect a more general masculine reserve in talking about such matters to a relatively strange man than their overall lack of significance. However, in this example as in the first illustration, I see questions of gender, questions to do with being a woman or a man in our society, as being very much tied up with actual and expected positions in the families. In both cases, although they would appear to represent different ends of society, being a woman is very much bound up with home and family matters, even where she be in full time paid employment, while being a man does not seem to depend so crucially upon positions and responsibilities within the home.

Thus the many and varied differences and inequalities between women and men in our society are not primarily to do with differences in sexual organs or differences in terms of genes or hormones but more to do with the very widespread and deeply held notions as to what is the appropriate place for members of each gender and that these notions revolve, very approximately, around distinctions between home and work and the private and the public. I say 'approximately' because closer examination often reveals these apparently straightforward distinctions to be less clear cut than they might at first seem. The latter distinction between the public and the private is, in particular, a very complex distinction. Generally, the term 'public' refers to matters outside the home, the spheres of the economy and political life. Women may reach the highest political offices but the language and imagery which we use to describe the public life remains heavily masculine: 'men of affairs', 'chairman', 'the harsh realities' and so on. Yet many working-class and middle-class men do not feel 'at home' at their places of work and see their main interests as lying in home, in family and in leisure and conversely many women make significant contributions to the total earnings of households. The distinction between the public and the private is a difficult one but, at least, continues to have some relation to the way in which we understand gender differences in our society and continues to have some kind of relationship to the more familiar distinction between the home and the workplace.

In this chapter I intend to concentrate on the home and the family and to explore the way in which gender differences and inequalities are shaped by expected patterns of behaviour in the home and, conversely, how these patterns of domestic behaviour are influenced by wider ideas about what it is to be a 'man' or a 'woman'.

I do not intend to explore, at any great length, the many and varied differences between men and women or the various ways in which these differences often cluster together to produce continuing and deep-rooted patterns of inequality between the sexes. (For some recent surveys see Oakley, 1981c; Whitelegg et al., 1982; Morgan, 1984.) Let us simply note, by way of illustration, the concentration of women employees in work situations and jobs at the lower end of the class structure, the presence of sexual harassment at work and the threat or presence of sexual violence in the streets or the home and the different representations of men and women in advertising and the media. My question in this chapter has a narrower focus: what have these inequalities to do with the family? How have sociologists approached the question of the supposed links between gender differences (or changes in these differences) and the family?

Sources of the questions

1 The sociology of the family

The study of the family has not always been a central interest for sociologists and this is particularly true in more recent times. Paradoxically, this may have been due to the fact that earlier scholars assumed the family to be a universal feature of all human societies, based upon the biological facts of human reproduction and meeting fundamental individual and social needs. For many it would seem that the family was such an obvious fact of life that it did not require close or critical examination. Others however argued that these assumptions about the family were misleading and certainly over-simplified (Thorne and Yallom, 1982).

Where sociologists have been interested in the family it has often been in the relationships that are assumed to have existed between the family and the process of industrialisation. For some, the growth of an industrial society was seen as a threat to the institution of the family, breaking up traditional ties, loyalties and obligations and failing to provide any effective or satisfactory substitute for these informal systems of care and mutual support. For others, more optimistically, the family has been seen as adjusting to a changing society, concentrating upon the tasks that it seemed to do best such as the rearing of young children and the provision of a source of emotional support for adults, a kind of haven from the growing stresses of everyday life, and allowing for greater freedom, equality and individuality among its members. One important measure of this was an apparent growing equality of the sexes within marriage.

Implied in this argument is a contrast between the traditional or patriarchal family of the past (associated with pre-industrial and early industrial society) and the democratic, egalitarian or symmetrical family of our own times. In the latter, there is more scope for individualism and expression of emotions and decisions are reached through discussion rather than being imposed by the breadwinning head of the household. While many changes were seen as being related to these changes in family structure and authority – fewer children per family as a result of more effective means of birth control being one of the most important – considerable emphasis is usually given to the increasing opportunities for employment outside the home on the part of women. Throughout industrial societies married women have increasingly undertaken paid employment (see Table 2.1) in a wider range of occupations and positions and for a greater proportion of their adult lives. Women now account for 43 per cent of all employees, ranging from 5.5 per cent of workers in mining and quarrying to 54 per cent in services (Central Statistical Office, 1984, p. 61).

Table 2.1 Estimates of labour force: men and women (millions)

| | females | | | males | all persons |
	married	non-married	all		
1961	3.9	3.9	7.7	16.1	23.8
1971	5.8	3.4	9.2	15.9	25.1
1976	6.7	3.3	10.1	15.9	26.0
1979	6.8	3.5	10.3	15.8	26.0
1981	6.7	3.7	10.4	15.9	26.3

Source: Central Statistical Office, 1984, p. 58.

Increasing employment opportunities provide a woman with a status and identity outside the home; she is not 'just a housewife'. She has an independent source of income and hence is less dependent upon her husband and this, it is argued, increases her bargaining power and influence within the home. Since the Second World War there has been a constant stream of research and argument around the effect of women's employment upon relationships within the home but the basic belief seems to be one of a steady move towards more egalitarian relationships within the family, especially between husband and wife.

This, then, has been one major influence on the study of the relationships between gender and the family: the concern about the effect of the married woman's employment outside the home on relationships within the home. However, these trends in research and theorising have not been unchallenged. For one thing, the historical account has been questioned as being much too simple. History cannot be neatly divided up into 'before' and 'after' boxes, the one labelled 'pre-industrial' and the other labelled 'industrial' (Harris, 1983). However, the main source of criticism of this view – and the source of a whole new set of questions concerning the relationship between family and gender – came from feminism.

2 Feminism

In recent years feminism has made a considerable impact on most areas of study within sociology. (See, for example, the chapters on work, health and welfare in this volume.) In relation to the study of marriage and the family, feminist critics have argued that this model of growing equality between the sexes is, at the very least, much too simple. They point out, for example, the often limited understanding of what is entailed by 'decision making' within the family. Women may have an equal or even greater voice in deciding about holidays or new furnishings but when it comes to considering some more crucial matters, such as moving house in order to further the husband's career, then her voice does not necessarily carry equal weight. Further, it is pointed out that while there has been a significant increase throughout industrial countries in the time spent by married women in paid employment outside the home this has not been accompanied, to anything like the same extent, by greater participation on the part of men in the home. They may also point out the limited range of employment opportunities that continue to be open to married women, the persistence of all kinds of inequalities in relation to welfare, insurance and taxation and the persistence of wife-beating and other forms of domestic violence.

But feminism has not simply argued that we have good reason for scepticism about the supposed growth of egalitarianism within the home. Feminism has been concerned with the wider patterns of disadvantage and inequality – in politics, in education and the labour market for example – and with explaining the source of these persisting and deep-rooted patterns. In seeking for an explanation of these patterns, they have directed attention back to the home and to the family. The family is seen as being a major source, if not *the* source, of female oppression within an industrial society. There are many debates and controversies as to how this is actually supposed to work (Finch, 1983, pp. 1–11; Oakley, 1981c; Randall, 1982) but the emphasis is to some degree placed upon the fact that the husband still derives considerable benefit from the unpaid labour of his wife (even if she is additionally involved in paid work outside the home) and that the responsibilities associated with rearing small children still rest centrally with the mother. Husbands may be seen pushing prams or even changing nappies, but it is the mother who more often than not has to take her child to the doctor, to be home when the child returns from school and generally be available as a caring and 'responsible' mother.

Case studies

What these two contrasting perspectives have in common is a concern with what is generally called 'the sexual division of labour'. Some other aspects of this will be treated elsewhere in this book (see, for example, the chapter on work) but the term is often understood as having three related aspects:

a) The divisions and distinctions between men and women in employment outside the home; for example, the divisions in gender terms between senior management and secretaries or between textile workers and coal miners.
b) The divisions in terms of tasks and responsibilities within the home; who does the ironing or nappy changing, who is responsible for planning the household budget or repairing broken domestic appliances?
c) Finally, the division between these two areas themselves, the workplace and the home and the continued tendency for women to be associated with the latter and men with the former, despite the many changes that have taken place in both spheres.

Thus, sociologists of the family argued that significant changes in the labour market in terms of the participation of married women in particular led, in their turn, to important changes in the relationships between men and women within the home. Feminists, on the other hand, were more sceptical and argued that conventional notions about women, particularly within home and family, limited their participation in economic and political life in the wider society. In this section I shall look at some case studies which consider the effect of the household structure on involvement in paid employment and on the way in which assumptions about gender continue to structure the division of labour within the home. Of crucial importance here is the question of parenthood and this will be the subject of a separate sub-section.

1 Gender, family and participation in the labour market

While there has been an increasing participation of married women in paid employment outside the home and while this participation is being spread increasingly over a wider range of occupations it is also the case that female employment continues to have its own special features. Thus, female employment tends to be more likely to be on a part-time basis (especially for married women), to be concentrated in a few specific sectors of the economy (most of a routine manual or non-manual nature) and generally in positions with little responsibility or status. How far, we need to ask, is the specific nature of women's position in the labour market derived from her position in the home?

Note, however, the way that I have framed the question in such a way as to present women as 'the problem'. It might seem that I am taking the position of men as 'normal' and not requiring explanation. Hence, it is desirable to turn the question around and ask how far the position of men in the labour market may be explained by their position in the family and the home.

Another set of questions may ask whether there is any difference *in kind* between the labour force participation of men and women. Do they have different kinds of attachment to or involvement in the workplace? Again, we must be careful to avoid framing the question from the standpoint of men only, from seeing the way in which men participate at work as being normal and rational while seeing the ways in which women behave at work as being in some ways peculiar and requiring an explanation. Both forms of behaviour (if indeed there be different forms of behaviour along gender lines) need exploring and explaining.

Let me provide an example. Sarah Wells decided to take a job in a bookshop after working at home as housewife and mother to her three children for 15 years. Her husband, Len, helps a little more around the house as a result of this decision and probably helps more than many husbands in a similar situation. Nevertheless, the situation is an unstable one. Sarah finds it difficult to cope with the demands of what, in effect, are two jobs. 'I get in such a state sometimes. I just feel I want to get back to normal living.' If her husband *helps*, Sarah still has to do all the day-to-day domestic planning and to assume overall responsibility for the home. Although both seem to accept the conventional division of responsibility – the male breadwinner and the female housewife – they both also slightly resent the apparent and probable illusory freedom of the other. Yet there has been some change; Sarah feels more independent in herself and is less likely to defer quietly or passively to the views of her husband.

This example is taken from Pauline Hunt's *Gender and Class Consciousness*, 1980, pp. 102–179, a study based upon detailed interviews with thirty-six men and women in Staffordshire. This case, and some of the others reported in the study, throws some light on the relationships between gender, home and labour market participation. Men and women, for the most part, start with fairly deep-rooted and basic assumptions about their respective positions and responsibilities in life. From the point of view of the woman we see a kind of spiral taking place. She is likely to enter marriage fully expecting to leave paid employment as soon as she starts to have children. Later (in Sarah's case, some considerable time later) she may return to the labour market, relatively untrained and with a background of domestic rather than industrial experience (Hunt, p. 101). She is still expected to bear a full load of domestic work and responsibilities, even if her husband also increases his level of helping. Her earnings are often regarded by the partners as 'extras' thus maintaining the idea of the central importance of the man's wage. Employer and trade-unionists may regard these experiences and practices as 'normal' and frame their employment policies and demands accordingly. Thus the labour market becomes even more restrictive.

This is not, in Hunt's study, the whole story. Her book refers to gender rather than simply women and the study indicates that men's positions in and experiences of the labour market are also shaped by their experiences and expectations within the home. Len, for example, started out with career aspirations (he works in a laboratory) but over the years the work has become less exciting, more a simple means to an end, the home and family. He feels he *has* to work but derives little satisfaction from the fact.

One of the advantages of a small-scale study, sensitively written, is that it can bring out all the contradictions and ambiguities of everyday life. Some women, Hunt points out, are often more militant at work than men but more in terms of 'humanistic' issues to do with the quality of working life; their relative inexperience of industrial life may be a positive advantage in some cases. Some men derive satisfaction from trade union activity rather than the work itself, although this too may be combined with a relatively traditional view of the division of labour between men and women. There is one couple, in Hunt's example, who chose to 'reverse roles' yet who still retained very clear notions about bringing up little girls and little boys. Hunt is arguing not so much that we can *explain* the different kinds of participation of men and women in paid employment by reference to home and family but rather that it is important to see home and work as essentially connected institutions, connected in all kinds of subtle and complex ways, however the popular understanding may separate them.

The interconnectedness of work and home is brought out in another study aimed to explore fatherhood and the degree of support for the idea of paternity leave (Bell *et al.*, 1984). Most of the 282 fathers who were interviewed in this survey took some time off during the time when their wives went into labour and gave birth to their child, a quarter suffering some loss of pay as a result. Most of them favoured the provision of paid leave at this time.

It is clear that work, or in some cases lack of work, affected decisions and attitudes around fatherhood. The complexity of the relationship is shown by a small section of the sample where it appeared that fathers withdrew from the labour market altogether during their wives' pregnancies. It cannot be said, in some simple sense, that the impending birth of a child caused the husbands to withdraw from the labour market. In some cases it would appear that they were in unsatisfactory jobs anyway and that the pregnancy tipped the balance in favour of home rather than work. What we are looking at here, as in so many other social processes, is an *interaction* between two different situations (home and work) rather than a simple case of the one affecting the other.

Generally, however, it would be wrong to read too much into this survey. Although most of the fathers took time off this did not necessarily mean a full time immersion in domesticity; there was often a female relative (mother or mother-in-law) to help. Moreover, the survey does not indicate any massive challenge to the traditional model, outlined by Hunt. While most of the men favoured paid leave at the time of the birth of the child, the expectations in this respect were relatively modest (5 to 10 days) and a majority of the fathers were opposed to the idea of mothers with small children going outside to work. What is suggested is that there is some kind of strain in our society resulting from the fact that the birth of a child often comes at the same time as the fathers' greatest involvement in paid employment and that fathers like mothers, if not to the same extent, feel some kind of tension between home and work.

2 Gender and the domestic division of labour

Hunt's study as we have seen was as much to do with the division of labour between women and men within the household as it was about the division between home and work. Hunt, acknowledging her inspiration from the feminist movement, sought to show the connectedness of the two spheres.

The feminist movement also stimulated a much greater willingness to look at the household itself, in particular focusing upon the economic activities within the home, or especially upon those activities which have economic significance even if they may not be specifically recognised as such. In particular, attention has been focused upon those clusters of activities around the word 'housework' and 'housewife'.

Oakley's work on this subject (Oakley, 1974) shows, again, the way in which such problems are formulated. She begins her study with a critique of the way in which sociology, a subject dominated by men, had traditionally asked questions about the society they were studying and the way in which, in asking those questions, they tended either to make assumptions about women (all women are dependent upon men, women tend to be more emotional and so on) or to ignore them altogether. Her study of housework not only managed to bring to the reader a sense of the experience of one of the most widespread but most ignored activities in the country but also demonstrated that these activities could be studied *as work*, in much the same way as it might be possible to study life in the office or on the conveyor belt. Certainly, her study showed that the women she interviewed regarded what they were doing as work and as hard work at that. Many indeed claimed that they worked harder than their husbands. Many of their likes and dislikes about their work were very similar to the preferences expressed to industrial sociologists examining situations closer to conventional work places. Thus the women disliked the routine and monotony of much of their work; ironing in particular came under attack. On the other hand, they liked the sense of being one's own boss and being able to plan one's own working schedules. Tasks which involved meeting people outside the home (shopping) or some degree of creativity (cooking) were also preferred.

Although Oakley focused on the women, the book is also about the division of labour in the home. Thus most of the women expressed some degree of identification with the role of the housewife, that is that they saw it as their main responsibility, as something that they had learned from their mothers and that was particularly identified with being a woman. They speak of housework as 'my work' and their answers to questions show relatively little participation on the part of their husbands. (Few husbands would be prepared to change a nappy, for example.) Oakley was one of the first sociologists to draw attention to a distinction that has been the experience of women all over the country: men may sometimes *help* in the home but women have the daily *responsibility*.

It might be argued that Oakley's study, published in 1974 and based upon research in 1971, is a bit of history. Surely with the influence of the women's liberation movement, things have changed since then? A more recent study, based on work carried out in Middlesbrough in the early 1980s suggests that this is not the case. Using a mixture of postal questionnaires and more detailed interviews, Rosie Collins found very little to suggest any substantial modification of the picture presented by earlier researchers (Collins, 1985). Here too, women were to be found most heavily involved in domestic labour, a fact only marginally changed if the wife were in paid employment herself. Here too, there was a clear division of labour in the home; washing, ironing and mending were clearly 'women's jobs' while men were chiefly responsible for repairs and the maintenance of the property. Right across the social spectrum, women and men alike seemed to accept the gender division of labour as something which was natural and relatively unchangeable. 'It's horses for courses, that's what I believe in' responded one male subject. Husbands may now possibly be more willing to change nappies (39 per cent in this survey) but the fundamental split remains: men may *help* in the home but women have the *responsibility*.

3 Gender and parenthood

In discussions about the equality of the sexes it is likely that someone will come up with the argument: 'when all is said and done, it is the woman who has the baby'. This is often spoken with that tone of finality that suggests that there is no further room for argument; a biological fact becomes a social norm. How far have sociologists, examining the division between home and work and the division of labour within the home, incorporated the question of parenthood into their analyses?

In many ways, it can be said that there has been some recognition. Hunt, for example, is far from being alone in recognising the birth and presence of small children as a major factor in tipping the balance between home and work as far as the mother is concerned. Oakley, Collins and others recognise that 'housework' is not all of a piece and that a significant distinction is to be made between those tasks most conventionally identified with housework – washing, cleaning, cooking etc. – and those more directly to do with child rearing and child care. Often these two aspects may contradict each other as when a screaming child breaks domestic routines or when a tidied room is reduced to chaos in minutes.

Nevertheless, perhaps because it is something so obvious, it has been argued that the actual experience of motherhood has been relatively ignored by sociologists. A recent researcher, Mary Boulton, certainly felt this was the case; although something like 80 per cent of women are also mothers, she felt on the basis of her survey of the literature that psychological, biological and much sociological research tended to ignore what it actually felt like to be a mother. Mothers, in other words, were not being allowed to speak for themselves (Boulton, 1983).

This was something which Boulton attempted to rectify. Again, hers was a small survey (twenty-five working class and twenty-five middle class women from two areas of London) but the size of the sample was more than compensated for by the depth of the interviewing and her skillful analysis of the data. For example, she attempted to distinguish between a person's *immediate* response to motherhood–did they find it frustrating or pleasurable? – and a mother's more *considered* response, based upon careful reflection.

It was one of her most important conclusions that a sense of the meaningfulness or otherwise of motherhood (derived perhaps from the dependence of the child, or from one's personal hopes and fears for the future or from a sense of pride in one's children) was not necessarily the same thing as a sense of enjoyment of motherhood.

Beyond this, Boulton's study does provide us with a vivid sense of the complex and contradictory feelings associated with being a mother. She presents a comprehensive account of what was enjoyed and what was disliked in housework and considerable insight into the 'responsibility without bounds' (Boulton, p. 78) the sense that motherhood is an all embracing but ill-defined sense of responsibility. What does emerge here, even more strongly than in some of the earlier studies, is that motherhood, or rather the way in which maternity is shaped and defined in our society, is a key to understanding the position of women in contemporary society. Enjoyed or not, the *responsibility* is clearly seen as a role for the women; once again there is very little evidence of father's detailed involvement in the work of childcare. It would seem that this fundamental difference extends to grandparents; grandfathers seem to be much less able or willing to talk about this subject than grandmothers (Cunningham-Burley, 1984).

Conclusion

The aim of this chapter has been to show how sociologists have tackled that area where the study of gender overlaps with the study of the family. The general conclusion must be that, while there may have been considerable changes in the public participation of women over, say, the past one hundred years, this does not appear to have been matched by any significant corresponding changes within the home. That, in other words, the study of the different positions of men and women in society as a whole must continue to focus upon their relative positions within the home.

Two further points, about the way in which sociological research is conducted, are in order. In the first place, this study provides a particularly apt case study of the way in which values enter into sociological research. A major emphasis, in the sociology of the family, had been to argue for some move towards a growing equality within the home between men and women. These findings were not necessarily incorrect, in terms of the way in which the questions were selected. Thus if you ask questions about 'help' in the home and interpret these responses to mean a growing involve- ment on the part of men in the business of being husbands and fathers in the household, then the findings are probably correct and the conclusions justified. However, the feminist movement prompted sociologists to ask further questions about who has the ultimate responsibility for certain domestic tasks and asked us to look much more closely at some of the basic assumptions upon which domestic life was being conducted.

Secondly, it is worth reminding ourselves of the difficulties involved in studying the family. These stem from the fact that the family and family relationships are often, as we have seen, regarded as being part of the private part of our lives; indeed the very idea of privacy in our society is closely bound up with the home and the family. We often do not have ways of studying families directly in the way in which, say, observers may study factories or schools. We have to rely upon interview material, usually carried out with, sometimes unrelated, individuals. It has sometimes been argued that the sociology of the family was the sociology of wives simply because it was women who were most likely to be interviewed. Skilled interviewing, as demonstrated in different ways in the work of Oakley and Boulton for example, may tell us a lot. But we still, firstly, lack material of comparable richness about men in the home and men as fathers and, secondly, about the *interactions* between women and men within the household. It is, however, such inter- actions that may contain vital clues to the ways in which gender differences and inequalities are maintained in present day society.

Finally, it is worth remembering that this chapter has focused on one small area of a very large topic area; the study of the social origins of the differences between women and men. To say that the study of family relationships, relationships between husbands and wives and between mothers and fathers contain important clues to understanding the continuing inequalities between men and women is not to say that the family is the sole cause of such inequalities. Clearly we have to look at many other factors in understanding this. Within the home itself we have to look not simply at the sexual division of labour but also at the processes of socialisation, the processes by which boys and girls learn behaviour appropriate to their gender within the family. We need also to look at sexual relationships both within the home and within the wider society. We need to look at the labour market and at the practices of senior management and trade-unionists. We need to look at education and the media. And finally we need to see how all these factors are connected. However it is unlikely that, in seeking to provide a fuller more comprehensive understanding of the positions of women and men in society, the family and the household will ever occupy less than a central place.

Suggestions for further reading

On gender in general

There is, by now, a very large body of literature on gender and on women in particular. One of the best points of departure remains Oakley, A. (1972), *Sex, Gender and Society*, (London: Temple Smith). Evans, M. and Ungerson, C. (1983) (eds.), provide an interesting cross section of debates in *Sexual Divisions: Patterns and Processes*, (London: Tavistock).

On the sociology of the family

Anderson, M. (1980) (ed.), *Sociology of the Family*, (2nd edn.) (Harmondsworth: Penguin) provides a good introduction to some of the main concerns while Thorne, B. and Yallom, M. (1982) give particular emphasis to gender issues in their collection of critical articles, *Rethinking the Family*, (London: Longman). The case studies mentioned in this chapter include Hunt, P. (1980), *Gender and Class Consciousness*, (London: Macmillan), Boulton, M. G. (1983), *On Being a Mother*, (London: Tavistock) and Oakley, A. (1974), *The Sociology of Housework*, (Oxford: Martin Robertson). Other aspects of parenthood are treated in Backett, K. C. (1982), *Mothers and Fathers*, (London: Macmillan) and McKee, L. and O'Brien, M. (1982) (eds.), *The Father Figure*, (London: Tavistock). More specific treatment of a variety of family topics is to be found in Rapoport, R. *et al.* (1982), *Families in Britain*, (London:

Routledge and Kegan Paul). Ray Pahl's *Divisions of Labour*, (1984) (Oxford: Blackwell) is an important and recent study.

On women and feminism

Most of the above-mentioned studies will, of course, deal with these issues in some measure but more specific treatment is to be found in Oakley, A. (1981), *Subject Women*, (Oxford: Martin Robertson); The Cambridge Women's Studies Group (1981), *Women in Society*, (London: Virago) and Whitelegg, E. *et al*. (1982) (eds.), *The Changing Experience of Women*, (Oxford: Martin Robertson, Open University).

Of works dealing specifically with *men*, Tolson, A. (1977), *The Limits of Masculinity*, (London: Tavistock) remains the best of a small field.

Resources

The *Equal Opportunities Commission*, Overseas House, Quay Street, Manchester provides leaflets and information sheets about a variety of topics to do with gender and has a helpful library and information centre. *The Feminist Library*, Hungerford House, Victoria Embankment, Charing Cross, London WC2N 6PA (01-930-0715) is recommended, as is *The Fawcett Library* located at the City of London Polytechnic. The Family Policy Studies Centre (previously called the *Study Commission on the Family*) publishes a variety of papers and fact sheets to do with the family (3 Park Road, London, NW1 6XN).

A variety of statistical information on matters to do with gender and family is provided by the *Office of Population Censuses and Surveys*, St. Catherine's House, 10 Kingsway, London, WC2B 68P.

Questions for Discussion

1 Is the family based household the cause or the consequence of gender inequalities in society as a whole?

2 The growing participation of married women in paid employment outside the home has not been balanced, to anything like
the same extent, by a growing participation of men in the home
and in parenting. Why do you suppose this is? What measures
or programmes would you suggest to change this situation?

3 Discuss the likely effects of the following upon gender relations
within the family:
   a) Long term high *rates* of unemployment within a particular
      region, say Merseyside or the North-East;
   b) Long term unemployment for men; for women;
   c) Early retirement for men; for women.

4 Why does the image of the 'ideal' nuclear family (two parents,
daughter, son) remain such a popular one with advertisers and
the media?

Chapter 3

Work, non-work and unemployment – a discussion

Colin Bell

> Recognition of the importance of work . . . helps, more than
> any other technique for living, to strengthen the ties between
> reality and the individual; in fact, the latter is firmly linked by
> his work to one facet of reality: the human community . . .
> The job of earning one's daily bread brings personal
> satisfaction when it has been freely chosen; that is, when
> through sublimation it allows the individual to give rein to his
> personal leanings, to instinctive impulses previously repressed
> or particularly intense for reasons of temperament.
>
> Sigmund Freud, *Civilisation and its Discontents*.

Introduction

What is remarkable about the word 'work' is the extent to which,
in our kind of society, it has come to apply only to 'paid employment'. That means that some activities are seen as 'work' whilst
others are not. Why do we refer to women who are wives, otherwise more than fully occupied with domestic labour, as going 'out
to work'? Raymond Williams, in his valuable lexicon of *Keywords*
of our times, states that 'the specialization of work to paid employment is the result of the development of capitalist productive
relations'. He continues that

> to be *in work* or *out of work* was to be in a definite relationship
> with some other who had control of the means of productive

effort. *Work* then partly shifted from the productive effort itself to the predominant social relationship. It is only in this sense that a woman running a house and bringing up children can be said to be not *working*. At the same time, because the general word is necessary, a person may be said to do his real work on his own, sometimes quite separately from his *job*. Time other than that spent in paid employment is significantly described as 'your own time', 'free time', or as 'holiday' (the old word for a day of religious festival), or as 'leisure time' . . . it is significant of the narrowing specialization of work that we now have 'leisure-time activities', often requiring considerable effort but not described as *work*, which belongs to our 'paid time'.

Williams, 1976, pp. 282–3

These are useful distinctions that are nicely made by Raymond Williams. How, though, are they changing? It must be stated first of all that almost any sociological source on work, non-work and unemployment is out of date. All were produced before the current deep recession and though we can ask and speculate we do not really know, with any precision whether for example, the current experience of unemployment is different to that, say, of the 1930s. Virtually no current sociological text takes today's basic lack of work seriously – but they will have to in the future. Meanwhile I too must rely on slightly dated material. There is, though, much sociological research on unemployment and its consequences in the making. For instance, there are major projects being conducted from University College, Swansea, on the impact of the dramatic decline in the steel industry in Port Talbot (the investigator is Dr Chris Harris) as well as in Sheffield (the investigators are Professor John Westergaard and Alan Walker). I will refer to the work in which I am involved in studying the West Midlands with Lorna McKee in more detail later. I mention this to point up the problems sociologists have in getting up-to-date materials.

Work and industrialisation

The outlines of the relationship between work and the processes of industrialisation are fairly well known and must be understood as an essential background. I will risk some (over-)generalisations. Industrialisation in the first instance saw a dramatic growth in employment in the manufacturing (or secondary) sector and a decline in agriculture (or the primary sector). This is factory employment, increasing specialisation of tasks, a fine division of labour – a decline of craft based employment and a rise of the assembly line. The image of 'the dark satanic mill' will evoke what I mean for nineteenth century Britain. In the twentieth century employment in manufacturing first steadied and then declined. In 1960, 35.8 per cent of the total employment in Britain was in manufacturing, in 1975 30.9 per cent and now (in 1984) it is thought to be around 25 per cent. There was an increase in employment in the service (or tertiary) sector – office work, bureaucratic work, and paper work. This increase was happily believed to be going to absorb the consequences of the decline in manufacturing – or deindustrialisation as it is sometimes known. And yet the increase in the service sector has also steadied and indeed may also be declining. Some hold out further hope for a fourth or quaternary sector as being the basis of a 'post-industrial' society. It would be 'knowledge based' and be centred around the 'micro-electronic revolution' – or the 'chip'. This is the so-called 'second industrial revolution' to which I will return at the end of this chapter.

We should note the changes in 'prime-movers' – or sources of power through the period of industrialisation – from human and animal power, through water power to the age of steam, and then to electricity – remember Lenin's definition of communism as 'Soviets plus electrification', to nuclear power and now micro electronics. Each does seem to have associated with it some characteristic organisation and form of work. But this should not be allowed to obscure the extraordinary continuity of the 'relations of production'. We must remember that Britain industrialised the capitalist way and is also deindustrialising the capitalist way. I am pointing to the continuing importance of *class* and to ownership of the means of production, and to the (increasingly difficult) search for profit during the era of monopoly capital that no amount of fanciful speculation about the 'chip' must be allowed to obscure.

There are two other useful generalisations – or foci of attention that I want to introduce at this point. There were once easily held beliefs that as industrialisation progressed the 'amount of alienation' (understood here as feelings in the heads of workers about their essential meaninglessness, powerlessness, anomie and lack of autonomy rather than as an objective situation that applies to all workers under the capitalist mode of production regardless of their feelings) would first rise but then decline as technological change gave them back their control (and dignity) in the work place. The change can be illustrated by considering craft workers such as carpenters or coachbuilders being replaced by mass production assembly lines in car factories in turn being replaced by high technology production such as oil-refineries thought of as in some way typical of 'stages' in industrialisation. However, the important insights of Harry Braverman (1974) in his book *Labor and Monopoly Capital* (which has the pointed sub-title, 'the degradation of work in the twentieth century'), are an important corrective to these views. Though far from being uncontentious, the 'deskilling' thesis has focused sociological attention on the labour process — particularly in white collar work. It leaves the worker performing only a fragment of a whole task. Deskilling in the workplaces has been widely noted by sociologists of work.

The second useful generalisation is to state strongly that what we are seeing currently is the emergence of a new international division of labour. Capitalism was perhaps always best understood as a 'world system' and many have related an understanding of the class system and of work in countries like Britain to their imperial activities. Asked simply, was the British working class – our proletariat, a kind of superproletariat on the backs of black and brown colonial proletariat? Did that blunt the revolutionary potential of the British working class? Recently though, not only has the empire struck back, but it looks very much as if manufacturing jobs have been 'exported' to the so-called Third World, for example to Hong Kong, Singapore and the Philippines. That is known as the new international division of labour. There are many who would now argue that the world economy is undergoing a profound structural change which is forcing companies to reorganise their production on a global scale. This not only implies the relocation of production to new industrial sites in the developing countries but also through what are euphemistically called 'accelerated rationalisation measures' (meaning unemployment) at the traditional sites of industrial manufacture – like here in Britain. That is the context of deindustrialisation, deskilling of the labour process and massive unemployment and represents an acute crisis for the older industrial countries. It may well be a process that is largely independent of the policies pursued by individual governments and the strategies of expansion adopted by individual firms. The most persuasive analysts of this process (Fröbel, Heinrichs and Kreye, 1980) do indeed argue that the conditions currently prevailing in the capitalist world economy mean that the efforts of individual countries to devise economic policies to reduce industrial unemployment in the industrialised countries or to accentuate a balanced process of industrialisation in the developing countries are doomed to failure (see Moore, Chapter 5).

Labour markets

Let us now change tack and approach the problem of work, non-work and unemployment from another direction. Even during the period of full-employment not all work was equal – some jobs were more equal than others. By this I mean much more than the level of pay. Take manual employment in the manufacturing sector for instance. Some jobs were unionised, were relatively secure in that unemployment was unlikely, were safe in that industrial accidents were comparatively rare – the Factory Acts applied and were enforced. Other jobs were much more spasmodic, dirty, nasty and dangerous – ununionised backstreet sweatshops are still with us. And so is 'outwork' or 'homework' paid by the piece. Immigrant females working at home for long hours and low return out of sight of factory inspector, public health officer, shop steward and tax inspector alike. I am introducing you to a fundamental *dualism* of the capitalist economy that cuts across the very nature of work.

There is another 'primary sector' – understood here are good jobs that are, to exaggerate, occupied by a white, male labour aristocracy – printers on Fleet Street. There is also a 'secondary sector' with unpleasant jobs, to exaggerate again, that are likely to be occupied by blacks – both male and female – foundry workers in the metal trades. There are certainly at least two segregated labour markets which limit competition for jobs in the primary sector from those in the secondary sector. In addition the best jobs in the primary sector are filled from what is called the 'internal labour market' – by internal promotion, and are consequently forever beyond the reach of those in the secondary labour market. To that can be added the process which is known in Birmingham at least, 'the lads of dads' syndrome whereby, especially under the current conditions of acute shortage, apprenticeships, the only route into the skilled labour force, are given to the sons (not daughters of course) of reliable fathers (see Roberts, Chapter 10). That effectively excludes, not to put too fine a point on it, most West Indians and Asians in the labour force.

There are then fundamental divisions in the labour force – cross-cutting dualisms in the labour market: between good and bad jobs, between the genders and by ethnic groups. Let me as simply as I can add this part of the argument to some of the points I was making earlier. Employment under capitalism never increases or reduces evenly. Just as uneven development is always present so is uneven recession. The 'new international division of labour' itself will have an uneven impact. Take metal manufacture – foundry work, in the West Midlands in England, once the heartland of the post war boom. It is now in a state of collapse and is one reason why the recently prosperous West Midlands now has the fastest increasing unemployment rate of any region in the country. During the boom years many Asians were drawn into the foundry industry. The geographical location of immigrants in Britain is a fossilised impression of the manufacturing and service prosperity of the 1950s and 1960s – naturally they went where the jobs were. They were recruited to do the nastiest jobs – and some are very nasty, but by industrial and political action at the point of production, in the foundries at least, eventually got access to the better jobs. And now they have done so the foundry trades themselves are going and Asians are becoming disproportionately unemployed. They are not to be found in the few growing areas of the economy – indeed many blacks are overly concentrated in jobs such as those in the once fast growing health and welfare sectors, that are facing cutbacks through massive, government induced, reductions in public expenditure.

The informal economy

What I have been remarking on so far is usually referred to as 'the formal economy'. It is legal, by and large, regulated, measured, taxed and enters the official statistics. The 'bottom-end' of the secondary labour market overlaps, as I have already implied, with what I now want to refer to as 'the informal economy' – unregulated, untaxed, sometimes illegal, unrecorded. The question that is being asked by many observers – from sociologists to the Inland Revenue, is whether as 'the formal economy' declines does 'the informal economy' increase? Before we can begin to get some purchase on the question we must be clearer as to just what we are talking about.

In an influential article 'Britain in the decade of the three economies', Jay Gershuny and Ray Pahl explore the implications and the future of the informal economy. They point out that much of the informal economy is work which goes on in and around the house and housework: cooking, childcare, decorating, gardening and so on. We should note that much of this is often referred to as 'women's work'. This might be, they claim, though how we can really be sure I do not know, as much as 35 per cent to 40 per cent of the Gross National Product. There is also 'fiddling' and regular criminal activities. This is sometimes called 'the hidden economy'.

Gershuny and Pahl (1980) make a three-fold distinction in order to get clear what they mean by the informal economy. There is they claim:

1 *Household economy*: production not for money, by members of a household and predominantly for members of that household, of goods or services for which approximate substitutes might otherwise be purchased for money, e.g. garden produce and DIY.

2 *Underground, hidden or black economy*: production, wholly or partly for money or barter, which should be declared to some official taxation or regulatory authority, but which is wholly or partly concealed, e.g. jobs 'on the side'.

3 *Communal economy*: production, not for money or barter, by an individual or group, of a commodity that might otherwise be

purchasable, and of which the producers are not principal consumers, e.g. 'care work' in the community.

Their argument, and it is one that must be taken seriously, is that much economic activity – work in other words, that once took place in the formal economy now is to be found in the informal economy – with sewing machines, power drills and food mixers we get nice clothes, great bookshelves and super food – if we have the skills. This last point should not be missed for it could well be that as the labour process in the formal economy is becoming 'deskilled', so in the 'informal economy' there is a 're-skilling' with, it would usually be suggested, a consequent increase in personal satisfaction (understood here as the opposite of alienation induced by the industrial process). To continue a central theme of this chapter, Pahl at least has wondered whether this represents a shift out of 'employment' into 'work'. As he puts it, 'it is *work* with goods purchased in the formal economy which is the clue to an alternative world of economic activity'. This does not lead he argues, 'to decline in the *consumption* of final services but rather the *substitution of informal household production of services for the purchase of services from the formal economy*'. (Pahl, 1980, p. 4).

So below the dual labour market of the formal economy there is an informal economy that is flourishing uncontrolled and perhaps uncontrollable. We, as yet, know very little in detail and with any reliability about the informal economy in any systematic way. It is clear that there is no simple relationship between it and the formal economy. And it is not an 'easy option' for the unemployed – an alternative, as it were to conventional paid employment. Indeed it would seem from my own empirical investigation in Inner Urban Birmingham that being 'in work' – as usually understood, is a key resource for activities in the informal economy. It is the source of materials and social contacts – the latter plays the part of capital in the formal economy. We must not forget the lack of resources and the social isolation of the unemployed.

One final point about the informal economy is about *time*. There is a famous paper by E. P Thompson (1967) called 'Time, work-discipline and industrial capitalism' in which he discusses the emergence, along with industrial capitalism of 'modern' conceptions of time – time related to the factory and the machine rather than the sun and needs of animals. The paper contains a marvellous discussion of the spread and availability of precise watches and clocks. Thompson reminds us that attention to time in labour depends in large degrees upon the need for the synchronisation *of* labour – precise time and the regularisation of labour go together. This happens, unevenly as always, through the latter part of the eighteenth and well into the nineteenth century. 'We are', he tells us, 'concerned simultaneously with time sense in its technological conditioning, and with time-measurement as a means of labour exploitation'. My point is that it can be suggested that the growth, if indeed that is what it is, of the informal economy has led to a re-evaluation of *time*. In the classic phrase, 'it paid me to take a week off work to paint the house'. At the very least we can agree with Ray Pahl's modest claim that 'the way work gets done and the way people get by and use their time, tools and other resources in everyday life is changing' (Pahl, 1980, p. 17).

Unemployment

To focus directly now on unemployment let us turn to Raymond Williams again. There is actually a debate about when the term was first used and when we came to use the term in its modern sense – the 1830s is most people's judgment. There are other related words, as Williams puts it:

> On the one hand industry developed from the sense of a
> general quality of diligent human effort to its modern sense of
> productive institution. On the other hand *unemployed* and *idle*,
> which were general terms for being unoccupied with anything,
> developed their modern senses of being 'out of paid
> employment', or of being 'in employment but not working'.
>
> Williams, 1976, p. 274.

And this happens 'because it represents the specialisation of productive effort to paid employment by another which has been an important part of the history of capitalist production and wage-labour'. This suggests, and it is a very important point, that not only did the rise of capitalism create our understanding of unemployment in its modern sense but that unemployment is an essential part of the capitalist mode of production. The current very high rate of unemployment then should not be understood as qualitatively different – nor as a temporary aberration, but rather as a continuation and growth of a phenomenon *always* present under capitalism, that is to say that it is only quantitatively different. Does, for instance capitalism need a 'reserve army of labour'? People who can be sucked in as the economy expands and spewed out as it contracts? Married women do seem to act as this kind of reserve army and are not traditionally regarded as 'unemployed' at all. Immigrants from the colonies – many of whom were specifically recruited and brought to this country to fill jobs that could not be filled from the local (white) labour supply – do seem to occupy this role too (see Moore, Chapter 5).

I will need to introduce you to the way social scientists (and policy makers) currently 'categorise' unemployment. Unemployment is now usually understood as a 'flow' – out of work, into unemployment and, hopefully, back into work. The speed of this flow – and whether all move through at similar speed is a matter of much debate and, as yet relatively little actual empirical sociological research. The idea of 'an unemployed flow' is usually contrasted with the idea of an unemployed stock but naturally enough, perhaps, this does lead to accusations that it obscures the presence of a very significant number of long-term unemployed. The best study of 'the unemployed flow' – that of W. W. Daniel (1981) for the Policy Studies Institute, is based on a sample of those who had registered as unemployed six weeks after their registration. During that six weeks one third found work and it is intended that they will follow this 'cohort' in order to understand better the nature of 'the unemployment flow'. One third were women – but as he laconically remarks 'registered women are not representative of all unemployed women'.

What are the characteristics of the 'unemployed flow'? It is predominantly composed of younger workers – even excluding the 16 and 17 year olds, 36 per cent of men in the sample were aged 18–24 and 63 per cent were aged 18–34. The less skilled and lower paid are substantially over-represented among the 'unemployed flow' relative to the working population. And despite the newsworthiness of large factory closures, small firms and small establishments contribute disproportionately to the 'unemployed flow'.

They also usually had had relatively very short periods of service in their most recent jobs. It would seem as if about half of those out of employment are family heads. And one of the major consequences of this is that the proportion of *children* affected by unemployment is higher than the proportion of females. As Adrian Sinfield puts it:

> Those worst and longest hit by unemployment have been compelled to pay a harsh tax on behalf of the rest of society in the fight against inflation. By allowing the numbers out of work to rise, and by cutting back benefits and other forms of help, the state, supported by the rest of society it would appear, is effectively saying to the unemployed, its conscript army in the war against inflation: 'with your help and at your cost, we shall win the war.'
>
> Showler and Sinfield, 1981, p. 238.

The consequences for the organisation of the family of the unemployment of the male household head is the subject of a major piece of sociological research that has been conducted from the University of Aston in Birmingham by myself and Lorna McKee funded by the Social Science Research Council (now the Economic and Social Research Council). We may well eventually have answers to such questions as to whether or not a husband's unemployment may cause his wife to take up employment or to leave it and how the wife's employment may affect her husband's likelihood of working. Are men with working wives under more pressure to find jobs? Do they have better social contacts and networks through which to find them? Does unemployment lead to any re-negotiation of the social division of labour between husbands and wives? Does it alter patterns of childcare? Or, is it the case as one informant told us 'that being unemployed is a *full-time* job'? As yet we really do not know. These are live areas of current sociological research that will perforce receive a great deal of sociological attention during the 1980s.

The future of work

Any speculation about the future of work, non-work and unemployment is almost uniquely fraught with difficulties. Take for instance the issues raised by the 'chip'. Is this just a quantitative change in techno-innovation or far more dramatic? Virtually every commentator agrees that the impact of the 'chip' on employment and opportunity structures, on the organisation and control of work and consequent commitment to work is changing – yet they disagree on almost every particular. Will the decline in employment in manufacturing accelerate decline in the service or tertiary sector of employment? What will the introduction of word-processors, say, do to the distribution of skills and the whole 'deskilling' process particularly of office work? What are the implications for the employment of women of such changes – some have estimated that there could be a drop of 20 to 70 per cent in the number of secretarial jobs in Britain by the end of the century. Will there be changed career progressions – men for instance displacing women in supervisory positions?

The optimistic position is that the 'chip' will *free* workers – for other jobs and a shorter working day, week, year and life. The bleaker scenario is that the 'chip' will simply displace workers who will never find paid employment again. That may of course from certain perspectives be no bad thing given how dirty, dangerous and boring many jobs are. Perhaps work has always been an over-rated commodity and as has often been remarked 'if work was such a good thing then the rich would have kept it to themselves'. If, on the basis of the micro-electronic revolution we really are moving from an economy characterised by low productivity and high employment (LOPRO-HIEMP) to one that exhibits high productivity and low employment (HIPRO-LOEMP) then it must be accompanied by massive political intervention to redistribute the fruits of all that productivity to those without employment. Of that there is, as yet, no sign.

Suggestions for further reading

General background

Abrams, P. and Brown, R. (1984) (eds.), *UK Society: Work, Urbanism and Inequality* (2nd edn.), (London: Weidenfeld and Nicolson). Chapter 3 by Richard Brown on 'Work' pp. 129–197 remains the best single source of information about work in Britain set in a tight sociological framework.

Nichols, T. (1980) (ed.), *Capital and Labour*, (London: Fontana); contains some important discussions and applications of 'the Braverman thesis' on the 'deskilling' of labour.

Williams, R. (1976), *Keywords: a Vocabulary of Culture and Society*, (London: Fontana). See particularly the entries under the headings Work, Labour, Unemployment and Career.

On unemployment

Fagin, L. and Little, M. (1984) *The Forsaken Families*, (Harmondsworth: Penguin). A timely and disturbing report on the effects of unemployment on family life in Britain.

Showler, B. and Sinfield, A. (1981) (eds.), *The Workless State*, (Oxford: Martin Robertson); contains seven chapters on such topics as employment in the 1980s, the political economy of unemployment, and since 1945 the international context.

Sinfield, A. (1981), *What Unemployment Means*, (Oxford: Martin Robertson). A very readable straightforward account of the experience of unemployment by Britain's leading authority – easily the best available summary of what we currently know.

On the 'chip' and employment

Note: All this literature is rapidly out-dated but two good sources that also provide a framework for understanding the debate are:

Conference of Socialist Economists (1980), *Micro-electronics: Capitalist Technology and the Working Class*, (London: CSE Books). Available from 55 Mount Pleasant, London WC1X OAE.

Council for Science and Society (1981), *New Technology: Society, Employment and Skill*, (London: CSS Report). Available from CSS, 3/4 St Andrew's Hill, London EC4V 5BY.

Accounts of work

Beynon, H. (1984), *Working for Ford*, (Harmondsworth: Penguin). This now has a quite justifiable classic position in British sociological literature.

Fraser, R. (1968) (ed.), *Work: Twenty Personal Accounts*, (Harmondsworth: Penguin). Twenty anonymous personal accounts – all worth reading. This volume has a conclusion by Raymond Williams on 'The Meanings of Work'.

Fraser, R. (1969) (ed.), *Work 2: Twenty Personal Accounts*, (Harmondsworth: Penguin). Twenty more anonymous personal accounts – all worth reading. This volume has a conclusion by Alvin Gouldner on 'The Unemployed Self'.

Terkel, S. (1972), *Working: People talk about what they do all day and how they feel about what they do* (New York: Random House). A truly great documentary based on one of the best tape recorders around.

Resources

Material on unemployment is regularly available from *The Unemployment Unit*, Tress House, 3 Stanford Street, London SE1 9NT and *The Unemployment Alliance*, c/o National Council for Voluntary Organisations, 26 Bedford Square, London, WC1B 3HU.

There is a study group called *Work and Societies in the Eighties* (WASTE for short) at 9 Poland Street, London W1V 3DG, who provide a series of interesting papers.

New Society provides regular articles, facts and comments on trends in employment and unemployment.

Questions for discussion

1 In what ways is 'work' different from 'paid employment'? Discuss this with particular reference to what you did last weekend and your mother does every day.

2 a) Advise the Inland Revenue how the 'informal economy' could be measured. Pay particular attention to problems of definition.

   b) Consider the ethical issues involved in advising the Inland Revenue about the 'informal economy'.

3 In his foreword to Showler and Sinfield (1981), Peter Townsend
writes that:

> In societies governed by the work ethic the psychological
> and social consequences of being denied an opportunity to
> fulfil a principal role assigned by virtue of membership of
> those societies are severe and have to be made known if
> measures are to be taken to prevent unemployment or
> diminish its severity . . . it will require courageous
> leadership – in the social sciences, no less than in politics –
> to teach that motivation is culturally induced and is not
> something narrowly dependent upon the wage-rate or any
> alternative income offered by the State. People want to work
> because they are taught from childhood to fulfil themselves
> and earn their keep, and contribute to the community's
> needs; and the work they do is often necessary justification
> for their families and for themselves for their lives. That is
> why unemployment is such an appalling and undeserved
> indignity.

Discuss this statement.

4 What kind of employment structure would you expect to see in
Britain bearing in mind 'the second industrial revolution' based on
micro-electronics?

Chapter 4

Social inequality: sociology's central issue

Sylvia Walby

Introduction

The existence of social inequality presents sociology with its central issue. Why do some people live in riches and others in poverty? Is Britain less unequal than it was fifty years ago? Do people have the same position in society as their parents? Why does inequality provoke attempts to change it at some times and not at others?

The unfairness and injustice of an unequal distribution of resources in society has led to countless attempts to explain this state of affairs and offer either remedies or justifications. The study of social inequality is often seen as the core of sociology; central to its theoretical development, and to its practical relevance. Sociologists have ranged from seeing stratification as a social evil to be eradicated by social and political action, to seeing it as necessary for the efficient ordering of society. It is a highly political field of enquiry and one which engenders fierce controversy. Often social class has been seen as the basic type of social stratification, but today the importance of inequality based on sex and race is more widely recognised.

The study of social stratification is one of the longest existing areas of sociological enquiry; it has deep rooted traditional questions and disputes. Yet it is also responsive to current social and political questions: the issues and themes are derived both from the theoretical tradition, and from the burning topics of the day.

Selection of research questions

I want to focus first on looking at why stratification theorists have asked the questions that they do, and then at how they try to answer them. I am going to examine only work on Britain here, although the comparison of forms of inequality between countries has been important in sociology. Some of the most enduring questions of social stratification analysis had their origins in the founders of the discipline of sociology in the nineteenth century. These questions include whether there is a connection between material position and political consciousness and action; a polarisation between the working class and the middle classes or a convergence; greater political militancy or apathy by the working classes, and so on. One of the fundamental questions then, is, how do changes in the social division of labour affect social inequality and forms of political consciousness and action? This is the time-honoured question of social stratification.

But sociologists are not just asking the same old question. While it has certain classic underlying aspects, sociologists have always applied these to the current issues. Sociologists have always been excited by the political alignments and questions of the day and sought to explain the relationship between these and the changing social division of labour.

Affluent Workers

Around the 1960s we had investigations into whether a decrease in Labour voting was to be attributed to the increasing affluence of some segments of the working class, and their adoption of the lifestyle of the middle classes together with the middle-class political view of the world (Goldthorpe and Lockwood, et al., 1969). Some of you may think that this is an extraordinary question at the moment! I think this goes to show the contemporary relevance of many of these questions, in that the issues of interest do change. During the 1950s and '60s, and into the '70s the issue of the impact increasing affluence was having on the working class was a burning topic of debate not only among sociologists, but among a range of social commentators and, indeed, politicians. At that point in history the commonly held expectation was that economic expansion would continue into the foreseeable future, and the impact that this affluence brought was of considerable interest. Hence there were many studies including the classic one by Goldthorpe and Lockwood *et al.* (1969) which carefully investigated whether the working conditions, standard of living and attitudes of the more affluent sections of the working class were becoming more like those of the middle class. Would the higher level of wages lead to greater contentment with the *status quo* and would this lead to higher levels of Conservative voting? Was automation restructuring the working class? Was the size of the 'real' working class shrinking? And what was the 'real' working class anyway? Were groups of workers such as technicians and clerks whose numbers were growing apace working class or middle class? (Dahrendorf, 1959.) Would automation lead to increased levels of protest against class relations, or would it lead to the incorporation of workers into the ethos of the enterprise?

Would automation lead to greater or less alienation of workers from management? (Blauner, 1964.) What was the relation between industrial politics and class politics? (Tourraine.) Did militancy in one sphere lead into militancy in the other? Or did the relatively limited economic demands typically made by trade unions in Britain mitigate against a transfer of industrial militancy to a wider class politics? Why was Britain different from other countries, for instance France, which has a more turbulent political history? These and many more questions exercised sociologists of the 1960s.

Labour process debate

While these questions were initially derived from contemporary issues, they were refined and reformulated by sociologists in the light of a body of pre-existing knowledge. This enabled us to draw on information and theories derived from other cases in order to explain the puzzle currently at hand.

On some occasions the impetus for a new debate comes from a particularly compelling piece of analysis which provokes excitement, controversy and further research. Such an impetus is well illustrated by the impact of Braverman's book *Labor and Monopoly Capital* (1974). Braverman argued that work was being deskilled in the drive by capitalist employers for control and profits. He looked at the way both the skilled manual crafts and skilled clerical work were being superceded by jobs which were much simpler; he argued that the complex work tasks which took years to learn and which gave workers pride in, and control over, their jobs were under attack by management. The new, so-called 'scientific' management was splitting each skilled job into several jobs each of which involved only a fragment of the tasks of the previous one. The management did this in order to both pay lower wages and to gain greater control over the labour process. Braverman's work led to a renewed interest in the details of jobs, and of the labour process, than existed previously.

His work met with a lively response, even 'Bravermania' from other researchers. Some tried to show that management strategies were more diverse than this and sometimes involved giving workers 'responsible autonomy' (Friedmann, 1977); others that Braverman had underestimated the significance of worker resistance to deskilling (Elger, 1979); and still others that he had underestimated the significance of gender (Beechey, 1982), and many other groups with an interest in the labour process. Thus the debate as a whole generated a much more sophisticated and complex understanding of changes in the nature of jobs themselves and the social relations in which they are enmeshed (see Colin Bell's chapter in this volume).

Middle class

The growth of middle level occupations, such as clerks and technicians has fuelled the controversy as to whether the class balance of Britain is shifting towards the middle class and away from the working class. The proportion of people in non-manual occupations has grown at the expense of manual occupations and there has been an increase in the number and importance of jobs requiring formal educational qualifications. Is Britain (and indeed most industrialised western countries) then becoming an overwhelmingly middle-class nation (Poulantzas, 1973)? Does this explain the recent electoral successes of the Conservative Party?

Some have doubted this and argued that many of these so-called middle level positions are really rather lowly, involving routine, repetitious tasks which should be correctly classified as working-class. This debate has raged, in particular, around clerical work (Lockwood, 1958; Crompton and Jones, 1984; Abercrombie and Urry, 1983). Typing and form filling in large offices under close supervision for relatively poor rates of pay was hardly the stuff of a responsible middle-class job (Braverman, 1974; Crompton and Jones, 1984). But is this typical of these new positions? Don't some of them require years of training, and carry considerable respon-sibility for the organisation of the work of others? Managers and professionals could be considered to fall into this category. Some sociologists have tried to solve this debate by dividing middle level occupations into two. One is called the service class, in view of the way in which this group of workers serves the functions of capital, the other is seen to be part of the working class (involving the routine clerical workers) (Abercrombie and Urry, 1983).

Other sociologists, such as Stewart, Prandy and Blackburn (1980) have commented that clerks do not stay clerks all their lives, so it is inappropriate to put the occupants of these positions in one class on the basis of their temporary occupational status. These writers go on to challenge the concept of class as a set of occu-pational slots, and argue instead that the focus should be on groups of people with similar job histories.

How have sociologists researched these questions? Some have engaged in detailed empirical studies of particular occupations. One of the classic early studies was that in which Lockwood investigated the position of the 'black coated worker', as he called clerks. This involved a close examination of the work and market situation of the clerk and to some extent their beliefs, looking for similarities and dissimilarities with typical working-class and middle-class occupations. He decided that while the market situation of the clerk in terms of earnings and benefits was not much better than that of a skilled manual worker, their position in the enterprise distinguished them from the manual workers in terms of work situation.

Some sociologists have devoted their creative energies to working out which are the appropriate questions and criteria to utilise to distinguish between social classes. It is no good describing an occupation in greater detail unless you know what are the relevant things to making a distinction between classes. So we have theoretical debates about what would count as a distinction between social classes. Is it a difference in position in relation to the relations of production (a typical Marxist position)? Or are market rewards such as level of wages more important (a typical Weberian position)? How important are educational qualifications, and if they are, is this because of the advantages they bestow in the labour market or because of their status and prestige? Is class position the same as prestige ranking? Is a class described by economic position? Or is it a political actor which has to be made by history?

Sociologists have thus had to decide what they meant by class before they could decide whether people or occupations with particular characteristics constitute a different class from another set of people or places.

I have been trying to suggest that the issue of class boundaries is one to which sociologists of stratification have devoted a lot of energy. Whether or not individuals move across such boundaries in the course of their own lifetimes or as compared to their family's origin thus becomes an important question. How much upward and downward mobility is there? Is it sufficiently common and far-ranging to alter the way people think of themselves as a member of one class or another? (Goldthorpe, with Llewellyn and Payne, 1980.)

Gender

Sociologists are responsive to social and political currents in their selection of interesting questions to study. Most of these studies I have described have been born of a concern with industrial militancy and voting (or rather non-voting) for the Labour Party, as some sort of proxy for class action.

The recent (well, recent in the lives of most established sociologists) revitalisation of the women's movement has caused this to be questioned. Stratification theory was criticized as being merely the study of inequalities between men, wrongly excluding those be-

tween women and men, and between women and women. Stratification theory was not the mainstream of sociological thought but
merely 'male-stream' (O'Brien, 1981).

This critique was taken up by those involved in or sensitive to
the enormous political energies of the women's movement. The
ferment outside sociology gave rise to a questioning, typically by
young women sociologists, of the way 'their' discipline treated
gender inequality. The political activists and theoretical writers
were not always the same people, rather there is a complicated and
indirect way in which sociology was affected by the ferment of
contemporary feminism.

How had stratification studies got away with ignoring gender
relations for so long? Why had they not taken gender inequality
seriously before? The 'conventional' sociologists argued that
studying gender was not really relevant for stratification studies
because they could work out a woman's position in it by looking
at the position of the family in which she lived. A woman's life
chances, they argued, were crucially determined by the household's
situation, and the position of the household was determined by the
male 'breadwinner'. In so far as women did have paid employment
this was too limited for it to significantly affect the position of
herself or her family unit. Hence a woman's position in the class
system could be derived from that of her husband or father and
there was no need to look at women themselves (Goldthorpe,
1983).

In view of the considerable participation of women in paid work
today this defence of the conventional view might seem rather
dated. Most women will spend many years in paid work and the
number of years the 'average' woman spends out of the labour
market for child (and husband) care is rapidly shrinking. Further,
increasing numbers of married women are earning as much as or
more than their husbands (Stanworth, 1984).

However, a more serious criticism of the 'conventional' view is
that it ignores inequality between husbands and wives together. It
is merely theoretically wiped out of existence by the practice of
taking the family (or rather household) as the unit of stratification
and assuming that equality reigns inside it. The importance of
social inequality within the family has been a major concern of
many of the new feminist sociologists (Delphy, 1984).

There has been a plethora of attempts to integrate the new insights derived from feminism into stratification studies. Some have focused on the importance of women's paid employment and examined the implications of this for analyses of paid work and for the class location of the family.

So, some sociologists have been investigating whether gender makes a difference to the nature of occupations; for instance are conditions of employment worsened if women typically fill a job rather than men? Other sociologists have asked what difference it would make if both husbands' and wives' jobs were taken into account when determining the class position of the family? What happens if a women from one class married a man from another class location? What are the characteristics of these 'cross-class' families? (Britten and Heath, 1983.)

My own work has been concerned with the inequalities between women and men in work. This has included questions as to why women perform less paid work than men and more unpaid housework, and why women are more likely to become unemployed than men (Walby, 1983, 1985).

Race

Sociologists have asked a variety of questions concerning the existence of racial as well as class and gender inequality. Why is there ethnic inequality? Why is there racial discrimination in a civilised society? Why are you more likely to have a low paid job if you are black than if you are white? Why are you more likely to be unemployed if you are black rather than white? Why is it easier to immigrate to and settle in Britain if you are white than black? Do black women suffer from racism differently from black men?

Sociologists have asked questions not only about the forms of racial inequality but also about the bases of them. Who, if anybody, benefits from racism? Is it employers who are able to take advantage of cheap labour? Or do white workers also benefit by being able to take the pick of the jobs and leave the low paid and more unpleasant forms of work to others? Is racial inequality primarily a particular form of economic disadvantage? If so, is it really a specific form of class inequality? Who is the ruling class in a racist society? Is there a link between racism in Britain and its colonial past? Is racism primarily due to this imperialist heritage, or does it rather have real bases in present institutional arrangements from which other groups benefit?

Sociological accounts of racism in Britain have had some impact on popular understanding. For instance, sociological reasoning was behind the attribution of one of the causes of the Toxteth riots to the high rates of unemployment among black youths. A further excellent account of sociologists' attempts to grapple with the problems of racism is to be found in Robert Moore's chapter on racism in this book.

Comparative stratification

So far I have only looked at stratification in Britain, yet one major field in British sociology is that of comparative stratification, and a set of comparisons which do not always refer back to Britain. This is an important element of stratification studies and gives us a helpful perspective on contemporary British stratification even if this is not explicit. For instance, the British route to industrialisation with its implication for patterns of stratification is not the only one, and indeed not the most typical one. Some societies experienced violent revolutions and dramatic changes in the forms of inequality, while others industrialized more slowly and evenly. Why should Russia and China have had major revolutions, while India did not? Indeed why should countries as near to Britain as France have a history of dramatic political change while its neighbour, Britain has a much more placid past? (Barrington Moore, 1966.)

In Britain inequality is organised around class, sex and race, while in other places and times the very forms of inequality are different; caste, for instance, or slavery. In a caste system people are born into their position in the social hierarchy, although there are none of the biologically distinguishing features of sex or race.

Some sociologists have argued that all these forms of inequality can be understood if we examine the organisation of production in these societies, while others have argued that there is no one underlying pattern and explanation.

Theoretical differences

I said at the beginning of this chapter that stratification theory, if not sociology as a whole, has sometimes been characterised as a debate between the ghosts of Marx and Weber; but I did not say much more about it. What is this debate about, then? One important difference emerges over the definition of one of the basic concepts used in stratification studies: class. Traditionally Marxists have defined class in relation to the means of production while Weberians have introduced elements of market position and of lifestyle as well. Hence the greater concern shown by Marxists about changes in the workplace, as evidenced by the labour process debate; and the greater interest by Weberians in lifestyle.

Traditionally Marxists have seen changes in the forces and relations of production as the source of social change, while Weberians have seen motors of social change in a much wider range of factors. Marxists have been concerned with a rigorous theorising of the underlying social structures, Weberians more concerned to emphasise complexity and diversity. Marxists saw a much clearer connection between changes in class structure and political action than did Weberians. To the traditional Marxist cry of: why don't the working class see, and act on, their real interests? Weberians would deny such a clear cut set of distinct interests and see no imperative to political action stemming from simple material exploitation.

However this division of the debate into two clearly laid out opposing positions is in many ways a caricature of the actual discussions. In practice the issues are more complex and the sides of the theoretical divide much less clearly drawn. For instance many modern Marxists place a considerable degree of emphasis on the place of ideological practices in social theory and do not succumb to vulgar economism; while many Weberians would argue for the central place of the division of labour in their view of the world. Many Marxists would acknowledge the importance of the mediations of the labour market in the struggle between workers and employers; while Weberians often conceptualise contemporary Britain as a capitalist society. Indeed some sociologists today argue that the clear distinction between Marxist and Weberian positions is out of date, and that modern writers on stratification draw fruitfully on both traditions simultaneously (e.g. Abercrombie and Urry, 1983).

Methods

Computers have revolutionised the methods of recent stratification studies. It is no longer necessary to rely on small, and perhaps unreliable, samples, or to restrict questions to those easy to ask. It is now possible to apply the power of machines to complex mathematical tasks and to large amounts of data that would take a mere human for ever to do. These new techniques have been especially important in the analysis of social mobility, which needs a lot of complex data about a lot of different social positions over time for large numbers of people to be analysed. In these analyses it is necessary to trace the movements of individuals between different occupations over time. In order to pick out the complex patterns information is needed on large numbers of people.

A recent classic of this type is the Oxford study in which the social mobility of 10,000 men was documented and analysed (Goldthorpe with Llewellyn and Payne, 1980). The underlying questions included whether men stay in the same social class as their fathers for all their lives, or whether they move up or down; and, how much mobility do men experience in their lifetime? Why do these questions matter? They matter because of two main issues: firstly, that of how open British society is; secondly, because mobility may affect the traditional relationship between material position and political action, in that if a person moves between different positions in the division of labour this may be expected to prevent the build up of loyalty and political commitment to a party or organisation.

In this study 10,000 men were carefully selected so as to form a representative sample of British men and asked a series of questions about their lives, and especially occupations, and those of their fathers. Sampling the population in order to get a representative sample is an art in itself. For instance it is no good having a sample with lots of men living in the south, even though this would have been easier for this southern based research team, since the greater affluence of that part of the country and its greater availability of higher level occupations would have skewed the results, giving an impression which was not true for Britain as a whole. In one crucial way their sample is not representative, however. They interviewed only men, yet purported to speak of Britain as a whole. This was justified by old-fashioned arguments about women's class position which are generally today seen as invalid (Stanworth, 1984). Yet there have been substantial changes in the position of women in the division of labour in post-war Britain which are now seen to affect their class position. Women's increased participation in paid work during this period, has not, however, meant an improvement in the typical sorts of jobs that women take. This paradox is itself an interesting issue for sociologists.

Goldthorpe and his co-workers have shown that there is more social mobility than had previously been thought to be the case, especially of upward mobility into the 'service' class (that of top managers and professionals). Yet this has not led to any increase in the relative mobility rate, which they take as the more fundamental indicator of the degree of openness of British society in that the chances of a man of working-class origins rising to a service-class position are so much less than that of a son of service-class father assuming the same position. Goldthorpe *et al*. conclude from this that the attempts to overcome social inequalities by the liberal and social democratic reformers of modern Britain have failed, and that only a process of class conflict can lead to a true reduction in the social inequalities. All this work would have been very much more difficult, if not impossible, without the assistance of computers, and special statistical procedures.

Conclusion

Sociology helps provide answers to the age old questions of why there is social inequality, and why people in different circumstances believe it to be right or wrong, and take appropriate action. And indeed, helps to evaluate the possible strategies for reducing social inequality in a rigorous and systematic way.

Suggestions for further reading

Braverman, H. (1974), *Labor and Monopoly Capital*, (New York: Monthly Review), Part I is a famous and provocative account of the degradation of work today.

Cockburn, C. (1982), *Brothers*, (London: Pluto Press). This ironically titled book is about male workers who are no friends of women who wish to do the same work – printing.

Crompton, R. and Jones, G. (1984), *White Collar Proletariat*, (London: Macmillan). This provides an account of the latest debates over the class position of clerks.

Delphy, C. (1984), *Close to Home*, (London: Hutchinson). It's women's oppression which is a bit too close to home for men as husbands and fathers, in Delphy's view.

Giddens, A. (1982), *Sociology: A Brief but Critical Introduction*, (London: Macmillan). An account of sociology which interprets it as the study of social stratification.

Goldthorpe, J. (1978), 'The current inflation: towards a sociological account', in Hirsh, F. and Goldthorpe, J. (eds), *The Political Economy of Inflation*, (Oxford: Martin Robertson). This paper powerfully demonstrates the necessity for an analysis of our economy in sociological terms. In it Goldthorpe takes a problem conventionally seen as 'purely economic' inflation and demonstrates that a sociological analysis of the competing social forces is a much more convincing explanation.

Heath, A. (1981), *Social Mobility*, (London: Fontana). What social mobility is, and why it matters.

Marx, K. (1967), *The Communist Manifesto*, (Harmondsworth: Penguin). Why not read this stirring polemic on class struggle for yourself?

Westergaard, J. and Resler, H. (1976), *Class in a Capitalist Society*, (Harmondsworth: Penguin). An account of inequality in a class divided society.

Resources

There are a lot of Government publications which document various forms of inequality. For instance, *The New Earnings Survey* will tell you which groups of people earn more than others; the *UK Census 1981* will tell you how many people are in which occupations, socio-economic groups, and social classes (Government publications such as these can be found in your library or are available from HMSO, 49 High Holborn, London WC1V 6HB).

The annual report of the Equal Opportunities Commission has tables showing how unequal women are in respect to wages, appointment to important bodies and so on (reports are available from Equal Opportunities Commission, 2 Quay Street, Manchester M3 3HN).

Political parties and trade unions are usually pleased to give you leaflets putting forward their views on what is wrong with the stratification system and how to put it right.

Conservative Party, Central Office, 32 Smith Square, London SW1.
Labour Party, 150 Walworth Road, London SE17.
Liberal Party, 1 Whitehall Place, London SW1.
Social Democratic Party, 4 Cowley Street, London SW1.

Questions for discussion

1 Is social inequality ever fair? Are rewards ever equal to effort? Should effort or need be the basis of the distribution of resources?

2 Is class more basic to stratification theory than other forms of inequality, such as gender and ethnicity? Give reasons for your answer.

3 What advice can sociology offer to political movements?

4 How do you expect the British pattern of social stratification to be affected by a period of prolonged high unemployment? Compare this to the changes in the period of 'affluence' in the 1960s.

Chapter 5

Immigration and racism

Robert Moore

In 1958 there was a violent encounter in Notting Hill in which white youths assaulted blacks. At the trial of the white youths Lord Justice Salmon said:

> You are a minute and insignificant section of the population who have brought shame on the district in which you lived and have filled the whole nation with horror, indignation and disgust. Everyone, irrespective of the colour of their skin is entitled to walk through our streets with their heads erect and free from fear.

Such a statement seems hardly credible today when the law seems no longer to protect black people. Evidence has been accumulating which shows that police are reluctant to admit even to the possibility of racial attacks. When complaints of crimes are made, even when witnesses are available, the police have been known to recommend private prosecution by the black victim (Lambeth 1981, IRR 1979). Furthermore coloured victims and their families are likely to be of interest to the police as potential illegal immigrants. Black victims have therefore become reluctant to seek police help. Racism has been shown to be part of the everyday culture of the Metropolitan Police (Smith *et al*, 1983; Banton, 1984) and in 1979 police in Southall went out of control and themselves rioted in a black community. Many people were beaten, and property destroyed by the police, a number of whom were carrying illegal weapons (National Council for Civil Liberties, 1980a, 1980b;

Campaign Against Racism and Fascism, 1981). The police also killed a white school teacher, Blair Peach. No police officer was ever brought to trial for this crime. The investigation into the Brixton 'riots' of 1981 by Lord Scarman showed not only the extent to which racist thinking permeates establishment thought, but an almost complete unwillingness to challenge police accounts of events. (Barker and Beezer, 1984.) Joshua and Wallace in *To Ride the Storm* (1984), give an historical account of the black experience of policing in Britain, as well as an analysis of how the black community of St Pauls in Bristol felt that they were defending themselves against police attack in the 'uprising' of 1980.

How the circumstances have changed between 1958 and 1984 is only explained in part by this chapter, which concentrates especially upon the effects of immigration policy. Among other questions that need to be considered are the relevance of the history of policing as described by Joshua and Wallace and the degree to which police attitudes reflect something other than, or beyond popular attitudes. Is racism more or less common amongst police? This is a question that can be posed and explained by both sociologists and psychologists.

But what about the police claim that they only reflect public attitudes? Does it stand up to criticism? For example if 'x' per cent of the public were thieves or embezzlers how would we regard 'x' per cent of policemen and women being such? Issues such as these belong to the realm of politics, belief and morality and cannot be answered by reference to data or sociological argument.

The rise of racism and inter-racial violence has been matched, albeit in a laggard manner, by changing perspectives on what is known as 'race relations' in Britain. It seems customary for sociologists to review the whole literature of a given field before commenting upon recent developments. I break with this custom and assume a familiarity with elementary 'facts and figures' (a guide to the basic literature is given at the end of this chapter). I confine the discussion to what I believe are important issues for sociological theory and confine myself also to those issues that I am most competent to discuss. These factors lead me to miss out a discussion of education and not to discuss the material on black viewpoints and responses. That I do not discuss the Notting Hill Carnival or the education of Sikh children is not because I do not think them interesting or important; they are too important for me to make amateurish comments.

In a sociological study it is worth looking at the ways in which ideas have developed in a particular field. If you look at Deakin's *Colour, Citizenship and British Society* (1970) you will see that 'colour' is defined as the problem in terms of the responses it invokes from the white public and policy-makers. The *structure* of British society was taken as given and not in itself seen as part of the problem. Solutions to the race problem therefore lay in the direction of social policies that reduced the effects of white prejudices in, for example, housing and employment, and which also ensured justice for non-whites. Such policies would reduce the possibility of ghettoes forming in the cities and of non-whites being confined to menial jobs. This in turn would lead to a reduction of what whites saw as being part of the problem ('they' live in ghettos, etc.).

The political climate would be changed by Government commitment to equality and justice. This is simply an extension of the idea of citizenship embodied in the welfare state to all groups in society. In the new climate of opinion mutual understanding would grow and hostilities decline. It was largely assumed in the late 1960s that social scientists would provide information helpful to the development of social policies appropriate to these goals. A few dissenting voices were raised, but they were ignored. A good example of such voices can be found in Donnelly's *Justice First* (1969), especially the essay by Anne and Michael Dummett. It may all seem common-sense stuff today. But when it was published *Justice First* was so outrageous that it was not reviewed or discussed in the press – which was, at the time, eager for anything on 'the race problem'.

What now constitutes the 'sociological perspective' upon immigration and race in the UK? I can answer this by contrasting current topics and themes with the themes of the 1960s.

From immigration to migration

The earliest post-1960 works on race relations in the UK were concerned, by and large, with settlers from Commonwealth countries, especially the West Indies, India, and (then) East and West Pakistan. It was soon discovered that many from the Indian sub-continent were not settlers at all but male members of families coming to the UK and returning home in rotation. This was changed by immigration legislation and regulation which through its threats to all immigration and the hopes for dependent families joining men in the UK turned the rotating migration into a permanent settlement. Pioneering work such as Peach's *West Indian Migration to Britain* (1968) concentrated on the 'push' and 'pull' factors in Commonwealth countries and the UK which facilitated the migration.

Five years later the title of Castles' and Kosack's *Immigrant Workers and Class Structure in Western Europe* (1973) foreshadowed the nature of the debates to come. But crucially their work set Britain's immigration in the wider context of the mass migration of workers to North-West Europe from the Mediterranean seaboard, ex-colonies and the Third World. This changed the rather parochial focus of British work and forced us to realise that our immigration was part of a much wider movement of labour (see, for example; Paine, 1974; van Houte and Melgert, 1972; Marshall, 1973; Cohen, 1980). Castles and Kosack and the writers who followed them showed that migrant workers did jobs for which there was no labour available or which locals would not do. They assisted the upward social mobility of native workers as well as making Europe's post-war economic miracle possible. But whilst migrants played an anti-inflationary role in the European economies they were not simply 'cheap labour', they were also *controllable labour*.

A crucial feature of European migrant labour was its rightlessness. The migrant had no vote, restricted freedom of employment, limited rights to social security and other benefits, restrictions upon housing and trade union activities. They were, ultimately, disposable. If a worker is no longer needed by an employer, or a whole economy, their lack of rights enables them to be discarded with ease. The fact that the sending country raised the adult worker, that he needed few services in Europe and had no family for whom the state needed to make provision, but that he nonetheless worked and paid taxes led Castles and Kosack to assert that migrant labour was the aid that poor countries gave to the rich.

British immigrants, however, werę quite different; they were citizens with all the rights and obligations that this entailed, fully entitled to play the market for jobs and housing, to vote and join trade unions, to collect sickness benefit and enter an NHS hospital. The contrast between European migrants and British migrants was to provide a clue for sociologists because from 1962 onwards, and from 1965 especially, British Governments set about systematically stripping the Commonwealth citizen of rights, first the right to enter the UK and then the right to family life. Finally in 1971 the mainly non-white Commonwealth immigrant was reduced to the status of a disposable migrant worker. White Commonwealth citizens meanwhile acquired the almost unlimited right of entry and settlement (we no longer even count them), thus finally and unequivocally establishing the racial basis of 'immigration' policy. Immigration politics were never about *numbers* in a 'crowded island'. Since 1971 through regulation and judicial decisions the right to enjoy family life has been further eroded. Persons who entered legally have been redefined as 'illegal immigrants' with a consequent loss of rights to defend themselves in court and exposure to instant removal. Blacks now find it advisable to carry papers which prove their right to be here. The respective rights of men and women have also been altered so that today a wife cannot confer the right to settlement and citizenship upon her husband. British women living in the EEC are much better protected, for example, they have the legal right to have their husbands with them, whatever their nationality. My book *Slamming the Door: the Administration of Immigration Control*, written with Tina Wallace, tells this story in detail up to 1975 (Moore and Wallace, 1975).

In a book entitled *The New International Division of Labour* Fröbel, Heinrichs and Kreye (1980) have widened the analysis yet further to show the effects of new developments in technology and communications that have made it much easier to export many jobs to Third World countries. Here the workers may be even more rightless and subject to direct control and perhaps state repression. They are not only cheap labour and controllable but 'superexploited' labour which is simply consumed, used up and discarded. It is not surprising that many of these workers are women in the 16–25 age group. At 25 they are worn out and ready for replacement (Sivanandan, 1979; Counter Information Services, 1979; Fröbel, Heinrichs and Kreye, 1980, Part III). There is then a 'new international division of labour' which partly explains rising unemployment in Europe. To take an extreme example a worker in a British electronics factory loses a job; this job is done by a woman in Taiwan. The microprocessor made in Taiwan is imported into the UK and built into a machine that puts another worker out of a job. Castles, Kosack, Fröbel and Cohen have forced us to look not only to the international dimensions of migration and job movement, but at the logic of capital. A firm can reduce its costs by replacing people with machines, sending jobs overseas, using women, immigrants or children in the home country. We need to see the use of migrants as just one of a possible range of strategies for employers (see Bell, Chapter 3).

Three questions might usefully end this section: the wider perspective on the use of migrants, immigrants (and especially black and female migrants) makes us view studies of racial discrimination in a new light. Instead of being a 'social problem' might not racial discrimination be useful to certain interests and *normal*? In other words racial, national, gender and age differences may be mobilised to serve interests. The elimination of discriminatory treatment destroys the usefulness of the differences. In what kind of a society can such differences become more or less valuable to particular interests?

Secondly, note that in the 1960s there was a paradox: the UK needed immigrant labour but governments felt it necessary for political reasons to reduce black immigration. With rising unemployment and economic stagnation in the 1970s and '80s the political and economic come into harmony. Is it a coincidence that at this point a policy of repatriation comes on to the European and British agenda?

Thirdly, what light does what I have called 'the wider perspective' throw upon what is commonly called the problem of the second generation? How can industry be sure of a supply of cheap, compliant labour if the racial groups which they have previously used have other ideas as a result of their upbringing in the UK (or Holland, or Germany)? Plainly a useful discussion of how schools and the education system work could begin from this point.

Having seen that immigrants and migrants may come from many parts of the world and that people may be discriminated against because they are young or female, or because of their nationality or skin colour, we ought to pause to consider the term *race*. To a biologist race means a breeding population: hence in the case of humankind the biologist can only refer to 'the human race'. Attempts to classify humankind into race on a biological basis have not been successful. They have concentrated on human physical characteristics but, for one thing, the variations within 'races' may be greater than the differences between them. Different shapes of nose or cross-section of hair have no meaning beyond differences of shape. Biological distinctions are not what are at issue when either the public or social scientists refer to race. Differences between groups – say skin colour – become socially significant when they become the basis for actions or attitudes between groups or individuals. That race is a social concept, not a *biological* one, is easy to see when one considers how an Indian would be regarded in South Africa and the USA. It is quite an instructive exercise to look at the way people of 'mixed race' are treated in different societies because it illustrates the *flexibility* of the idea of race. A good definition from a sociological point of view was given by John Rex:

> We shall speak of a race-relations structure or problem in so far as the inequalities and differentiation inherent in a social structure are related to physical and cultural criteria of an ascriptive kind and are rationalised in terms of deterministic belief systems, of which the most usual in recent years has made reference to biological science.
>
> Rex, 1970, p. 39.

It is not biology but the belief in it that makes the idea of race a reality in its consequences.

Sociologists then go on to ask about the function of beliefs and the interests served by inequalities. We have already seen some of the possible social functions of racial beliefs and how they might relate to patterns of political, social and legal inequality. But you will note that Rex also refers to 'cultural criteria'. This is a reference to a seemingly more rational view that recognises the discredited nature of pseudoscientific ideas about race.

Biological arguments were used to defend not only unequal treatment of groups but the unchanging and *natural* basis of the inequality. Ideas about the connection between biological differences in human 'races' and social inequality have been entirely discredited (UNESCO 1969) and only a tiny and unrepresentative group of scientists still hold to these ideas. Racists therefore need other ideas. For example customs, religion, food and dress distinguish peoples and provide a set of differences which provide a basis for defining the boundaries between them. These differences, racists argue, are as unchanging as biological differences. More sophisticated racists would say that conflict and inequality are based on these rather then biology as such. Some would go further and argue that culture embodies an idea of race or nation, and that conflict along *these* lines is natural.

Cultural differences might indeed be a feature of conflict as may be seen in Belgium and Northern Ireland, but we do not normally refer to these as racial conflicts. We may well treat people differently according to how they hold their fork but to say that this kind of consideration is *all* that race relations comes down to is to do violence to the truth. Cultural differences have been most widely asserted to be significant in conditions which we recognise as already being racial conflict.

Race in the social consciousness and its consequences for society interest sociologists. How does the concept of race fit in with another important dimension of inequality, namely class?

Race and class

The wise sociologist hesitates to venture upon a simple exposition of the current state of sociology in this area. It is likely to be an excursion through a minefield.

Frank Parkin (1979) suggests that the class and race issue has been mishandled because ethnicity, 'tribal loyalties' and race were seen as archaic features, bound, like religion, to wither away. When such factors persisted nonetheless they were treated as 'complicating factors', spanners in the works of an otherwise clearly understood class structure. He sums up the situation by saying:

> Ethnic conflict would now appear to be as normal a feature of advanced industrial societies as class conflict, even though its theoretical treatment is still at a relatively primitive stage.

Parkin, 1979, pp. 32–33

There is a simple view which says that ideas about race are false ideas, encouraged by those who wish to deflect the population from asking questions about the failure of social and economic policies. Blacks may be blamed for housing shortages, unemployment and crime. Racial divisions at work prevent workers uniting to defend their jobs and conditions of work against bosses (Cohen, 1980). What is needed therefore is an unmasking of these false ideas and their functions. Blacks are *really* part of the working class and could take their place in the conflict between classes if 'black and white unite and fight'. This view is not without merit. Blacks have been scapegoated and they are, largely, a part of the working-class.

There is a second, slightly less simple view, which sees black workers as a 'sub-proletariat'. They are in a different class position from the working class, they are subordinate to it and as much exploited by other workers as by employers. This is a view adopted by many immigrants and by migrant workers in Europe. They do the worst jobs for the least pay and experience discrimination not only from employers and landlords but from white workers and trade unions. Sometimes they encounter outright hostility, as when white workers seek to break strikes involving blacks. Indeed, white workers have never given unequivocal support to black workers in any wholly black dispute (Moore, 1975). They feel themselves therefore to be *outside* and *below* the working class. This may be enhanced by the separation or segregation of housing and lack of common membership of working men's clubs, chapels, PTAs and by language. The accumulation of differences from the native working class makes them so different that even the sociologist must treat them as separate. If, however, you believe classes to be discontinuous categories then an accumulation of small differences cannot move a group or individual across a class line – even if he or she feels they have so moved.

Some of these difficulties may be resolved by understanding how a black worker belongs to more than one set of relations of domination. The immigrant has been forced to leave his country because of the poverty resulting from the relationship of his home country to Europe. Thus a Jamaican peasant living on marginal land alongside the lush plantation of a western company may feel compelled to leave soil and kinsfolk in order to seek a better life in the UK. He is one of the propertyless colonial poor. The colonies have contributed to the relative prosperity (by world standards) of even the poorest in the metropolitan countries. Thus members of the European working classes have been indirect exploiters of the colonial poor. Sometimes they were direct oppressors too appearing as soldiers or as settlers who took the locals' land.

When immigrants came to Europe they joined the propertyless working class of Holland, France or the UK. They shared the basic inequalities and deprivations of working-class people, the same conditions at work. But they did not fully shed their colonial status. It was this which brought them to Britain and enabled them to be employed in the lowest positions in the labour market and to be discriminated against by employers and other workers. *Race* provided the unmistakable mark of their status. Workers normally experience the reality of class in its clearest form in relations at work. For many blacks their first experience of class exploitation in Europe was of racial discrimination at work – *but* discrimination that may have been regarded as legitimate by white workers. Paradoxically, for many blacks their first experience of the class structure was also their first direct experience of the fact of race. Thus the rise of black consciousness and class consciousness amongst blacks is closely related.

The low esteem of the black worker and the inheritance of a colonial tradition (and colonial imagery in white minds) means that the second generation of blacks bears the burden of history, as modified by the British experience and their response to it, and remain part of the two intersecting systems of domination even though they are not displaced peasants.

In this section I have so far referred to blacks as if they were all men, it is very important to remember that half the population is female and that women occupy various (usually subordinate) positions in systems of domination based upon gender. Therefore most migrant women are at the intersection of three systems of domination.

Phizacklea and Miles (1980) in their study of Willesden, give a much more practical illustration of these problems by asking whether migrant workers will be more likely to organise around colour, class or ethnicity. They reject colour as a basis for organisation because of the cultural distinctiveness of migrant groups.

Consciousness of colour does not transcend differences between, say, Bangladeshis and Trinidadians. Each might view the other with suspicion or hostility. We seem to be a long way from the day when all non-white immigrants and their descendents in the UK refer to themselves as 'blacks'. When they do so they will be making a statement about their position in society. Will this be a statement about 'race' or class?

Class might provide a basis for unity and the evidence suggests that black workers are willing to join trade unions and vote Labour – if these are class conscious acts. As workers they have stood up to employers in industrial conflict – the most elemental form of class action. But, conclude Phizacklea and Miles, white exclusionary and discriminatory practices have often forced them into ethnic solidarity (pp. 34–38). In *Racism and Black Resistance in Britain* I describe some of these conflicts, including the Imperial Typewriters dispute. In this case white workers were organised against Asian workers who were therefore forced to organise as an Asian workforce, relying on the resources of the Asian community rather than their unions (Moore, 1975).

Perhaps it is a mistake to try to find one answer to the question of where blacks are located in the class structure. It is a very complex and vigorously contested theoretical question. 'On the ground' we have to accept highly contingent situations with colour, class, ethnicity and perhaps gender providing the bases for action.

Phizacklea and Miles referred, as we have seen, to racial exclusion. The idea of exclusion features in the analysis by Frank Parkin referred to at the beginning of this section (Parkin, 1979). Parkin explains social closure as, 'the process by which social collectivities seek to maximise rewards by restricting access to resources and opportunities to a limited circle of eligibles' (p. 44). Race, language and social origin all form the basis for closure against outsiders. Closure operates *downwards* by creating categories of less eligibles or inferiors who are denied access to (usually economic) opportunities. We are familiar with this in terms of social class and the institutions of exclusion in the UK.

The excluded may respond by trying to *usurp*, or take away, the privileges of the excluding group. In its most extreme form a politically powerless class forms a political party with the intention of wresting power from the power-holders. This could lead to revolutionary change. The structures of power are themselves transformed. But the powerless may find their power limited, even when they are organised, and thus only be able to *modify* their position by using such power as they have. Although they may only be able to negotiate improved circumstances, this nonetheless entails taking some power away from power-holders who would not concede voluntarily. The basic structures of power, however, remain the same. This latter, non-revolutionary, outcome is what has been acheived by most trade unions and the Labour movements of Europe. But these working-class movements often find exclusion easier than usurpation.

According to Parkin, class in its Marxist sense is one important example of exclusionary closure – namely that based upon the expropriation of surplus value. But excluded classes may also practice exclusion themselves and this is the case of the European working classes *vis-à-vis* migrants. Governments created the conditions for the development of the excluded class by making migrants relatively rightless.

In most respects it is simpler to keep down those who are already weak and below you in the power structure than it is to take power from those above you. Being in work and earning a living wage has been the experience of most post-war European workers. It is a privilege of a kind – and seems even more so today. But maintaining privilege means that few others share it. The mechanisms that were formed to win a measure of advantage for the disadvantaged become instruments for excluding the even less advantaged. This explains why European trade union and Labour movements did so little to encourage migrant workers to join them and why it became easy for migrants to be defined as an economic threat. They could be seen as potentially undercutting wages (a traditional role for a migrant) and doubly threatening because they were non-union labour. Actually this latter point is far from the truth – can you explain how such a stereotype took hold?

Parkin points out that the state which first excluded and made minorities vulnerable faces a problem if it then wishes to incorporate the minority into civil society (p. 96). Eugene Dionne (1982) carries this line of argument further into its practical outcome in the politics of the USA and the UK. In the 1960s and 1970s racial discrimination (other than that practised by the state in its immigration policies) became defined as a problem – in part (and especially in the USA) because blacks were beginning to demand equality. The problem was defined largely by white middle-class people who saw discrimination as irrational and leading to conflict as well as being inherently 'unfair'. To preserve social tranquillity racial equality must be assured. But equality had never been on the British political agenda before and it was simply wrong to argue that race relations reform entailed extending the equal opportunities enjoyed by whites to blacks.

In response the poor and excluded whites say 'What about us – you never promised us equality?' Thus policies of racial equality are seen as reverse discrimination, favouring the blacks. A policy of positive discrimination raises the issue even more acutely: why has there been no positive discrimination in favour of working-class children in education, or 'equal opportunity' provision in employment? The potential for conflict is even more acute when the economy is declining, unemployment rising and the social services shrinking. Race thus threatens the political consensus in which the native population has learnt to accept as legitimate a relatively high degree of inequality.

Race promises to put equality upon the political agenda but what has happened in the UK according to Dionne is that voters who traditionally vote Labour for economic reasons started to switch to the Conservatives because of their hostility to immigrants whom Labour seemed to be favouring. The Labour Government under Wilson and Callaghan responded not by tackling the whole question of social inequality but by adopting policies to defend the economic standards of employed working-class men – their political base – and entering into a 'Dutch auction' with the Conservatives over who could be tougher on black immigration. Traditionally the Labour Party has neglected the very poorest, just as the trade unions have neglected the unemployed and ununionised. How could either defend blacks therefore and hope to hold its traditional support?

The work of Parkin and Dionne has led us from class to politics, but it is important to understand the connections. We might ask ourselves how adequate Dionne's analysis is, does it enable us, for example, to make sense of Labour governments both attacking the citizenship rights of blacks and legislating against racial discrimination?

From integration to criminalisation

In the previous section we saw how sociologists might analyse the position of blacks in the class structure and how the issues raised might have put equality on the political agenda. We also know that this did not happen, for the reasons outlined. If blacks are not to be equal, how are they to be treated?

Politicians have left the public in no doubt about this. Tina Wallace and I have described this in our evidence to the Scarman enquiry:

> From the mid-1960s onwards discussion of immigration was dominated by 'the numbers game'. The most important feature of this was that each party tried to show how it had been more successful than the other in reducing the number of Commonwealth immigrants entering the United Kingdom. This concern with numbers later extended beyond new immigrants coming into Britain to the number of dependents entering and even to the number of births to black families in Britain. It also inspired a public debate about illegal immigration and the numbers of clandestine entrants. Both the legislation and the tone of its enactment has threatened the black community. A clear and resounding message has gone out, that Britain does not want black people – regardless of party. The message is unambiguous and threatening . . .
>
> Moore and Wallace, 1981, p. 1.

The effect of this on officials in their dealings with blacks is serious enough. Its effect upon an uncritical popular press will be seen below. But the effects upon the police has been even more significant:

> Given the pattern of legislation and especially the attitudes expressed by leading politicians, it is hardly surprising that many members of the police force see themselves as a last line of defence against the threatening horde of black invaders. When the police define their role as one of defending Britain against a threat they are clearly able to justify to themselves discriminatory and rough handling of those who constitute the threat.
>
> Moore and Wallace, 1981, p. 6.

The police involvement in the process of immigration control and checking on blacks in Britain has led to passport raids, and checking the citizenship status of the victims of crime. Reports of violence against blacks and heavy policing (over-reacting to minor incidents usually with a great show of force) are now widespread and commonplace (Institute of Race Relations, 1979; London Borough of Lambeth, 1981; Humphry and John, 1971; Humphry, 1972).

It was probably such heavy policing that sparked the disturbances in Bristol. The mishandling of a minor matter turned into a wider conflict on the streets. Since the early 1970s however juries have shown themselves less than ready to convict, especially when police evidence has been inadequate, confused or possibly fabricated. The first most important acquittals were in the Mangrove case in December 1971. This has been followed by attacks on the jury system and the question 'Can you get an unbiased jury in a black area?' When the police ask this question they have usually meant 'Can we be sure of getting a conviction?' There are tactics to deal with this, like bringing charges at a level just below that entitling the accused the trial by jury. How the charges were tried after the Southall police riot can be seen in the NCCL report (National Council for Civil Liberties, 1980a).

It is relatively easy for a sociologist to understand how conflict between blacks and the police has arisen, and in the 1960s senior police officers were also aware of the hazards that lay in the future and have now been realised. A very useful sociological concept is that of 'criminalisation' (Becker, 1963; Cohen, 1972; Young, 1972). Let us take a simple example: suppose the suburban police concentrated their efforts upon offences against the Litter Act, and minor motoring offences (dirty windscreens, empty washer bottles, and so on). Many people would be charged and prosecuted – thus providing statistical evidence of a crime wave in the area. More police would be drafted in and more crimes detected. Eventually the locals would begin to object, and argue or answer back when apprehended. Arguments might lead to blows and arrests for offensive language, resisting arrest, threatening or assaulting police officers. Faced with this tidal wave of crime and a press outcry about 'crime on the streets' the police would have to concentrate even more resources in the suburbs and perhaps call out the Special

Patrol Group . . . . Of course the police do not behave in this way in suburbia. But a similar *process* takes place in areas where blacks ('the alien wedge') are to be found on the streets. Until recently the 'Sus' laws usually provided the basis for stopping and arresting and creating a crime wave. Street robbery with violence when practised by black youths was redefined as 'mugging' and thus mugging became a black crime. For a detailed account of the development of mugging as a (black) crime and public and media responses to it see Hall *et al.*, (1978).

The 'fact' that blacks are involved in a crime wave justifies police actions and attitudes. The best known recent outcome was seen in 'Operation Swamp' in Brixton when plain clothes and uniformed officers saturated the streets in a stop and search operation which was a major contributory factor in the Brixton riots. The police were criticised for this action and there have been demands since for more accountability of police forces, especially the Metropolitan Police. In what looks like a deliberate attempt to orchestrate public opinion the Metropolitan Police replied by publishing criminal statistics in which about 5 per cent of crimes (robbery with violence) were broken down by the race of the offenders (not, for example, by the offenders' social class, employment status or housing conditions). Such data when treated in headlines like 'Black Crime: the Alarming Figures' help to reinforce the equation Black = Crime which would enable the police to resume the heavy policing criticised by Scarman and others. Asked to justify this treatment of part of the crime figures a senior police officer said that it was in response to public disquiet. What he did not say was that the press had for some weeks built up public disquiet through the use of data selectively 'leaked' to them by the police (Pierce 1982). For many, if not most blacks, the image of the police uppermost in their minds is that of hundreds of uniformed officers escorting Martin Webster on his one-man racist march. The experience of Asians with the police are described and analysed in *Racism and Black Resistance in Britain* (Moore, 1975, Chapter 4).

In response to this account it could be said that blacks are simply on the receiving end of treatment that has always been meted out to the poor and deprived. They are now the victims of rapid inner-city decay and dislocation (Community Development Project, 1977). In other words, this is still a class issue, not a race one. To raise this question, however, is rather different from asking whether blacks will integrate or be assimilated; the debate has to be located in the context of institutionalised social conflict. Three points could be raised in the discussion; firstly, is it accidental that blacks occupy this alleged class position? Secondly, would criminalisation have been so easy had the state adopted a different stance on non-white immigration? Thirdly, however much of the argument about class one may concede, does not race remain an added and unique element which amplifies and intensifies the conflict?

This final section underlines the point made by Parkin that the state provides the framework in which the working class practises exclusionary policies against minorities. If minorities are not only excluded but regarded as actually or potentially criminal then the ground is prepared for even more extreme mobilisation against them. If they are *racial* minorities then it is relatively easy for racist and neo-Nazi groups to seek recruits. But it is not the National Front or similar organisations that created the conditions in which they themselves flourish. The rise of fascism, increased violence and the development of a stronger state, with a general loss of civil liberty and human freedom may already be on the Research agenda for British sociologists.

Suggestions for further reading

There is no single text which gives an adequate introduction to problems of race, racism and immigration.

Guides to the literature

There are two good guides to the literature:

Madan, R. (1979), *Coloured Minorities in Great Britain: a Comprehensive Bibliography 1970–77*, (London: Aldwych).

Walters, H. (1976), 'Guide to the literature on race relations in Britain, 1970–1975', *Sage Race Relations Abstracts*, vol. 1, no. 2, pp. 97–105.

On immigration, race and racism

Hiro, D. (1971), *Black British, White British*, (London: Eyre and Spottiswoode) is a good introduction to the immigrants and their history. This may be read with Watson, J. (1979) (ed.), *Between Two Cultures*, (Oxford: Basil Blackwell) and Wilson, A. (1978), *Finding a Voice*, (London: Virago).

For a very useful book of readings see Husband, C. (1982)(ed.), *'Race' in Britain*, (London: Hutchinson).

Resources

Sage Race Relations Abstracts besides providing an abstracting service also publishes bibliographical articles on a wide range of topics within the field and it therefore should be consulted.

Book reviews and lists of books received should be consulted in *New Community* and *Race and Class*.

The Runnymede Trust's Race Relations Bulletin (monthly) provides 'facts and figures', reports of current events, documents, and other current information.

Students should regularly peruse the following journals: *Race Today*, *Race and Class* and *New Community* which should be available in public libraries.

Teachers might like to read the journal *Ethnic and Racial Studies*, and Street-Porter, R. (1978), *Race, Children and Cities*, (Milton Keynes: Open University Press) which might raise useful questions about their wider objectives in teaching race relations.

For information write to:
Commission for Racial Equality, Elliot House, 10–12 Allington Street, London SW1E 5EH.
The Institute of Race Relations, 2–6 Leeke Street, King's Cross Road, London WC1X 9HG.
The Race Today Collective, 74 Shakespeare Road, London SE24 OPT.
The Runnymede Trust, 37A Grays Inn Road, London WC1.

Questions for discussion

1 How important are *class*, *race* and *gender* in understanding social inequality in contemporary Britain – are they mainly distinct or overlapping factors, for example? Do they operate in a sufficiently open and public way for you to be able to put together a dossier of material dealing with them?

2 Do you agree with the view that understanding race and race conflict is a matter of *instinct* and therefore not amenable to sociological analysis?

3 This chapter might be thought to be unsympathetic to the police. How would you reinterpret the evidence from a policeman or policewoman's point of view and what problems of organisation and attitudes would you indentify for the police in their relations with the black community? Discuss how, if at all, these problems could be resolved in the *mutual* interests of the police and the community.

Chapter 6

Oil mills and ironing: understanding Third World development

Janet M. Bujra

Everyone has some idea of what development means, because 'development', like many other terms used in the social sciences, is a word we use in everyday conversation, with the rather vague and general meaning of progress or change. It is when we try to define what it means in particular situations that problems arise. Change which is seen as progress by some may be experienced as deprivation by others. An all-round improvement in the conditions of people's lives is very difficult to achieve, and the means to securing it are a source of much disagreement amongst social scientists, planners and politicians. I want to look at this debate in relation to the Third World, looking first at general issues, then considering two specific case studies of development in Africa.

Let me begin by giving you an example of *how* differently 'development' can be defined by people who are caught up in the process of change. This example draws on a case study of a conflict between the Government and villagers in one region of Senegal in West Africa (Adams 1982). Most Third World Governments these days are eager to promote 'development', but the Senegalese Government's conception of what would be good for the villagers, *and* count as 'progress' for the country, came up against the villagers' own ideas and plans for change. For the villagers, 'development' meant *working for themselves but cooperating together in new ways* to produce more. 'That's what I call development', said one of their leaders: 'free, independent small farmers working together'. Government officials had quite other ideas: 'Without

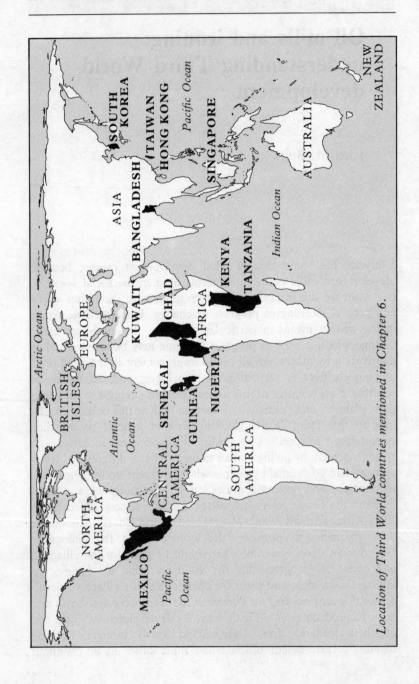

Location of Third World countries mentioned in Chapter 6.

government control', they insisted, 'there is no development . . .You need *modern technology* . . .It is to be hoped that God will help us to be like Europe or America' (my emphases).

The only thing that everyone agreed on here was that 'development' meant greater material prosperity and that this in its turn meant higher levels of production. The Senegalese are not the only ones who define development in this way – indeed we could say that the predominant meaning of development these days is 'economic growth' or increasing the capacity of a given country or region to produce more goods per worker, per unit of time. It is certainly true that countries vary considerably in their level of economic development, or productive capacity. One way in which this is measured is by dividing the annual value of total production in a country by its population size – a measure called *per capita GNP* (Gross National Product). The World Bank produces a league table along the lines of Table 6.1 which enables us to see the stark contrasts between countries like Bangladesh and Chad where the average person survives on around £200 a year, and the very richest countries like the USA or West Germany with average annual incomes in excess of £20,000 – or Kuwait, the richest of all in these terms, over £35,000 per person per year!

Measuring levels of economic development in this way is something about which development experts disagree[1], but everyone

Table 6.1: League of GNP

country	GNP per capita in US dollars: 1979
Bangladesh	90
Chad	110
Tanzania	260
Senegal	430
Nigeria	670
United Kingdom	6,320
United States	10,630
Germany, Fed. Rep.	11,730
Kuwait	17,100

Source: adapted from World Bank 1981, Table 1.
Approximate sterling equivalents above are at 1979 values.

concurs in the view that development should mean less poverty and deprivation in the world. It is only in the last hundred years that humankind has been able to conceive of *planning* to eradicate poverty. Before that, economic change and development certainly took place, but its benefits were enjoyed by only a tiny minority in society, whilst for the unnumbered millions, economic change was something which simply 'happened' and over which they had no control.

If, in the world today then, development is generally defined as *planned economic change*, then you might be forgiven for thinking that the relevant experts would be economists. What (I suspect you are thinking) could a sociologist possibly add to the solid facts of economics? It is true that the economists have invented very useful indices by which economic development may be measured (like the proportion of the national product devoted to manufacturing, the growth of domestic investment relative to consumption, productivity levels, capital intensivity and debt servicing ratios) but when it comes to prescribing how to *achieve* development, the economists are as divided as the rest of us! In development studies, sociology is to be seen as one partner amongst many in what is essentially an interdisciplinary exercise, bringing together economists, geographers, political scientists, lawyers, engineers, historians and students of culture. The special claim which sociology makes in this collective enterprise is that it takes a *broader view* of development than any of the other disciplines, and that it looks beyond surface events and phenomena to uncover underlying relationships. For example, a sociologist would argue that the 'hard', 'objective' indices of the economists were merely abstract ways of talking about *social relationships*; some equal, some unequal – relations for example between producers and consumers, between farmers and the Government, between industrial workers and their employers. Moreover sociologists would insist that these are not the only kinds of social relations relevant to understanding the course of economic development – that one might have to look as well at relations between husbands and wives, between political parties, or between devotees of one religion as opposed to another. Social relations of these kinds, whether enduring or in a state of flux, exert a profound influence on the process of economic change, in some cases limiting its scope and dictating its objectives, in other cases smoothing its path and generating new goals.

Like other theorists of development, sociologists aim for explanation, not for its own sake, but in the expectation that better understanding will yield better results in the real world. Like other theorists they eschew simple solutions. Let me give you two examples of such instant panaceas. The first is the suggestion that what is needed to promote development is – as was argued by the Senegalese officials quoted above – the introduction of 'modern technology'. It is not difficult to show, with specific examples, that modern technology – by which we mean machine production, automation – may in some cases lead to economic difficulties rather than development. For example, when Canada offered Tanzania a fully-automated bread factory, its costly buildings were more suited to a cold than to a hot climate, its projected output threatened existing small bakeries in the capital employing two hundred people, and this complex machinery entailed continuing Tanzanian dependence on Canada for spare parts and technological know-how (Coulson, 1979, pp. 179–183). Some years ago the Americans donated an up-to-date fish processing factory to Somalia designed to process forty tonnes of fish and lobster a day. Unfortunately local fishermen, whose fishing boats were dhows or dugouts, were catching only a fraction of that amount. Consequently the factory ran at far less than capacity, whilst generating heavy bills for maintenance and repairs (MacManus, 1978).

Modern technology does of course offer higher levels of output per worker given the right context, but it can be quite inappropriate where relatively unskilled labour is in abundant supply whereas technicians and spare parts are not, and where the technology itself has to be expensively imported. Even where this is not the case, one still has to ask: who is going to benefit from increased production? The answer can be disconcerting, as we shall see presently.

The second example of instant solutions is the idea that *money*, especially in the form of foreign aid, can solve the problems of economic backwardness. Guinea, in West Africa, has borrowed on a large scale from socialist countries but has achieved little in the way of industrialisation or raising the standard of living of its people. Mexico's heavy borrowing from western countries caused a crisis in the world banking system in 1982 when she was unable to keep up interest payments. And whilst Mexico is now generally described as a 'newly industrialising' country, it is also the case that 'the gap between rich and poor in Mexico is one of the most flagrant in the entire Third World' (*World View 82* p. 130). Conversely countries like Singapore, Hong Kong and Taiwan have become highly industrialised with relatively small amounts of foreign aid. Sociologists would argue that an explanation of these very different outcomes requires an examination not only of the economic structures of the individual countries but also of their political, cultural and social systems and an understanding of their historical development.

As the examples offered above show, the concern with economic development is today generally directed towards Third World countries. As a global issue, however, it first surfaced in the attempt to rebuild the shattered economies of Western Europe after the Second World War. Nowadays sociologists are to be found working in many international development agencies which had their origins in that post war period – bodies as diverse as the World Bank, UNESCO, the International Labour Office, the World Health Organisation or the various relief agencies. And the sociology of development is becoming an ever more popular academic subject.

Let me now give you an example of the kind of questions which are raised in sociological studies of development. I draw here on work carried out by a Nigerian social historian, Anthony Nwabughugu (1982). By uncovering long-forgotten episodes in colonial history, Nigerians are demonstrating that the past may have a message for future development planning.

Women say no to oil mills in colonial Nigeria

Oil palm trees produce many useful things. From their fruit comes fibre for fuel and oil which is used for cooking, whilst its kernels and oil may be processed to make soap, margarine, candles and cosmetics. Oil palm products are part of everyday life in Nigeria, being used in the home and bought and sold by local traders. Since the nineteenth century they have also been exported to Europe in response to an increasing demand for vegetable oils. By the early twentieth century Nigeria was one of the world's most important exporters of palm products, and before the discovery of vast reserves of fuel oil in the 1960s they were one of Nigeria's major exports.

Attempts by the colonial Government to expand the production of palm oil and kernels date back to the 1920s, when it was under pressure from British firms involved in the trade who saw their interests threatened by competitive production in the East Indies. The establishment of oil mills to process the fruit by mechanical means seemed an obvious means to improve both the quality and the quantity of exportable palm products, whilst also augmenting Government revenue. Early initiatives foundered on the reluctance of entrepreneurs to risk capital in setting up mills; later attempts confronted quite a different problem.

Between 1948 and 1950, when oil mills were at last being built, there were extensive riots in the areas affected – riots led by women. Hundreds of women, singing, dancing, and chanting 'We are as strong as iron', drove away labourers on the oil mill sites, set fire to buildings and damaged tools. When their leaders were arrested they marched to the prison, overpowered police, released the prisoners and set fire to the Native Court. Nor were these women prepared to listen to those notables of their own communities recognised by the British as 'native officials' – indeed they assaulted two such men in the course of the riots. A colonial official reported in alarm that: 'It is becoming increasingly obvious that with projects such as Pioneer Oil Mills . . . the women must be consulted. They are the greatest potential source of trouble in the villages and are well organised' (quoted Nwabughugu, p. 77).

Why did women react with such hostility to modern technology? It was in fact women who had always processed the oil palm fruits by hand. They depended on palm produce not only to supply their own families, but also, by selling kernels and some of the oil to traders, to earn a cash income independent of their husbands. 'Any attempt to deprive them of this right', they insisted, 'will be visited with anger' – anger against the authorities whose plans for the mechanisation of processing threatened women's livelihood, and anger against their menfolk, even husbands, who collaborated with the Government's scheme. Where women did not attack the mills they refused to supply them, or allow men to supply them, with palm fruit. In the end, the violence of the women's response led to the collapse of the Government's scheme. As Nwabughugu concludes, 'In a short time many of [the mills] fell into disuse, leaving the traditional method of extraction and the hand presses dominant in the oil production in Eastern Nigeria' (p. 79).

As an abstract economic plan the Government scheme had much to recommend it – large-scale, automated production of a time-consuming and tedious hand process. But to be successful, plans for mechanisation must be appropriate not only to goals but to context. In the end, the coercive power of Government (colonial officialdom with its police and its courts and its 'native' function-aries) was pitted against the solidarity of 'well organised' women. Women's intransigence here was effective not only because their individual economic interests were threatened. The pre-existing relations *between* women, as kinsfolk, neighbours and friends, often engaged in mutual help in production and trading, were a source of political as well as economic strength. At the time, colonial officials were inclined to blame this failure on poor communication and to talk of the need to keep up 'the propaganda'. The fact is that there was *no* discussion of the plans with those most likely to be affected, women. Women's work, mostly carried on at home, was 'invisible' to colonial officials, until women exposed it by their anger.

Failure to communicate is often a factor when development plans go astray. In the Senegalese example quoted earlier this took an extreme form – Senegalese officials could not speak the language of the peasants they aimed to persuade, and were forced to use the ex-colonial language, French, and an interpreter! A failure to inform or to discuss plans with those affected, or *their* failure to listen or to comprehend, is in fact symptomatic of underlying differences of interest over the question of development. Women in Eastern Nigeria aimed to defend their only source of income; improving the quantity and quality of palm products so as to boost exports was a matter of indifference to them if they were to be forced out of production. To the Government, however, and to a loose alliance of other interests (mill owners, export financiers) this was the central concern. Clearly, when we talk about 'development' in the sense of *producing more*, we have to ask: who will benefit by the increase in production?

The colonial Government saw the expansion of exports as the key to economic development in Nigeria. Many independent governments have taken the same line, promoting the traditional Third World exports of basic raw materials and foodstuffs in order to pay for the capital goods (machinery etc.) with which to create an industrial base.[2] Meanwhile, one of the most heated debates in development studies has centred on the extent to which international trade benefits the Third World. On the one hand there are those who point to Taiwan or South Korea as success stories in the push for 'export led growth'. Critics of this view argue that it is primarily via international trade that developed capitalist nations exploit the Third World, selling manufactured goods to it dearly and buying its raw materials cheaply. Colonialism was the political shell within which this unequal relationship developed, but it has outlived the demise of empire. Such theorists talk of 'export dependency' creating 'underdevelopment', and may argue that 'self reliance' is a better recipe for real development.

In accepting that development is primarily a process of economic change then, sociologists insist that it is not just an economic question. Economic change cannot usefully be considered in isolation from wider issues – of political power within and between nations, of cultural differences, social inequalities and the relations between men and women. I want to offer you a second example of this broader view that sociologists pursue – this time taken from field research that I am planning to do myself in Tanzania. This will also give you an idea of the way in which sociologists of development carry out their work.

Domestic service in Tanzania

Tanzania is a country with which I am already familiar, having previously carried out research there and having taught at the University of Dar es Salaam. I also speak the national language (Swahili) reasonably fluently. This research is designed to explore one aspect of a more general issue: the new forms of social relationship which accompany processes of economic development. The two major kinds of social relationship with which I shall be concerned here are the relations between men and women and between social classes. Having stated the general problem you may be rather surprised to hear that what I am actually going to study is domestic servants in one of Tanzania's larger towns. Let me explain how these larger issues can be illuminated from this particular perspective.

In the colonial period, when Tanzania was under British rule, there was very little in the way of industry, but workers were in demand for the country's small plantation sector, for jobs in the docks and on the railways and at the lowest levels of the administration, and to work as domestic servants. Tanzania was basically an agricultural country, however, and agriculture was dominated by independent small peasant farmers, producing primarily for their own livelihood. The main burden of work on peasant farms was shouldered by women – all the hoeing and planting and weeding and most of the harvest work too. Men had their specific tasks – mainly work like ground clearing, house building, keeping wild animals away from the crops and so on. But women's labour was more vitally required over a longer period than men's, and hence, when taxes were imposed on the African population, forcing them to earn cash incomes, it was not women but men who went off· to be migrant workers. And when Europeans wanted servants there were only men around to employ.

Since independence in 1961, Tanzania has aimed to develop both its industries and its agriculture. This has meant an intensification of work for women on peasant farms, and an increasing sense of resentment amongst women at all the burdens they have to shoulder – increased cultivation as well as child rearing, cooking, carrying water and home care. Tanzanian sociologists have suggested that it is this resentment which is behind an increase in the number of women beginning to migrate to towns (Mascarenhas and Mbilinyi 1983, p. 122). In addition young women are beginning to accompany husbands to town whereas previously they would have remained behind. In towns they seek ways of supplementing their husband's fairly low wages. It is in this situation that there has begun to be a shift towards a female labour force in domestic service.

Now why should this change be of interest to me as a sociologist, and what relevance does it have to the question of economic development? In all societies we know of, men and women play different parts or roles. Thus in our society we expect miners to be men and nurses to be women, and we are disconcerted when men want to be midwives, and shocked when we read how women toiled underground in the early part of the nineteenth century. If there is one kind of work we associate above all with women, it is work in the home, or what I call the 'Three Cs' – cooking, cleaning, and caring for children and other members of the family. When women go *out* to work, we most commonly find them doing similar tasks. This is why we are not surprised to find that the vast majority of domestic servants in nineteenth century Britain were women (Burnett 1974, p. 136) – that seems both 'natural' and obvious to us.

However, to say that in all societies men and women play different roles does not mean that exactly the *same* sexual division of labour pertains. One example of a pattern very unfamiliar to us is found amongst the Kikuyu people of Kenya, where women carry all the heavy loads and men are believed to be physically less capable of doing so.

Finding men as domestic servants, cooks and cleaners in Africa is surprising to us, but at least in this case we can understand *how* the unfamiliar practice came about – it evidently had to do with the pre-existing sexual division of labour in agriculture which meant that in the colonial period men were 'free' to travel to search for paid work whereas women were not. But having recognised that men can, in certain circumstances, do domestic jobs, we are led to think again about our assumption that domestic work is 'naturally women's work'.

This brings us to consider the matter in quite a different light and to ask where people get the *skills* to do certain jobs. We assume, if not that women are *born* caring or home-making people, then at least that these capacities are a consequence of their upbringing. Now Tanzanian men are not born with an aptitude for dusting or washing up, nor did their mothers teach them these skills. So where did they get them? The fact is that they had to be learnt on the job. At this point it is as well to consider whether their mothers *could* have helped them to acquire the requisite skills. In colonial Tanzania the employers of servants were mainly Europeans, though sometimes Arabs or Asians. *Their* domestic routines and technologies were far removed from those with which people from Tanzanian villages were familiar. So in fact, no matter what sex these earliest domestic servants had been, they would still have had to *learn* skills such as ironing or dusting, or cooking strange foods in strange utensils on strange stoves. The skills of the job were not simply *transferred* from the home situation to the work situation. Now this is something we might not even have thought about if women had always done this work in Tanzania as they did in Britain.

By extension we cannot assume that Tanzanian women are becoming domestic servants *now* because they are more 'naturally' able to do the work – we need to find some other explanation. Various ideas suggest themselves. On the one hand the availability of female labour may have increased, consequent upon changes in the agricultural sector. On the other hand the standing of domestic service relative to other jobs may have declined, creating a shortage of male workers. Domestic service has always been viewed as a demeaning occupation, allowing employers to exert a day-long control over servants' lives. But whereas in the past wages seem to have been comparable with those in other unskilled occupations, they are now abysmally low. Given the gradual expansion of other forms of employment with somewhat better wages and conditions, shifts of labour would be inevitable, and employers would be obliged to seek domestic servants from amongst those new to urban areas, unfamiliar with more industrial occupations and ignorant of comparative wages and conditions. Women are merely the newest wave of rural immigrants, fresh for exploitation.

Some of the data which I would need to test out these ideas will be available, in the form of national statistics on migration and occupational change, but (as I already know) these are very limited. So I shall be concentrating my effort on one urban area of Tanzania where domestic servants can be studied at first hand. By seeking out and making friends with these people, I can directly observe their lives and work, as well as finding answers to my questions. Were they born in the town or in some other area of Tanzania? What led them to leave home? Why did they seek work as a domestic servant? Who taught them to do the job? Under what wages and conditions are they employed? – and so on. Some of the questions I want to ask will emerge naturally in the course of ordinary conversation, others will have to be formulated more care-fully as part of a questionnaire or survey. The answers are interesting to sociologists for two reasons: firstly because they provide individual case studies which illustrate how people survive the vicissitudes of life; and secondly, by aggregating the replies, one can build up a general picture of servants' lives. The response of men and women servants *may* be quite different, which would help to develop my understanding of the general issue of sex-stereotyping in certain occupations.

I shall also be looking at the employers of domestic servants – and here we come to quite a different aspect of this study. The employers these days are only exceptionally Europeans – most of them are now Tanzanian Africans. When you get some people hiring, and others toiling as domestic servants you can be sure this is one manifestation of class distinction in society. Now Tanzania aims to be a socialist society which has no room for class inequalities – indeed its President, Julius Nyerere, has argued that 'traditional' (which is to say pre-colonial) African society was 'classless'. How is it then that in Tanzanian society today some people can afford to employ others to do household tasks for them?

A study like mine cannot of course answer this general question, but it can hope to illustrate certain aspects of the formation of different *'class cultures'* (ways of living and ways of understanding the world) in Tanzania. To what extent do the employing class here differentiate themselves from their servants, given that they may have similar rural origins? Let me give you two examples of the kind of behaviour I shall be looking at. First there are the domestic routines and technologies of the employers' homes – to what extent do they differ from those in servants' homes? As compared to 'servants' quarters', which usually consist of a single, bare room, employers' homes are obviously much bigger and they have more possessions (e.g. electric cookers and irons as compared to charcoal stoves and probably no iron). Are they also organised differently in the timing and level of performance of jobs like washing clothes and cleaning rooms and serving food? This question relates back of course to the issue of *skills* and where servants learn these, but it also raises the question of how the employing class sets its *standards*.

A second aspect of this question of class culture is the character of employer-servant relations. There is the tricky problem here of what sociologists call 'social distance' – the problem, in other words, of how servants, with whom the employing family lives in close proximity, are nevertheless 'kept in their place', discouraged from easy familiarity. The rationale offered for such aloofness is usually that over-familiarity encourages servants to 'take advantage' – in other words to become lazy and careless and perhaps to help themselves to the employers' property. My argument is that this rationale begins to be an ideological expression of class differences. 'Social distance' can be maintained by, for example, an insistence on respectful forms of address, a ban on 'idle chatter', a restriction of servants to certain parts of the house (generally the kitchen) for most of the day, and so on.

The member of the employer's family who generally has most to do with the servants is the woman of the household, which leads us to ask whether the solidarities of class and gender ever pull in opposite directions? Do mistresses feel more comfortable and familiar with female servants than with male? Do they have the same attitudes towards things domestic? Is there a sort of complicity set up between a wife and the female servant against the man who is husband and boss? Are there occasions on which this complicity must be denied and the class superiority of the mistress be reasserted?

You may be wondering what all this has to do with development – well, a lot more than might, at first sight, seem apparent! Firstly, if women's migration to towns in search of work begins to disrupt rural development schemes initiated by the Government, then these initiatives have to be rethought. It cannot simply be assumed that women will be ready to take on ever heavier burdens of agricultural work without fair reward. In many areas of Tanzania it is the established practice for men to sell the crops which women have produced, and for men then also to determine how the money is to be spent. Given this situation, men and women almost certainly have discordant views on what constitutes 'development'. Rural development efforts would be more successful if the extra tasks were more fairly shared, and women brought more effectively into decision-making and reward-sharing processes.

That is one side of the development question. The other side concerns the urban and industrial sector where labour migrants seek work. The existence of a category of domestic servants is not only an indicator of a class-divided society, it is also generally a society where industrialisation is in its early stages. The Tanzanians who employ servants are able to do so because servants' wages are extremely low (often much lower than the Government-specified minimum wage of just under £9 a week). People will work for these wages only when other more remunerative work is unavailable. Industrial jobs – in factories, workshops or mines, or in transport or the service sector – *are* better paid, but there are not enough of them to go round. Tanzania is not an industrialised society by any stretch of the imagination, and despite some modest expansion since independence, its industrial sector is still small. One of the most generally agreed characteristics of a 'developed' society is that it is industrialised. Women's work as domestic servants is thus a manifestation of the slow rate of economic development in Tanzania.

Other people's problems in far away places?

I want to end by asking why you or I should be concerned with questions of development in distant countries like Nigeria or Tanzania. One answer to this question might be that we cannot afford *not* to grasp at an understanding of what goes on in the Third World. Our world is contracting every day and we are vitally affected by events in far away places. One example of this was the effect on Britain and the world of the oil crisis of the 1970s, when Third World oil producers suddenly and drastically raised the price of crude oil. They did this in an attempt to improve their share in the profits from oil exploitation (previously enjoyed largely by Western multinational oil companies). The price rise sent shock waves through the oil-consuming economies whose industries had become dependent on supplies of cheap energy.

The second reason might be the way in which certain social phenomena in our own society are a direct consequence of *lack* of development elsewhere in the world. I am thinking here particularly of the immigration into Britain of unskilled workers from regions less industrially developed, like Ireland or the Caribbean or the Indian sub-continent. In periods when British industry was expanding, the immigration of such workers was quite economically advantageous to us, whilst in an earlier period the colonisation of these areas was also to our benefit. If we want to understand 'race riots' in Britain today, part of our answer must be sought in the background to immigration and in particular the way in which regions which are less developed tend to export labour to those which are more industrially developed (Robert Moore has more to say about this in Chapter 5).

The third answer might be that attempts to plan economic change are not simply a feature of Third World countries. Since the inter-war years the British Government has periodically funded the creation of variously named 'development areas' to encourage firms to establish themselves in regions of high unemployment and social deprivation. The idea is to give certain kinds of economic change a helping hand and to prevent other kinds of change occurring (regional economic decline with all its disastrous social consequences). So development planning also goes on in Britain and in other already industrialised countries, and the sociological insights which can be drawn from its study in Third World situations are very relevant to its practice at home.

Notes

1 Controversy focuses on the method of calculation and on the adequacy of the US dollar as a universal standard. More important, this mode of comparison ignores the differences between countries where income is distributed relatively evenly and those in which ordinary people suffer dire poverty whilst a tiny minority enjoy fabulous wealth (see question 1 below).

2 This, at least, is the rationale. In practice, given the unequal distribution of income in many Third World countries, much scarce foreign exchange is 'wasted' on importing luxury goods (e.g. cars, petrol, cosmetics, television sets) to satisfy the demands of the better-off.

Suggestions for further reading

Introductory texts often assume a familiarity with one or more of the disciplines which come together under the umbrella of development studies. It is better perhaps to start with a book that gives you an idea of how people in the Third World view their own lives such as Johnson H., and Bernstein H. (1982), *Third World Lives of Struggle*, (London: Heinemann/Open University). Roxborough, I. (1979), *Theories of Underdevelopment*, (London: Macmillan); is a relatively straightforward theoretical introduction whilst, Alavi, H. and Shanin, T. (1982), *Introduction to the Sociology of 'Developing Societies'*, (London: Macmillan); is a useful set of readings, some very dense and theoretical, others more readable.

Further reading on the two African case studies

Coulson, A. (1979), *African Socialism in Practice: the Tanzanian Experience*, (Nottingham: Spokesman).

Oyono, F. (1966), *Houseboy*, (London: Heinemann) (novel).

Review of African Political Economy (journal), Special issue on Nigeria, no. 13, (1979).

Rodney, W. (1972), *How Europe Underdeveloped Africa*, (London: Bogle L'Ouverture).

Shivji, I. (1976), *Class Struggles in Tanzania*, (London: Heinemann).

Williams, G. (1980), *State and Society in Nigeria*, (Nigeria: Afrographika).

Resources

UNESCO and the World Bank publish yearbooks containing useful statistics on Third World countries.

The journal the *New Internationalist* is a lively and readable introduction to both general and topical issues in development. Its stance is critical and radical. The *Guardian* newspaper includes a weekly page, 'Third World Review', which offers shorter articles, mainly from the same perspective. Information on particular Third World countries can be obtained from *embassies*.

The *Development Studies Association* (Secretary M. Veitch, Planning Centre for Developing Countries, University of Bradford, Bradford, West Yorkshire BD7 1DP) can advise on courses.

The Commonwealth Institute (Kensington High Street, London W8 69Q, Tel. 01 603 4535) and the Africa Centre (38 King Street, London WC2) mount exhibitions and cultural events.

Questions for discussion

1 Should we interpret the outcome of the oil mill scheme in colonial Nigeria as 'ignorant women standing in the path of progress'?

2 When and why did domestic service disappear in Britain?

3 See what you can discover about Hong Kong and its export-led growth. Would you describe Hong Kong as a developed country?

4 Several kinds of social inequality are mentioned in this chapter. After listing them, ask yourself what effect social inequality has on efforts to achieve economic development. Why do you think some writers argue that inequality actually promotes development?

Chapter 7

The sociology of health, illness and healing

Margaret Stacey

How I became involved

I became involved in the sociology of health and illness when I was what I would now describe as an unpaid health worker. I graduated as a sociologist in 1943 and was a mother of young children when the Platt Report (Ministry of Health, 1959b) on the welfare of children in hospital came out. That report suggested that mothers should go into hospital with their children to prevent the children suffering mental damage. As a young mother and a sociologist, I was fascinated about the progress of that report. It seemed to me to be a remarkably humane document, but it turned out that hospital staff were not really at all happy to have the mothers in the wards. The nurses in particular revolted against this. Parents, encouraged by psychiatrists (which is an interesting combination), formed voluntary pressure groups saying 'this report must be implemented: parents, particularly mothers, must be allowed into hospital with their children'. When I looked at the background to the report I realised that the psychology had been carefully researched, but not the sociology. The sociology of the family and what it would actually do to the rest of the family if the mother suddenly went into hospital with one child was ignored. There were no recommendations for anybody to replace her in the home. Nor did the report look at what the change would do for the division of labour in the ward, what it meant to the nurses to have the mothers there. These experiences and reflections led to the first series of studies in health and illness that I was involved in (Stacey *et al.*, 1970; Hall and Stacey, 1979).

So through children in hospital and my dual involvement as a mother and a sociologist I began research on the sociology of health and illness, and started the subject in University College, Swansea which did not have a medical school. Sociologists often get involved in research which relates to their positions in the world. Some of us are more open about it than others. Many of those people who researched the sociology of education in the 1950s had been upwardly mobile through the state educational system, but they did not make that very plain. Nowadays we are more prepared to confess our autobiographies and how they relate to the research we do (see Roberts, Chapter 10 and Burgess, Chapter 11).

Health and illness long ignored by sociologists

It is surprising that sociologists ignored health, illness, healing and medicine for so long. Social anthropologists recognised it earlier. The events of birth, death and suffering are central human experiences: the ways people in a society deal with these events are crucial to the social organisation of that society and to its belief systems. Different societies have a variety of arrangements tied up with birth. Nowadays we have all sorts of medical arrangements. All societies have ways of admitting people to membership such as christenings or going down to the registrar's office to turn the newborn into citizens; in all societies death involves social observances to mark that somebody has left the group. Suffering, whether of the mind or body, is treated in every society some way or another.

Healing in other societies and our own

Societies understand and treat suffering differently, classify sufferings in different ways and have different kinds of healers. The Gnau (of the south-west Pacific) that Lewis (1976) has talked about have really no clear divisions of labour except between the sexes and no clearly separate healers. They have nothing like doctors, nurses, opticians, dentists. If a Gnau thinks s/he is ill s/he just lies in the dirt or in a darkened hut, covered with dust and ashes, speaking in a lowered tone: that is to say 'I am ill'. Then people come and minister to the afflicted. It is no *one* person's responsibility to come; usually but not necessarily members of the family come. Whoever comes, they make the incantations, collect the herbs, do whatever needs doing to help the person who is suffering. They do not examine the patient; they take the patient's word for it that s/he is ill. The patient decides when s/he is better and then gets up and washes and rejoins the group.

Illness among the Gnau is usually caused by the hostile actions of neighbours or is a consequence of offending the sprits in some way. The illness behaviour is to cheat the spirits so that they think the patient is really dead. You will notice there are no specialist healers at all, the patients make up their minds whether they are ill or not and also when they are better. None of this going to the doctor as we do saying 'I think I'm ill, do you? And what is wrong?'. The issue of malingering, of cheating, of pretending you are ill when you are not, to get off work or school, simply does not arise.

That is a big contrast with the way we do things, but this example of an undifferentiated society shows how tightly illness and healing are tied in to the social organisation. It illustrates the first socio-logical principle that the way these major events of birth, death and suffering are dealt with is linked to the organisation of the society as a whole. Given that, it is really surprising that sociologists were so slow off the ground to look at these institutions.

It is also surprising for a second and quite different reason which is that in contemporary societies, in our society for example, the health industry is one of the largest employers of labour. This is true of the National Health Service (NHS) in Britain, of the European countries, and of the USA. Although American health services are fragmented in a variety of ways, together they amount to a really major industry: a unique industry that sociologists can no longer ignore.

Problems of studying a sacred area

One might hazard one guess why it took such a long time for sociologists to study health and healing: it is a really difficult area to research because it is a difficult area to be detached about. After all it is not easy to be objectve about the very people and the very scientific knowledge that you hope will save you when you have a serious accident or a serious illness, because we do put a great deal of faith in modern medicine. Historically it probably is the case that the sociology of religion really only developed when people's general faith in their religion was beginning to be shaken. There may be something similar about the sociology of health and illness. People are more sceptical about doctors nowadays, perhaps that has made it possible for us to be more inquisitive about healing.

Parsons' breakthrough

The founding fathers of sociology did not address the issue of medicine, or of health, illness and healing, at all extensively. (I say 'founding fathers' deliberately because sociology was founded by men and in the nineteenth century.) Durkheim looked at suicide, a very specific aspect of the many problems of health and illness, only one of the things that puts one at risk of death. Marx and Engels in looking at the conditions of the working class, looked at illness and suffering as part of their total misery and saw illness in terms of the development of capitalist industry and the associated urban developments.

Sociologists did not look systematically at problems to do with health and illness until the middle of the twentieth century. Talcott Parsons (1951) was the first major sociological theorist to look at medicine as a social institution. He was the first person to recognise that control of ill health was essential for the maintenance of the social system. He showed that if people are too ill too often, or (perhaps even worse) pretend to be ill when they are not ill, the social system will break down because people will not be producing goods and services. He talked about the way in which one can legitimately adopt the 'sick role' which includes an obligation to seek treatment and to get better. It is interesting that, although Parsons was writing in a capitalist society, sociologists in state socialist societies find the Parsonian analysis of the health system helpful. State socialist societies just as much as capitalist society are concerned to keep people in work and get them back to work. This link between continued productivity and ill health is there in both societies. That thought gives hints about why it is always difficult to get enough resources in the health service going to the non-productive, for example, to the elderly who are never going to produce again, to the severely handicapped, mentally or physically, who are never going to be able to produce (see Finch, Chapter 8 on the elderly). So Parsons was the first person who really looked at medicine, illness and treatment in relation to the functioning of the social system as a whole.

In Chapter 10 of *The Social System*, he provides good insights into what the health business is about. He recognises for example that the doctor/patient relationship is a sacred relationship, that it is subject to taboos (as religious practices are). This has to be the case because of the nature of the relationship. For example, we give doctors permission to investigate our minds and our bodies in ways that we would not even accord to our lovers (for example, while lovers may 'touch our hearts' they do not literally cut them open). We accord quite extraordinary intimacies to doctors and therefore the relationship has to be defined in some way as sacred, so that the social order may be sustained.

Parsons has been criticised for his failure to understand the historical development of the institutions of medicine, and their relationship to the class structure and the gender order, and also because his analysis is static. Particularly he has been criticised as an apologist for the medical profession. However, it has to be given to him that he recognised how important this area was about twenty years before other sociologists, and he began important debates and researches followed up for example by Freidson (1970).

Medicine: conservative or radical?

The point I would like to emphasise, and which Parsons saw, is that the institutions which are associated with medicine and with healing, not only reflect the kind of society that they are found in, but they also reproduce it, they are actively involved in keeping the society going the way it is. These institutions help to maintain the class structure, the gender order and the divisions between

experts and non-experts. But one can also argue, particularly now
that medicine really has got quite powerful tools at its command,
that the institutions associated with health and healing can originate
change, albeit perhaps insidious change. For example, in this
country we have had successive committees, composed mainly of
male doctors, making judgements about how and where childbirth
should take place (Ministry of Health (Cranbrook), 1959a; Department of Health and Social Security (Peel), 1970). Birth is symbol-
ically very important to any society, as well as being critical for the
individual mother and her family. In addition to upsetting a lot of
women, new medical arrangements for childbirth may create new
notions about what it is to be a citizen. If this is so people (in this
case doctors) who have got no real understanding of social relations
may be altering the future structure of the society by the arrangements they make. In another area, the debates about brain death
and keeping people alive on machines call into question what it is
to be a human being. Thus medical institutions not only reinforce
and keep going a society as it is but probably initiate change. We
have been insufficiently aware of this. Current developments in
fertility control, *in vitro* and *in vivo* fertilisation ('test tube babies')
and genetic 'engineering' whereby it may become possible to take
out genes from the foetus in the womb, alter and return them,
make it even more important to understand this (DHSS, 1984).

Sociology and social medicine

Sociology may have been late entering the area of health and
illness, but there is a long history of social medicine going back at
least to the early nineteenth century. It was associated with the
public health movement. Doctors were aware that there were social
facets to the ill health they had to deal with. They came to recognise
the importance of the environment, things like clean water and
clean air, and the safe disposal of rubbish and refuse. They also
thought about the importance of social relations. When they started
trying to stamp out venereal disease (VD) social relations could not
be avoided. In dealing with VD in the late nineteenth century
doctors began to make social maps of who had been with whom in
an effort to trace the origin of the disease in order to control it.

There has for long been a link between sociology and epidemiology. Epidemiology is that branch of medicine which deals with the distribution of disease in a population. It is distinct from clinical medicine which treats individual sufferers. Epidemiologists are interested in the prevalence and the incidence of diseases, for example, malaria, cholera and tuberculosis. Some years ago in a seminar Fred Martin used a marital metaphor to explain the rather uneasy relationship between sociology and medicine, especially epidemiology, social medicine or community medicine as it is now called. It is a terribly sexist way of expressing it but nevertheless he said medicine and sociology were joined at the outset in the post war period 'smiling in holy wedlock, but has it proved', he asked 'to be holy wedlock or wholly deadlock?' (Acheson and Aird, 1976, p. 17). He argued that in retrospect marital expectations had been fallacious from the beginning. No-one questioned that medicine was the male partner, kindly, benevolent but a bit of a chauvinist. However, he continued, it turned out that the bride was a dedicated member of the women's liberation movement and intended to spend her time in marriage not performing her duties along the lines laid down by her partner but in proclaiming the autonomy of sociology and denouncing medical domination. Be that as it may, one impetus for sociologists to study medicine came from social medicine.

Sociology and clinical medicine

Clinicians also played a part. By clinicians I mean the doctors who practice clinical medicine, who are concerned with healing in a one to one doctor/patient relationship (although of course they are backed up by many nurses, laboratory technicians and others, such as porters and domestics). Some of the clinicians began to 'court' sociologists. There have been changes in the nature of illness. Epidemic illnesses are largely controlled. Now many illnesses are long term and difficult to cope with. High-technology medicine has come in and clinicians have realised that there are social facets to this. So they have called in social workers to help them with the treatment and the management and they have called in sociologists to help them with the research. The sociology which resulted has since been referred to as sociology 'in' medicine, sociology being the 'hand maiden'.

Sociology and health administration

We have now moved on from there partly because there were other sources of encouragement. One came from the administrators who were principally concerned with mounting costs. In the NHS in Britain, in the national insurance systems in Europe and the private insurance systems in the USA, administrators were worried about rising costs. They were looking around for people who could help them to increase the effectiveness and the efficiency of the health service. They turned to various sorts of people, like operational researchers, but they also turned to sociologists.

Many sociologists had had a long-standing concern with administrative problems. They were concerned with equal opportunity and equal access to health services (see also Finch, Chapter 8). Brian Abel-Smith's history of the hospitals (1964) never really questions whether the development of modern medicine was a good thing, whether the development of the hospitals was a good thing. He assumes it was, although criticising corruption and inefficiency in hospitals. His theme is the increasing availability of hospitals to the mass of the people and how to make the hospitals competent and efficient. He represents the great concern with equal opportunity which is echoed contemporarily in the concentration on equality and inequality in health. Some of you will have heard about the Black Report (DHSS, 1980; Townsend and Davidson, 1982). It was written by a doctor, the then President of the Royal College of Physicians, that is, the most prestigious doctor in the country, along with a leading professor of social medicine and two sociologists. The report shows that we still have marked social class differences in the healthiness of the population. The gap between the working class and the upper class, as measured by the Registrar General's occupational scale, has not got any narrower since the welfare state began and may have widened. When it was published the Government were not sufficiently concerned to take action about the findings, nor are they today (1986). Nevertheless others continue to pursue a long-standing concern with equality and inequality in the health service, and with questions of common humanity.

A good deal of social science research is associated with these concerns; for example, the whole series of work Ann Cartwright has done in the Institute for Social Studies in Medical Care, about what patients felt like in hospital (Cartwright, 1964), about the new childbirth arrangements (Cartwright, 1979), about people hoarding their medicines and what happens then (Dunnell and Cartwright, 1972). Recently with Rob Anderson she compared what patients thought about general practice thirteen years ago with what they think about it now (Cartwright and Anderson, 1981). Although descriptive and totally a-theoretical her carefully representative excellent survey work is providing valuable cumulative data. Her work flows from the early interest in social justice, a school which continues and provides useful and important data.

Administrators as well as general practitioners and other health care professionals have been interested in the delivery of primary health care. Combining recent history with interview and observation Margot Jefferys led a team looking at the changes in general practice organisation in the NHS, the division of labour between doctors, nurses, health visitors and social workers and what the patients thought about it all (Jefferys and Sachs, 1983). This work adds dimensions lacking in strictly numerate survey work.

Patient protest

In the last 10 to 15 years a radical critique of the medical enterprise began to develop. To some extent the patients or their relatives got together and protested, as for example about children in hospital which I mentioned at the beginning of this chapter; parents of mentally handicapped children paying for research to be done is another (Morris, 1969). Cartwright's work provided a voice for the patient, but that is rather different from the patients providing their own voice. In the Cartwright work the patient's voice comes through paid interviewers and structured questionnaires.

Critiques of medicine

One early critique of medicine came from the deviancy movement (see Pearson (1975), *The Deviant Imagination*). Their concerns were mostly with mental illness and its treatment and link with ideas like Foucault's in *Madness and Civilisation* (Foucault, 1967). However, the first really systematic, theoretical radical critique of the medical enterprise came not from the sociologists as such, but from feminists, some of whom were also sociologists.

The feminist critique

Feminists such as Ehrenreich and English (1979), Gamarnikow (1978), Leeson and Gray (1978), Oakley (1981a), Ruzek (1978), Roberts (1981c), and Scully and Bart (1972–3) argued that the practice of medicine was an important instrument in the continued oppression of women. Feminists pointed out that medicine plays an important role in defining what it is to be a woman and how women should be treated: that a woman's notion of herself is redefined every time she visits her doctor. Her doctor has a high chance of being a man and 10 or 15 years ago this chance was even higher (Elston, 1977).

Ehrenreich and English (1974) wrote an exciting polemic (one of two from which their 1979 book developed) in which they show how in the nineteenth century upper-class women were said to be sick while working-class women were 'sickening'. Upper-class women had to be idle and were ill a lot of the time. Their well-to-do husbands paid the doctors many fees for attending their wives who were kept in this weak and dependent position. Working-class women on the other hand had to be tough. They could not go to bed when they had a period, they had to keep going, they had to carry the water, carry the coal, do whatever had to be done. They were sickening because they came from the slums, from the back-streets where disorder threatened and they brought death and disease with them when they entered the upper-class household. Their health was defined in a quite different way from the health of their well-to-do mistresses. Ehrenreich and English's work is not altogether as scholarly as one might like, but it gave a good jolt to male-dominated ideas of what medicine is about.

The neo-Marxist critique

Later again a radical critique emerged from the neo-Marxists. Much of this came from the USA, where the capitalist nature of the health industry is more obvious than it is in Britain. Neo-Marxists in the USA argued that the health empire (by which they understood the medical profession, the hospitals, the pharmaceutical and the hospital supplies industries) was deeply involved in the exploitation of the working class for profit. In some ways those neo-Marxists writing about health in the USA now are more like the early British Fabians than they are like European Marxists, as they are much concerned with social justice and the re-distribution of health and welfare services. A number of these strands emerge in a useful British book, Doyal with Pennell, *The Political Economy of Health* (1979), written from a neo-Marxist point of view but including some feminist concepts.

The cultural critique

More radical than critiques which focus on the distribution of health services are those, sometimes called 'cultural critiques' (see Ehrenreich, 1978), which challenge the efficacy of medical know-ledge and medical practice. Parts of the feminist critique do this as do critiques developed by those who judge alternatives to biomedi-cine to be less dangerous and more effective.

All these radical critiques came much later than the original development of the sociology of medicine.

The sociology of health and illness today

To sum up, the sociology of medicine, as it was then called, grew up under the patronage (and I use that word advisedly) of medicine and administrators and it grew rapidly. Beginning with small starts in the 1950s, it grew in the 1960s until it became the largest subsection of the British Sociological Association (BSA), with its own annual conference and its own journal. The change was demonstrated when in 1976 the BSA annual conference was devoted to the sociology of health and illness. Contrast this with the first sociological conference on health when almost all the papers were given by doctors. The position of the sociology of health and illness can now be said to be secured since the Rock Carling lecture normally given by a prestigious doctor, usually a clinician, was given by the sociologist Raymond Illsley (1980).

By now sociologists understand the importance of health and healing for social relations. The subject is taught in many sociology departments and outside medical schools. So sociology in medicine became the sociology of medicine, analysing medicine in the way it had long analysed education, industry, work and religion. It has now developed further, from the sociology of medicine to the sociology of health and illness or the sociology of health and healing. This reflects the major importance of many occupations in addition to doctors involved in health and healing. Although the doctors dominate the complex health division of labour they are numerically a small minority.

A rich field

So how to find one's way through the great deal of literature which is now available? There are contributions from every school of sociological theory (from Marxist to Weberian and feminist) and using every kind of method from interpretative to survey techniques and mixed observation and interview.

It is a difficult area as I hinted at the outset. It has a great advantage for study, which is also its great disadvantage: we all know a bit about it. Nowadays, all of us from the minute we are born, are involved in this great medically dominated, clinically dominated, health enterprise. Our birth is a medical event (this was not always so), our childhood is medically surveilled, including jabs at routine intervals, before school and during school life. We rapidly learn to go to the doctor the minute anything is wrong, to rely upon the doctor for advice as to whether we are really ill. We are all participant observers in this great enterprise and we mostly see it exclusively from the point of the patient unless we happen to be the daughters or sons of doctors or nurses. We have a considerable faith in modern medicine in some sense as in a religion. It is difficult to be detached about it.

How can we see medicine as a piece of socially constructed knowledge made by human beings, practised by human beings and historically specific? We do have to rely on the health service in times of need. Furthermore, there is a high emotional loading: we are all frightened of dying and frightened of being ill. This feature makes health and healing particularly difficult areas for sociologists to look at, but exciting and fascinating too. As sociologists we do have to see health knowledge and the organisation of health care as socially constructed, to examine what kinds of social relations are involved.

Cross-cultural and historical approaches

There are two separate ways in which we can begin to get some detachment. One is by looking at societies cross-culturally. I mentioned the example of the Gnau at the beginning of this chapter. Another way is historical, looking at how clinical medicine as we now understand it was established, how in the sixteenth and seventeenth centuries there were many different kinds of healers: bonesetters, tooth pullers, herbalists, empiricists, some of them women and some of them men; women who knew how to help others have babies, and how everybody, from highest to lowest in the land, believed in supernatural powers as well as in empirical powers. This was much like the situation in parts of the Third World now (Feierman, 1979). But, within a couple of hundred years biomedicine as we now understand it had become dominant. These changes went along with the rise of industrial capitalism. People like Jewson (1974; 1976) have shown how the knowledge and practices of doctors have changed. At first their medical knowledge was abstract, they were not at the patients' bedside. Doctors knew more about the stars than their patients' bodies. Later they developed bedside medicine and the patient became a 'case'. Later again the focus moved into the laboratory, where cells were sent for analysis. Now it was the disease and not the person that was looked at. Recently the medical gaze as Foucault called it has extended to social affairs (Armstrong, 1983).

Why did biomedicine dominate?

But there are puzzles. We are all inclined to attribute our better health, our longer lives to the successes of modern medicine. However, Thomas McKeown (for example 1971a; 1971b), a professor of social medicine, argues using carefully sifted evidence that this improvement in the nineteenth century was due to better standards of living, a cleaner environment, more food and family limitation so that there were fewer mouths to feed. He argues that it was not until the middle of the twentieth century that medicine began to have more than a few powerful weapons at its command at all. However, before this, in the nineteenth century, medicine managed to achieve a dominant social position. How? It seems that members of this occupation, who called themselves professionals, were able to persuade the bourgeoisie in the nineteenth century that they really had the message about good health and were worth special prestige and rewards because of that.

The likelihood is that it is only because of the deep social class divisions in the nineteenth-century society that modern medical knowledge ever developed at all. The nineteenth-century working class went into hospitals to be treated and provided the 'good clinical materials' on which the doctors could experiment and on which they could teach their pupils. Their upper-class patrons who previously had constituted the doctors' patients would not have permitted that kind of experiment. The movement of workers to towns led them to have recourse to hospital, so that the clinical material (that is, the patients) became available to the doctors. Here there seems to be another link between the development of capitalist industrial society and the development of modern medical knowledge and practice. In so far as we do now have an efficacious medical system which actually can make us better in a lot of ways, it is because of the work that was done in that deeply class-divided nineteenth-century society. Furthermore, the concepts of health and healing which were developed also fitted with that kind of society, with personal treatment of individuals, and with individuals being held responsible for their own health.

Revising the division of labour

In the early development of the sociology of health and illness study was concentrated first on the medical profession and later extended to other paid health workers and to the organisation of the hospital and of health care. I want to go back to sociological first principles of the division of labour and say we should go more widely still and be interested in the whole division of labour in health care, for there are more than paid workers involved (see Stacey, 1981, 1984). First we need to define what health is about. It is not just having jabs or getting cured when you are ill. It has to do with health maintenance as well as health restoration, with the care of the permanently impaired and care at the crucial points of birth and death. On such a definition we are all involved in health work all the time. All of us are in the business of maintaining our own health (or undermining it, depending on how well we look after ourselves).

Some people are also involved in looking after others although they are not necessarily paid to do it. At the University of Warwick we describe these people as unpaid health workers. Finch (Chapter 8 in this volume) also mentions the notion of unpaid workers. Some people are particularly designated as being unpaid health workers. Because of the gender order that we have in our society it is mostly the women, the mothers, who are the principal unpaid health workers. They are responsible for keeping the house clean, feeding the children and their husbands an appropriately balanced diet, understanding when professional care is needed, carrying out professional instructions. As Hilary Graham (1984) has shown mothers have a very considerable responsibility put upon them. They find themselves pulled apart as to whether they should have primary loyalty to their husband, or their children, their youngest child or their oldest child, as to which way their loyalties should go. They have quite a hard task relating to professionals too, who do not always value their experience sufficiently highly and do not always listen carefully enough to what they have to say. The difference between experience and expertise in the division of labour is an important one. All the paid workers, the doctors, the nurses, the physiotherapists, have been trained and have expertise of various amounts and of various kinds. As time goes on they also gain experience.

Unpaid health workers have a great deal of experience and experience of the particular patient (themselves or their relative). In *Medical Encounters* (Davis and Horobin, 1977) sociologists who have chronic illnesses show how their experience of the illness is such that they can really tell their doctor how to treat them. Mothers of children (and those fathers who really do a lot of child rearing) get to understand a great deal about their children's health. They may not have the medical jargon to convey their understanding to those with expertise, but they have the knowledge from experience. As Hilary Homans's work showed, women with their first babies lack experience and they do what they are told in antenatal care and afterwards. Women with their second child and subsequent children have had experience, they know what childbirth is about, they understand the health care system, they know how to weigh up what is sensible and what is not sensible in what they are being told to do by the professionals (Homans, 1980). Unpaid workers are extremely important in the health division of labour. It is impossible to understand about the health system without looking at them as well as the paid workers.

Theories to include the unpaid workers

The unpaid workers have hitherto been ignored in the health division of labour because they have been ignored in classical division of labour theories (whether Durkheimian, Weberian or Marxian). All of those theories were developed in the public domain, that is the domain of industry, the State, the market palce as I have argued elsewhere (Stacey, 1981). Health work, like education work, is done unpaid in the home (that is, the private or domestic domain) as well as paid in the public domain (for example, the sick are nursed in hospital and at home). We need to develop theories to cope with this which do not denigrate the unpaid or assume their work is 'natural', for it is a social arrangement, as much as paid work is. Furthermore the nature of health work is such that it is inappropriate to divide the labour into 'production' and 'consumption'. Health work whether in the domestic or public domain happens where people are working on the minds or bodies of other people. But the patients are not passive recipients of care, they are actors in the situation. Yet they often are dependent and rendered even more dependent because the paid workers exercise their power over the patients. Studying health work again shows we must revise the classical theories of the division of labour.

To conclude, the sociology of health, illness and healing has much to offer to health practice and to sociological theory. Its substantive subject matter is fascinating and of critical social importance. At the same time, insights from health and healing challenge much sociological theory and have contributions to make to other subject areas. We cannot understand contemporary society without understanding health knowledge and health care. The associated institutions actively maintain the deep class and gender divisions. Health care activities unintentionally trigger social change. On both those counts the subject area cannot be ignored.

Suggestions for further reading

On the development of the subject

Cookerham, W. C. (1983), 'The state of medical sociology in the United States, Great Britain, West Germany and Austria: applied vs. pure theory', *Soc. Sci. and Med.*, 17, pp. 1513–1527.

Claus, L. M. (1983), 'The development of medical sociology in Europe', *Soc. Sci. and Med.*, 17, pp. 1591–1597.

Elling, R. H. and Sokolowska, M. (1978) (eds.), *Medical Sociologists at Work*, (Transaction Books: Rutgers, N. J.)

Stacey, M. with Homans, H. (1978), 'The sociology of health and illness: its present state, future prospects and potential for health research', *Sociology*, 12 pp. 281–307.

On the development of modern medicine

Feierman, S. (1979), 'Change in African therapeutic systems', *Soc. Sci. and Med.*, 13B, pp. 277–84; contrasts and compares the state of beliefs and occupations in sixteenth- and seventeenth-century England with those of the contemporary Third World.

Jewson, N. D. (1974), 'Medical knowledge and the patronage system in eighteenth century England', *Sociology* 8, pp. 369–85 and Jewson, N. D. (1976) 'The disappearance of the sick man from the medical cosmology', *Sociology*, 10, 2 pp. 225–44; discusses the change in doctor patient relations with the rise of the hospital in the capitalist division of labour and the associated changes in medical knowledge.

Critiques

Doyal, L. with Pennell, I. (1979), *The Politial Economy of Health*, (London: Pluto Press); a neo-Marxist account with some feminist overtones.

Roberts, H. (1981) (ed.), *Women, Health and Reproduction*, (London: Routledge and Kegan Paul); brings together a number of feminist critiques of the medical profession and medical practice.

Townsend, P. and Davidson, N. (1982) (eds.), *Inequalities in Health: the Black Report*, (Harmondsworth: Penguin) is a Pelican edition of the Black Report with an introduction added by the editors.

For sociological accounts of being a patient

Davis, A. and Horobin, G. (1977) (eds.), *Medical Encounters: the Experience of Illness and Treatment*, (London: Croom Helm)

On the division of labour in health care

Graham, H. (1984), *Women, Health and the Family*, (Brighton: Wheatsheaf) (distributed Harvester); Graham draws together her own and other sociologists' data, official statistics and reports on these three topics.

Stacey, M. (1981), 'The division of labour revisited or overcoming the two Adams', in Abrams, P.; Deem, R.; Finch, J. and Rock, P. (eds.), *Practice and Progress: British Sociology 1950–1980*, (London: Allen and Unwin) pp. 172–90; the second part of this chapter discusses the theoretical errors revealed by an analysis of the division of labour in health care. The second part is developed in Stacey, M. (1984), 'Who are the health workers? Patients and other unpaid workers in health care', *Economic and Industrial Democracy*, 5, pp. 157–184 which relates this approach to conventional theories of professions and organisations.

Stacey, M.; Reid, M.; Heath, C., and Dingwall, R. (1977) (eds.), *Health and the Division of Labour*, (London: Croom Helm). A set of papers that emerged from the 1976 BSA conference includes further essays on the division of labour.

On the relationship between knowledge and practice

Armstrong, D. (1983), *The Political Anatomy of the Body*, (Cambridge: Cambridge University Press). An analysis of the development of medical knowledge in the twentieth century inspired by Michel Foucault.

Cartwright, A. (1983), *Health Surveys in practice and in potential: a critical review of their scope and methods*, (London: King Edward's Hospital Fund for London); is just what it says it is and a useful reference book also.

Dingwall, R.; Heath, C.; Reid, M. and Stacey, M. (1977) (eds.), *Health Care and Health Knowledge*, (London: Croom Helm). A second set of papers from the 1976 BSA conference which provides a sociological analysis of the relationship between knowledge and practice.

Resources

The Kings Fund Centre, 126 Albert Street, London NW1 will provide files on all major health service issues.

The Women's Health Information Centre, 12 Ufton Road, London, N1 5BT, Tel: 01 254 9094; is developing resources and publishes on women's health.

The Medical Sociology Newsletter is published three or four times a year. It contains news and notes, reviews and comments about publications and affairs in the health service. Available from Steve Platt, MRC Unit, University Department of Psychiatry, Royal Edinburgh Hospital, Morningside Park, Edinburgh EH10 5HF.

Social Science and Medicine is a Pergamon journal which carries articles by medical doctors and by social scientists in the areas of medical sociology, medical geography, medical psychology and medical anthropology.

The Sociology of Health and Illness Journal is published by the British Sociological Association and carries articles on the sociology of health and illness.

Questions for discussion

1 What grounds are there for arguing that beliefs and practices relating to health and healing are particularly difficult to study sociologically? Is this area not like any other social phenomenon sociologists might study?

2 How would you start trying to account for the remarkable success of medicine in achieving a high professional status in the nineteenth century when it had limited healing power?

3 Feminists have argued that medicine is an active agent in the continued oppression of women even though individual practioners do not intend this consequence. How good is the evidence that these feminists use and how do they structure their argument? Do you think there is anything in it?

4 Discuss the view that because health work by its very nature straddles the public and private domains it presents a serious challenge to conventional theories of the division of labour.

Chapter 8

The sociology of welfare

Janet Finch

Introduction: the sociology of welfare and solving social problems

Most sociologists are very used to the popular assumption that the main purpose of our work is to solve social problems. We find ourselves called upon to produce solutions to whatever is currently exercising politicians or receiving media coverage: drug abuse, juvenile crime, school riots, and so on. At the same time, we also get used to being told that the studies we do produce are no more than commonsense. We can reply of course that it is unrealistic to expect anyone to produce instant and reliable solutions. But more importantly, 'solving social problems' is not actually what sociology is about – or at least not in the way that problem-solving is often talked about in the media and by policy-makers. Sociologists often are very interested in precisely those areas of social life popularly defined as social problems, but our focus of interest may be very different. The purpose of this chapter is to identify the main features which would be present in a specifically sociological approach.

To make the discussion more concrete, I am going to use an illustration of an event which I am calling 'The Death of Lydia Brown'. It is an example of the kind of 'social problem' often highlighted in the media. The details are those commonly found in newspaper reports. At the end of this chapter, I will return to this case again, and discuss how a sociologist's account of this event might differ from a journalist's.

The death of Lydia Brown

Lydia Brown was an elderly woman of 76, found dead in her second-floor flat after the police had broken into it. It appeared that she had fallen and hit her head on the sink, sustaining a severe blow. A verdict of death from natural causes was returned. Apparently she had died several days previously, but no-one had raised the alarm.

The police were eventually notified by the milkman, who noticed that several bottles remained on the step when he went to collect the money. When asked why he hadn't noticed sooner, he said that he didn't do the daily deliveries himself: that was done by a boy who was with him temporarily on a youth employment scheme.

Neighbours said that they hadn't noticed anything because the flats were designed so that people did not walk past each other's front door. They said that she was a pleasant person, but she kept herself to herself. She was afraid to go out much, because she had heard on television all about old people getting mugged.

Her doctor said that he had been treating her over the past five years for various ailments and he knew that she sometimes became confused. He would have liked her to go into sheltered housing, as she wanted to herself, but there was such pressure on places. He felt that he could not justify recommending a home help, because now they are really only available for people who are physically incapable. She was able to look after herself, but a home help would have been a useful way of keeping an eye on her. She had said that she could always telephone her daughter if she needed anyone. When her daughter was traced, it appeared that she had been out of the country at the time of her mother's death: on a trip to the United States, in connection with her work in publishing.

This account is fictitious, but it is composed of elements commonly found in press reporting of such incidents. The essence of the media approach is a search for where the 'blame' should lie: should the milkman have acted sooner? Should the neighbours have been taking a more active interest? Why wasn't the daughter taking responsibility for her mother? A sociologist would want to look well beyond that in explaining why such an undoubtedly unfortunate event had occurred, and in examining what it tells us about contemporary social life.

Many of the activities designated as 'social problems' in practice concern those areas of social life which could broadly be covered by the term 'welfare', and the welfare institutions of the state and of other bodies (for example, charities) are often mobilised in attempts to resolve them. Until quite recently, sociologists in Britain have taken comparatively little interest in studying welfare, often being content to leave it to the more obviously 'applied' discipline of social administration, and regarding the study of social policy as rather peripheral to the central concerns of sociology.

However, especially since the mid-1970s, the influence of Marxism and of feminism upon the discipline of sociology (see Stacey, Chapter 7) have been very important in revitalising the sociological study of welfare, because they have suggested new kinds of questions. Among the questions which a Marxist perspective poses are: does welfare provision undermine the existing distribution of goods and material resources – or does it in fact support that distribution? Why does the state act as the provider of welfare and in whose interests? Is welfare provision always benign, and good for those who receive it – or does it seek to regulate and control individuals? The way in which these questions have been applied to particular aspects of welfare will be illustrated in the next two sections. Similarly, feminism has directed attention to such issues as: what do social policies assume about women's lifestyles and the pattern of relationships between women and men? Do social policies reinforce women's position as inferior and dependent?

Both these perspectives direct attention away from studying simply whatever happens to be publicly defined as 'social problems' at a given point in time, and towards questioning the basis of welfare provision, and the institutions through which it is provided. They also tend to emphasise the negative side of welfare: that welfare can control as well as alleviate problems; it can constrain people as well as liberate them; it can reinforce an unequal distribution of resources as well as being a tool for redistribution.

The following sections of this chapter outline some of the ways in which sociologists have developed the study of welfare, and of the 'social problems' which form a central theme of much welfare activity.

Sociological perspectives upon social problems

Any study of welfare can properly claim to be a 'sociological' study not simply because the researcher claims the label 'sociologist', but because it asks sociological questions and tries to find sociological answers. How do we recognise specifically sociological questions about welfare, and how can we begin to develop them for ourselves? I will try to answer this first by looking at the ways in which sociologists have approached the study of social problems.

In the last resort, there are no simple guidelines about what 'counts' as a sociological question, because the process of 'doing sociology' is a creative process and part of that creativity is developing the right questions – 'right', that is, in the sense that they will help to illuminate the particular area of social life which is the topic of the study. However, saying that there are no *simple* guidelines, does not mean that there are no guidelines at all. Sociologists in fact would differ about the kind of guidelines which we should follow in this matter. Burgess' chapter in this volume (Chapter 11) discusses the various approaches to sociological research and the creation of sociological knowledge in the study of education. The study of social problems is an illustration of similar issues. Some sociologists would argue that the distinguishing mark of a sociological study is the particular kinds of scientific methods which we employ: we act as detached observers of social life, using techniques which have scientific validity to study our subject-matter. This is broadly the approach taken by the American sociologist Robert Nisbet, in his very good discussion of the sociological study of social problems. He argues that:

> The primary objective of the sociologist is to uncover the causes of the problems, to seek their determining contexts and their relations to other areas of social behaviour
>
> Nisbet, 1966, p. 16

This approach to social problems falls into the tradition of sociological explanation which is often called 'positivist'. Explanation is based on the search for *causes* of social problems and features of social life are assumed to *determine* the actions of individuals. It also fits well with the structural-functionalist idea of society as a cohesive whole, in which the individual parts fit together.

This kind of approach to the study of social problems has a long history in sociology. An important early example is Emile Durkheim's classic study of suicide, in which he looked at whether the causes of this particular 'social problem' can be found in the organisation of social life. On the basis of the statistical evidence available to him, he concluded that rates of suicide are closely linked with certain aspects of social, economic, religious and family organisation (Durkheim, 1897). It is possible to take a similar kind of approach to any activity currently identified as a social problem: rates of juvenile delinquency can be shown to be linked with belonging to a large family, having only one resident parent, or poor educational performance. Poor educational performance itself can be linked with overcrowded housing, having parents who do unskilled manual work, or belonging to an ethnic minority group.

Establishing these kinds of links is one kind of exercise, and often a very useful one, but claiming that they are 'causes' of a particular social problem is quite different. There cannot be a simple cause-effect relationship, since some people who have all the features associated with delinquency or with poor educational performance never actually come before the courts, or they do well at school. Moreover, by looking at the links between the different characteristics of individuals in this way, we miss very important questions about how various social institutions, including welfare institutions, operate. For example, what are the stages in the legal process which ends in some young people being prosecuted, but others being filtered out? Or, how do selective processes operate in our educational system, and do they favour some young people rather than others? Behind these lie even more fundamental questions about why we have an educational system whose major purpose is to label some people 'successes' and others 'failures'; or why the criminal justice system punishes some kinds of human activity severely and leaves others entirely untouched. So the kind of approach which begins by tracing links between social problems and features of the individuals involved can be very illuminating if it leads on to these wider questions. But simply identifying the links cannot be treated as if it demonstrates 'causes' or provides explanations in itself; and it is unsatisfactory if it fails to question why social arrangements are as they are.

A somewhat different approach to the sociological study of social problems is one which focusses on the processes whereby different aspects of social life get defined as 'a problem'. So, instead of asking what causes the problem of drug-taking or teenage sex, we ask: how has it happened that either of these activities has come to be defined as 'a problem' at a particular point in time? The importance of this question can easily be seen by considering the wide variation in what counts as a problem in different societies, or in the same society in different historical periods, or in different strata of the same society. Large families, for example, have been highly desirable in many societies in the past, but now most governments treat them as a problem – or to be more precise, a problem if found among the poor, but not necessarily for more privileged groups.

This approach to the study of social problems sees the problems themselves as socially constructed – that is, what counts as a problem is itself a product of social processes and therefore an object of sociological study. It entails the exercise of what Wright Mills called the sociological imagination:

> The sociological imagination enables its possessor to
> understand the larger historical scene in terms of its meaning
> for the inner life and the external career of individuals . . . [it]
> enables us to grasp history and biography and the relations
> between the two within society.
>
> Mills, 1970, pp. 11–12

The essence of sociology is to develop an understanding of a particular area of social life which makes connections between the individual and the larger issues of social structure, and moves easily between the two. Wright Mills says that the essential distinction here is between the 'personal troubles of the milieu' and the 'public issues of social structure'. In the case of unemployment, for example, one needs to see that it is a personal trouble for the unemployed person, a problem for him or her which needs to be solved on an individual level. But where we have very large numbers of people unemployed, we cannot treat it as if it were *simply* a personal trouble, certainly not as if being unemployed were simply a result of some individual peculiarity or weakness: it is a public issue of social life, and the resolution of this 'social problem' can only be found in the wider economic and political structures of our society (Mills, 1970, pp. 14–15).

This kind of approach to 'social problems' is very different to the one often taken in the media and by official agencies, and may sometimes seem quite threatening to them. The 'problem' of poverty, for example, is often treated as if it were the result of some personal failings on the part of the poor, and can only be 'solved' by making the poor into different kinds of people. As William Ryan has argued, this is tantamount to 'blaming the victim' for his or her own fate:

> The 'multiproblem' poor, it is claimed, suffer the
> psychological effects of improverishment, the 'culture of
> poverty', and the deviant value system of the lower classes;
> consequently, though unwittingly, they cause their own
> troubles. From such a viewpoint, the obvious fact that poverty
> is primarily the absence of money is overlooked or set aside.
>
> Ryan, 1971, p. 5

Sociologists are inclined to ask precisely the kinds of questions about poverty which Ryan's approach indicates: why is poverty treated as a personal problem of the poor rather than a public issue of how resources get unevenly distributed? How does this process of uneven distribution actually operate? And why are certain characteristics (such as lack of thriftiness or having a large family) regarded as reprehensible when found among the poor but quite permissible for the rich?

Such an approach is obviously very different from producing quick solutions to popularly defined 'social problems'. That is not to say that sociologists are not interested in talking about solutions; but on the whole such conclusions would be based on asking rather different – and somewhat more uncomfortable – questions. A sociologist interested in poverty, for example, might well see the 'solution' as lying more in changing the lifestyle of the rich rather than of the poor.

Asking sociological questions about welfare

How do we go about asking sociological questions in the field of welfare? The previous discussion has illustrated the different kinds of perspectives which sociologists have brought to bear upon the study of 'social problems'. Although there are no simple guidelines, there are a number of common themes in the way in which different sociologists approach the study of welfare, and I shall now divide them into four types of questions. In indicating the types of questions which sociologists commonly ask, I hope that this will also be helpful to others who wish to develop their own sociological questions about welfare.

Firstly, a sociological analysis of any area of welfare needs to ask questions about the social context. Sociology should always recognise that its subject-matter is located by time and place, and ask questions like: what is it about this particular society at this point in time which produces this particular piece of welfare provision? A particular item of provision (for example, financial support for single parents) has to be set firmly in this kind of context. Similarly a popularly designated 'social problem' (such as mugging or alcoholism) cannot be treated as if it were an inherent and fixed feature of the human condition. This approach implicitly recognises that social life *can* be organised in many different ways, and comparison with other societies and other historical periods often helps illuminate our own arrangements. It can be very useful, for example, to look at how different systems of welfare deal with the care of the disabled, or with financial support for young children, or with the availability of abortion – not necessarily because we want to recommend that their methods are preferable (although that might be true), but to understand how such arrangements relate to the employment of women, or to population changes, or to the class structure of any given society.

Secondly, a sociological analysis of welfare usually needs to ask questions about who defines which areas of social life are treated as suitable targets for public provision, or what is to be treated as a social problem. This can lead into very complex areas of analysis, including such issues as the way in which power is distributed between politicians and officials, the effects of pressure groups and other kinds of struggles, and the extent to which the media define, rather than reflect, public issues. However, we can begin to ask this kind of question without needing to tackle these major issues head-on before we can even start. One useful starting-point is often to ask the simple question: for whom is this 'social problem' a problem? The 'problem' of truancy from school, for example, may be a problem for education authorities, but not necessarily for those who are absent, who may actually be making quite realistic assessments about what school can offer them further, if, for example, they are aged 15 and in the bottom stream (White, 1980). Truancy is a problem for education authorities because school attendance is compulsory by law, and they are the bodies charged with enforcing that. So looking at the 'problem' of truancy sociologically can lead us right away from explaining it by reference to the characteristics of the truants themselves, and to an examination of why school attendance is compulsory.

That leads into the third type of question which sociologists ask about welfare. This involves looking at the consequences of welfare and who actually benefits from it. That is not necessarily the same thing as looking at the overt intention behind a piece of welfare legislation: as sociologists we have to be concerned with the unintended as well as the intended consequences of social actions. Moreover, the overtly expressed intentions of governments may not always be an accurate reflection of their whole range of reasons for a particular piece of social policy. Recent innovations in training and education schemes for school-leavers have been presented by the government as assisting young people to get jobs, or better jobs, in the future; whereas this policy can equally be seen as a way of keeping them off the unemployment registers in the short term. So asking questions about the actual consequences of welfare, and who in fact benefits from it, can tell us a great deal more about social processes and social relationships than looking at the explicit intentions of particular policies.

Finally, sociologists need to be concerned with what is *not* provided and what is *never* discussed, as well as what is. In their study of poverty in America, Bachrach and Baratz have shown the importance of looking at 'nondecisions' as well as at decisions:

> Policy choices are frequently made in the absence of a clear-cut once-for-all decision. They simply 'happen' in the sense that certain steps are taken that are necessary but preliminary to a decision, and the sequence of steps acquires (as the saying goes) a life of its own.
>
> Bachrach and Baratz, 1970, p. 42

Various tactics – sometimes direct, but mostly indirect – can be employed to ensure that the area for potential decision never gets clearly defined, or never gets re-defined, and this allows the existing power structures to keep operating smoothly. Power resides just as much in the ability to keep issues off the agenda, as to get issues on to it.

So we may find out more about the social processes which underlie welfare provision by looking at what is taken for granted and never discussed, than we do by looking at its existing forms. Again, looking at arrangements in other societies can help us to focus upon what is taken for granted in our own, as Margaret Stacey (Chapter 7) shows in her discussion of health and illness in a different culture. For example, the care of young children whose parents are in employment is treated as a 'problem' of working mothers, to which a range of policy solutions are possible. But why are working fathers never considered as a problem? And why are parents seen as the people who ought to be looking after young children? Once we ask these questions, we can see that the provision of welfare services draws heavily upon prevailing ideas and values, which in principle could be capable of change. We can also speculate on the consequences if such questions were to be taken seriously, and thus we can begin to explore whose interests are served by keeping those particular issues off the agenda.

These four types of questions do not exhaust sociological approaches to welfare, but they do illustrate some of its important characteristics. Like any other area of sociology, the form which a particular study takes will be governed both by the subject-matter and by the theoretical perspective which a given writer adopts. The following section illustrates how these kind of sociological questions can be applied to a particular area, by drawing on some of my own recent work.

Community care for the frail elderly

The elderly have been a target group for welfare provision throughout the history of British welfare provision in the nineteenth and twentieth centuries, although the types of provision thought appropriate have varied considerably, as has official thinking about whether old age as such should be considered a social problem, and if so, what kind of problem it is meant to be (Macintyre, 1977).

The particular focus of my interest is that section of the elderly population for whom advancing age has brought a degree of mental or physical infirmity which makes it difficult for them to live as independent adults: I shall refer to them as the frail elderly. The numbers of elderly people in the population, especially the very old who are particularly susceptible to these infirmities, has been growing in the past two decades and will continue to grow by about a further 20 per cent, until the end of the century. As more women than men survive into older age, women form the great majority of the elderly population, especially in the older age cohorts: at the age of 75+, there are about two and a half times as many women as men (Central Statistical Office, 1984).

The frail elderly are a group who have usually been reliant on state or upon charitable provision, since few of them have the resources to buy care for themselves on a commercial basis. Historically, the state has provided for such people in residential institutions, but since the early 1960s, there has been increasing emphasis on different kinds of provision, partly because residential care is very expensive to provide, and partly as a result of studies which demonstrated the negative effects of institutional settings upon those who live in them, including Peter Townsend's study of residential institutions for the elderly (Townsend, 1962).

Alternatives to residential provision have been sought as various forms of 'community care'. This phrase in fact covers many different kinds of provision, ranging from state-funded domiciliary services (such as home nursing or meals on wheels) to the implication that it means 'the ill-defined cosy picture of a group of local people "caring" for their neighbours' (Tinker, 1981, p. 38). In recent years, there has been increasing emphasis on 'voluntary effort' in the provision of community care, as successive Governments have sought 'low cost solutions' for the provision of services, in an era of public expenditure cuts (for a fuller account, see Finch and Groves, 1980; 1983). Meanwhile, some academics and social work practitioners have enthusiastically promoted the idea of relying more upon 'informal caring networks'. This phrase refers to the provision of care by friends, neighbours or relatives, completely independent of State services and often unknown to them. It is claimed that substantial amounts of care for the dependent population are already provided in this way: a major task of State welfare should be to support and promote these networks rather than to replace them with more formal services (see, for example, Hadley and Hatch, 1981; especially chapter 6).

Different sociologists would raise different questions about this new emphasis on community care. The particular issues which I have been interested in exploring concern the implications for women in the shift from residential care to community care. From the range of sociological questions which could be developed, I shall focus here on two issues: the meaning of 'community care' and the supply of potential carers.

Any sociological discussion of community care must begin by examining carefully the meaning of the term, and drawing upon the existing body of sociological knowledge to examine what 'communities' are in contemporary British society. This is part of the task of placing the object of study within its social context. The concept of 'community' has been a notoriously slippery one when-ever sociologists have examined it. Margaret Stacey argued, as long ago as 1969, that 'it is doubtful whether the concept "community" refers to any useful abstraction' (Stacey, 1969b, p. 134). Bell and Newby's very useful review of theories of community indicate that there is very wide disagreement about its meaning, and that its use may often say more about what we might *like* the world to be like, than what it actually is like (Bell and Newby, 1971, especially chapter 2).

Nevertheless, the phrase 'community care' continues to be used in discussions of welfare provisions as if it was unproblematic. The implication usually is that some combination of friends, relatives and neighbours (possibly supplemented by volunteers previously unknown to the elderly person) will constitute the 'community' who will do the caring. How far does this match the reality of contemporary social life? A sociological analysis of the patterns of relationships upon which such care could be based almost certainly indicates that it matches rather badly. Philip Abrams' excellent work on community care and neighbouring shows that 'extensive and effective community care is uncommon and improbable in our type of society' (Abrams, 1977, p. 79), and that where such care is available, it is likely to be on the basis of kinship, religion or race, and not simple geographical proximity.

So a sociological analysis of 'community care' leads us to question the whole basis of such policies, and directs our attention to the unacknowledged consequences of pursuing them. These, presumably, are either that care is not available to the frail elderly outside residential institutions or specific state provisions; or that some care *is* available, but not from 'the community'.

This leads directly to the second issue upon which I want to focus: the supply of potential 'carers'. If one examines the evidence about who actually performs the daily (and sometimes hourly) tasks involved in caring for a frail elderly person, the answer is that it is usually female relatives: community care in practice means care by the family, and the division of labour within the family usually assigns that care to women (EOC 1982a, Family Policy Studies Centre 1984). Thus a further unacknowledged consequence of community care policies is that the unpaid labour of women is incorporated into provision for the elderly. If we ask why *that* is never regarded as a social problem, it can be seen that community care policies contain assumptions that women will be available in the home to provide this kind of service, where it is part of their natural role to undertake caring tasks. Whoever may be the beneficiaries of such policies, the women who provide the care in many ways are the losers, especially if they are excluded from paid work by the obligation to provide unpaid care.

In these circumstances, carers may experience considerable material hardship. A study of the effects of caring for an elderly handicapped relative has shown that married women carers, on average, had given up a job in which they earned £5,500 a year at 1982 prices. The amount of unpaid labour which they invested would have cost on average £3,000 if paid at the very low rates offered to home helps or ward orderlies (Nissel and Bonnerjea, 1982). So, at a conservative estimate, these women were losing £8,500 per year, and were entitled to no state benefits as an alternative, since their status as married women designates them the financial dependents of their husbands. This points to important questions about what counts as 'work' and whether that work is paid or unpaid which link with issues raised by both Colin Bell

(Chapter 3) and Margaret Stacey (Chapter 7) in their contributions to this book. In the case of carers, work is unpaid because these arrangements are regarded as quite appropriate for married women. Thus state policies maintain and reinforce traditional patterns of gender relationships.

A sociological analysis of community care policies therefore leads us to examine such issues as the relationship between social policies and the reality of the social context in which they are implemented; the unacknowledged (and perhaps unintended) consequences of such policies; who are, in practice, the benficiaries and the losers; and how welfare polices contribute to maintaining or undermining major patterns of social relationshps – in this case gender divisions.

Conclusion: thinking sociologically about Lydia Brown

In the light of the foregoing discussion of developing sociological questions about welfare, it is worth returning to the Lydia Brown case, to ask how a sociological account would differ from the one presented above.

Firstly, the journalistic account implies that the explanation of Lydia Brown's death is that it was a failure of community care: the neighbours took insufficient interest, the milkman should have been more conscious of his potential role in keeping an eye on elderly people, her daughter should have been more heavily involved in caring for her mother. But each of these suggestions implies a view of natural neighbourliness and the cohesiveness of community life which quite simply did not match the social reality of Lydia Brown's circumstances. In contemporary urban communities, milkmen are not necessarily the life-long friends of all the elderly people on their rounds, nor does natural neighbourliness inevitably flourish. The assumption that daughters will take day-to-day responsibility is unrealistic if they do not live locally. Even if they do, there is an unresolvable tension between that expectation and being in full-time employment, especially in work which demands considerable personal commitment.

Secondly, rather than blame the failure of community care, we might rather see the death of Lydia Brown as a failure of State provision. On one level, this means looking quite explicitly at the effects of public expenditure cuts, which meant that alternative provision was not available to her – neither sheltered housing, nor even the minimal provision of a home help. The processes whereby some individuals do get access to the limited facilities which are available, and others do not, are important too: here we would want to focus upon the doctor's role as gatekeeper to State services, which links with questions raised in Margaret Stacey's discussion (Chapter 7) about professionals in health care. One particular feature of interest in this case is an issue of gender: would an elderly man have been given sheltered housing and/or a home help more readily? That question could only be answered by examining carefully the ways in which doctors and other gatekeepers structure their priorities: but it may well be that they assume that elderly women can manage on their own at home more easily than elderly men with similar disabilities, because the home is seen as a woman's natural environment.

Finally, a sociological consideration of this 'social problem' as presented in the media would probably need to turn the spotlight back on to the media themselves. Lydia Brown, it is said, was afraid of being mugged if she left her flat, and this must have contributed considerably to her social isolation. But how great really were the dangers of being mugged, by comparison with the very real dangers of that isolation? A Home Office study in three inner city areas has demonstrated that elderly people are not especially at risk of being mugged: only 14 per cent of the victims were pensioners, as compared with 45 per cent of the victims aged 30 or under (Ramsay, 1982). Mugging is a very good example of how media treatment can encourage people to imagine that a social phenomenon is more prevalent than it actually is by creating what has come to be called a 'moral panic' (Cohen, 1972).

The study of welfare therefore is by no means peripheral to sociology: it brings us back to major and important questions about the organisation of social life. We may not be in the business of providing quick solutions to social problems as popularly defined; but in developing sociological questions about welfare, and in the exercise of the sociological imagination to pursue them, it is possible to offer an illuminating analysis about the 'problem' itself and the society which produces it.

Suggestions for further reading

On the welfare state and social policy in Britain

Bruce, M. (1968), *The Coming of the Welfare State*, (London: Batsford). An historical review of the development of the welfare state. A standard text in social policy.

Hill M. (1983) (ed.), *Understanding Social Policy*, (2nd edn.) (Oxford: Blackwell). A good introductory text on social policy, with contributions on all major institutional areas of welfare provision.

Titmuss, R. M. (1976), *Essays on the Welfare State*, (3rd edn.) (London: Allen and Unwin). A classic contribution by the 'founding father' of social administration as a discipline. Contains major essays on: national health service; pensions; the position of women; the social division of welfare.

Ungerson, C. (1985) (ed.), *Women and Social Policy: A Reader*, (London: Macmillan). A varied and useful collection of readings on women's relationships to health, housing, education and social services.

On the sociology of social problems

Manning, M. (1985) (ed.), *Social Problems and Welfare Ideology*, (Aldershot: Gower). A collection of articles on a variety of contemporary social issues with a good introductory chapter on the social construction of social problems.

Merton, R. K. and Nisbet, R. (1966) (eds.), *Contemporary Social Problems* (2nd edn.) (New York: Harcourt, Brace and World Inc.). A collection of American articles reflecting a range of approaches to the study of social problems. Nisbet's introduction is an important discussion, and David Matza's article on 'Poverty and Disrepute' is a very good illustration of the lively exercise of the sociological imagination.

Mills C. Wright (1970), *The Sociological Imagination*, (Harmondsworth: Penguin) is a classic of modern sociology. Chapter 1 sets out Mills' view of the sociological imagination and his key distinction between 'personal troubles' and 'public issues'.

Sociological perspectives on welfare

Gough, I. (1979), *The Political Economy of the Welfare State*, (London: Macmillan) has become a very influential text, in which the author develops an explicitly Marxist perspective upon the welfare state. Sociological analysis has been significantly influenced by the kind of questions he raises.

Mishra, R. (1977), *Society and Social Policy: Theoretical Perspectives on Welfare*, (London: Macmillan). A well-written book which summarises and evaluates the range of theoretical perspectives, mostly sociological, which can be brought to bear on the study of welfare.

Room, G. (1979), *The Sociology of Welfare: Social Policy, Stratification and the Political Order*, (Oxford: Blackwell/Martin Robertson). A more difficult text than Mishra, but useful for reference.

Wilson, E. (1977), *Women and the Welfare State*, (London: Tavistock). A lively and important book, in which the author raises questions about welfare from a feminist perspective.

On the elderly and community care

Charlesworth, A.; Wilkin, D. and Durie, A. (1984), *Carers and Services*, (Manchester: Equal Opportunities Commission). Report of a study of women and men caring for elderly dependent people.

Equal Opportunities Commission (1982a), *Caring for the Elderly and Handicapped*, (Manchester: EOC)

Equal Opportunities Commission (1982b), *Who Cares for the Carers?*, (Manchester: EOC). These two pamphlets together are the product of the study made within the EOC of available evidence about caring situations, especially as they involve women.

Family Policy Studies Centre (1984), *The Forgotten Army: Family Care and Elderly People*, (London: FPSC). A 'briefing paper' which brings together in very accessible form up-to-date evidence, mainly of a statistical nature, about the family care of elderly people.

Finch, J. and Groves, D. (1980), 'Community care and the family: a case for equal opportunities?' *Journal of Social Policy*, vol. 9, no. 4, pp. 487–511, sets out the arguments and evidence for the view that community care policies rely extensively on women's unpaid labour in the home, to the detriment of these women 'carers'.

Finch, J. and Groves, D. (1983) (eds.), *A Labour of Love: Women, Work and Caring*, (London: Routledge and Kegan Paul). A collection of articles on women's experience of caring for dependent people, of the tensions between that and their participation in the labour market, and the implications for women themselves.

Finch, J. (1984), 'Community care: developing non-sexist alternatives', *Critical Social Policy*, no. 9, pp. 6–18. An article which considers whether it is possible to envisage any form of community care for the frail elderly which would be non-sexist, and concludes on present evidence that it is not. This article has proved controversial, and further discussion of it is included in issue 12 of the same journal.

Jones, K., Brown, J. and Bradshaw, J. (1978), *Issues in Social Policy*, (London: Routledge and Kegan Paul). Chapter 7 gives a good outline of the arguments and evidence about both residential care and social policies.

Macintyre, S. (1977), 'Old age as a social problem', in R. Dingwall, C. Heath, M. Reid and M. Stacey (eds.), *Health Care and Health Knowledge*, (London: Croom Helm). A very good discussion, using historical material, of the variations in the way in which old age has been treated as a social problem.

Tinker, A. (1981), *The Elderly in Modern Society*, (London: Longman); provides a review of services for the elderly and an assessment of them from the viewpoint of social policy.

Walker, A (ed.) (1982), *Community Care: the Family, the State and Social Policy*, (Oxford: Blackwell). A collection of articles which provide a good summary of recent work on community care for a whole range of dependent groups.

Resources

The weekly magazine *New Society* carries many articles relevant to the sociology of welfare. *Community Care*, also weekly, is a magazine for people who work in the personal social services, and carries many useful articles illustrative of current issues in welfare provision.

Government publications of reports and other documents provide a useful source, especially the publications of the *Department of Health and Social Security*. These are obtainable through *Her Majesty's Stationery Office*, 48 High Holborn, London WCIV 6HB. A weekly catalogue of publications, called *Government Publications*, can be found in most major libraries.

Pressure groups active in the field of welfare produce much relevant literature, most of it in pamphlet form. Probably the most important of these, producing material which covers all aspects of income and welfare, is the *Child Poverty Action Group*, 1 Macklin Street, London WC2.

In relation to the elderly specifically, *Age Concern*, Bernard Sunley House, 60 Pitcairn Road, Mitcham, Surrey, produces much useful material. Also the *Disability Alliance*, 21 Star Street, London WC2 1QB which is a federation of voluntary organisations concerned with the disabled.

Questions for discussion

1 Discuss how you would develop sociological questions about the following areas of welfare provision:
   a) child care provision for the children of working parents,
   b) financial support for the unemployed,
   c) housing for the single homeless,
   d) day care centres for the mentally handicapped.
   What kind of information would you need to fully develop your analysis?

2 What case would you make against the view that sociology has nothing to contribute to the discussion of social problems, except what everyone knows from commonsense?

3 Collect a range of newspaper reports about incidents involving an aspect of welfare provision, and discuss how a sociological account of the event might differ from a journalistic one. For example, a social worker's decision about removing a child from its parents; an incident of alleged staff ill-treatment of residents in a mental hospital.

Chapter 9

The sociology of crime and deviance

Bob Roshier

Sociology's long involvement with the study of crime and deviance illustrates two fundamental problems that have already arisen at other points in this book (see, for example, Janet Finch, chapter 8): the nature of the relationship between sociology and neighbouring academic disciplines, and the extent to which sociology's academic status can be compromised by an expectation that it provide solutions to social problems. In dealing with these questions the sociology of crime and deviance has been, perhaps more than any other substantive area a battleground, not only for confrontations with other disciplines, but also for the endless civil war between protagonists of differing perspectives within sociology itself.

It is not at all surprising, of course, that disciplines other than sociology should be interested in crime and deviance. In the past century or more biologists, psychologists, anthropologists and others have all applied their favourite theories and methods to these areas. As we will see, the most significant confrontation has been between psychology and sociology. But, as we shall also see, the differences between the two have sometimes masked an even more significant, though unacknowledged, agreement at the more fundamental level of assumptions about the nature of human beings and the nature of crime.

It is no less surprising that the expectations of a sociology of crime and deviance should be that it provides solutions. Crime is surely a 'bad thing' that needs to be stopped, or at least reduced?

In so far as it consists (almost entirely, it is sometimes made to appear!) of elderly women being beaten up in the streets and having their pension books stolen, few would disagree. But, fortunately perhaps, it does not – it also consists of smoking marijuana, cutting fences at Greenham Common, over-zealous picketing and 'unfortunate' oversights on tax-returns. When these 'crimes' are considered, other questions have a habit of suggesting themselves as being of sociological interest – such as, for example, who defines what crimes are, how, and with what consequences? For this reason, as we shall see, recent sociologists have been highly critical of the policy-orientated 'causal-corrective' tradition, claiming that it has biased and stunted the development of the sociology of crime and deviance. In particular, they have pointed out that such an approach is based on two highly contentious assumptions about the nature of human beings and the nature of crime.

First, the quest for 'causes' of crime implies a deterministic view of human action, as opposed to the view that we possess 'free will'. Human beings are portrayed as the victims of forces inside and outside of themselves which determine their actions and are consequently amenable to correction by manipulation of these forces.

Secondly, the 'causal-corrective' approach, in taking for granted that crime needs correcting, implies that there is some kind of generally accepted authoritative basis for existing definitions of 'crime' – for example, that they are God-given, or can be derived from objective human or social needs. This 'absolute' view of crimes is in sharp contrast to the 'relativist' view which sees crime as being merely violation of rules which reflect the particular interests of particular groups of people (those with the power to see that their rules are enforced by the state's agencies).

We will see that it is differing positions in relation to these two dichotomies – free will versus determinism, absolutism versus relativism – that distinguish the historical schools of thought on crime and deviance. This chapter will look at this history in terms of three 'revolutions' (each, coincidentally, occurring in the sixth or seventh decades of the eighteenth, nineteenth and twentieth centuries) in the position taken in relation to either or both of these dichotomies. These changes have not, it is important to note, occurred through new evidence 'disproving' earlier positions, but rather through changing philosophical and ideological fashion. For this reason there is a degree of circularity in this 200 year, three revolution cycle.

Classical criminology

Classical criminology (a concern with the wider category of 'deviance' does not arise until later) is usually seen as commencing with the publication of Beccaria's 'On Crimes and Punishments' in 1764, but also includes the later contribution from Bentham. Their intellectual revolution consisted of a systematic attack on the cruelty, barbarity and extreme arbitrariness and irrationality of the system of criminal justice that was seen as dominating Europe at that time. Their contribution has consequently been much more towards reforming the operation of the legal and penal system. It is also the case, of course, that seeing human beings as having free will (as they did) leaves little to say about criminals as such (they are simply people who have chosen to commit crime).

However, classical criminology did propose a theory of human action. Human beings were seen as motivated by rational self-interest, governed by the utilitarian principle of seeking pleasure and avoiding pain. As individuals, people would reject the limitations on their freedom that would be involved in certain actions being outlawed as 'crimes'. But their rationality also enables them to perceive that if everyone gives up some of their freedoms (via some form of 'social contract') then they will benefit through increased order and security in social life. This mutual perception of benefit is not sufficient to ensure order however (it is always to an individual's advantage to break rules, especially when everyone else is observing them). Consequently penalties are required to deter criminal actions – the penalty being sufficient, but no more, to ensure observance.

Classical criminology thus postulated a free, but rationally self-interested human nature. The conception of crime was absolutist – crime represented the violation of rules which could be objectively derived from the requirements of the social contract: the severity of the punishment should hence be determined by the 'objective harm' done by the offence.

Although classical crimiology's acceptance of free will and consequent focus on crimes rather than criminals certainly differentiated it from the later positivists, it was not as free from causal-corrective concerns as some writers (see Matza, 1964) have suggested. They *were* concerned with controlling crime, and did propose a strategy (deterrence). In this respect they differed from traditional 'retributive' justice with its concern for 'just dessert' rather than crime control. Also, the pleasure-pain principle could be seen as an embryonic causal theory of human action (indeed, twentieth-century behaviourist psychology could be seen as the logical extension of it). But this must not be pushed too far – the spirit of classical criminology was very much more accepting of human freedom of choice than any of the later positivist theories.

Positivist criminology

Just over a century after Beccaria wrote 'On Crimes and Punishments' a new school of criminology emerged – in celebration of the triumph of science and technology and the apparently successful application of their methods to understanding human beings (following the work of Darwin). This new school became know as the 'positivist' school and its most famous proponent, Lombroso (Wolfgang, 1960), is normally considered to be the founder of 'modern' criminology. The original members of this school were mostly biologists, medical psychiatrists and psychologists. They believed that the application of the methods of these scientific disciplines would provide an explanation of what makes people into criminals.

The positivist school is usually considered to be quite distinct from later, particularly sociological, schools and there are indeed important differences between them. But there are also some significant continuities. It is important to be aware of these, especially if we are to understand the more recent sociological revolt against this kind of approach and its assumptions.

The first continuity was that all the schools of thought following the original positivists shared a new, fully deterministic conception of human beings. Criminal behaviour was 'caused' by forces beyond the control of individuals and these causes could be framed into deterministic theories. Admittedly the causes picked on were different for the different schools (as we shall see). Also they all tended to have a generally 'reformist' approach to treating criminals, i.e. criminals could and should be 'reformed' by the application of scientific technology. As Matza was later to put it (1969) they all shared a 'causal-corrective' approach to criminology.

A second continuity was one that also followed on from the earlier classical criminology: an absolutist conception of crime. In the case of positivist criminology though, this was often more by default than by stated theoretical preference. That is, they simply did not bother to question existing definitions of 'crimes', they took them as 'given' in their quest for causal-corrective theories. At least implicitly, then, they treated them as if they had some sort of commonsense absolute status.

1 The founding fathers and their legacy

The first edition of Lombroso's 'L'uomo Delinquente' appeared in 1876. His historical importance owes much more to the pattern of research he established than to his particular theory, which is now generally discredited. Lombroso concluded that criminals were a distinct 'atavistic' group of people (i.e. genetic throw-backs to more primitive human forms) who could be identified by physical stigmata such as facial and cranial deformities, excessively hairy bodies, overlong arms etc. His 'research' consisted of exhaustive studies and measurements of convicted criminals. Lombroso laid great emphasis on the scientific, empirically validated nature of his findings. Unfortunately, even by the narrow criteria of positivism, Lombroso's research was extremely shoddy – inconsistently carried out and monitored, inadequate use of control groups, unwarranted deduction from inadequate facts, and so on. Also, by the later editions of his book, even he was forced to concede that by no means all convicted criminals fell into his atavistic group. Later studies, using proper control groups, found no differences at all between criminals and non-criminals in terms of the physical characteristics defined by Lombroso.

But the basic, general features of Lombroso's work – the assumption that criminals are identifiably 'different' in some way from non-criminals has inspired (mainly psychological) research to the present day. Two more specific features – the assumption that the difference is 'pathological' in some way (i.e. something has 'gone wrong' with criminals) and is genetically determined – have also played a major part in subsequent theories. Even the idea that criminals are physically different continued to have influence long after Lombroso. For example, S. and E. Glueck (1956), writing after the Second World War, claimed that delinquents were more commonly of 'mesomorphic' (stocky, muscular) bodily build.

Genetics have played a part in recent theories such as Eysenck's (1970). He proposed that delinquents are more commonly of 'neurotic extrovert' personality, these characteristics being genetically determined. However, the genetic connection was established by the method of comparing identical with fraternal twins. The assumption is that since identical twins are genetically identical while fraternal are not, then if identical twins are more similar in terms of their criminality (i.e. are more 'concordant') then this suggests genetics play a part. However, it assumes that the *environment* for identical twins is no more similar than it is for fraternal – an assumption now regarded with some suspicion. A currently more favoured method is to compare adopted children with their adoptive and natural parents. If their criminality is more similar to that of their natural parents than to their adoptive then, again, this is taken as evidence of a genetic connection. Recent research along these lines (see Ellis, 1982) has found such a connection, though a small one, with no indication as to how it actually operates to produce criminal behaviour.

The most general and persistent legacy of Lombroso has been the continuing search for the 'criminal personality'. That is, trying to define particular personality types that are crime-prone (using personality questionnaires and without making any necessary assumption that the results are genetically determined). Although some loose connections have been suggested, no clear-cut personality types incorporating substantial proportions of officially-defined criminals and excluding non-criminals have been established.

It is probably fair to say that the legacy of the Lombrosian tradition of seeking the causes of crime in the individual make-up of criminals has not been very productive. This could, of course, be rectified by future development in genetics and personality testing.

On the other hand, it could be that the whole approach is fundamentally misguided.

2 Sociological theories: the Chicago School

The distinguishing feature of sociological explanations is that they do not assume criminals and delinquents to be 'different' in their individual make-up and characteristics from non-criminals. They are rather seen as any kind of person caught up in particular social and economic circumstances: the 'causes' are external to the individual. It should be noted that this does not mean that sociological explanations differ *simply* in that they see the causes in the 'environment' while psychological explanations see them as being in the individual. Indeed, some psychological explanations do see aspects of the environment (particularly, for example, the family) as being important. The crucial difference is that where psychologists have considered such environmental features they have tended to see them in terms of their producing identifiably different crime-prone personalities.

Nor has the idea of 'pathology' been entirely absent from sociological explanations, though it has taken a different form. Whereas in psychology the pathology was attributed to the individual make-up of criminals, in sociology it has tended to be attributed to the social circumstances surrounding criminals.

These features certainly characterised one of the earliest and most famous schools of sociological criminology: the Chicago School, most active in the period before the Second World War. The origins of most later developments in sociological perspectives can be traced back to the Chicago School, but their major contribution in the field of criminology was their study of 'criminal areas'. Professors Park and Burgess, and Shaw and McKay (1942) plotted the addresses of convicted delinquents over several decades and found them to be heavily concentrated in the inner, decaying residential areas of the city. Despite a high turnover of population, these areas remained the same over the whole period. They explained this by a kind of 'ecological' process of 'natural selection' (they flirted with biological concepts, but later abandoned them) whereby the most socially and economically disadvantaged ended up in the least desirable residential areas. These areas were characterised by 'social disorganisation' – the ineffectiveness of conventional agencies of socialisation and control. Delinquents then, were essentially 'normal' children, but who were growing up in deprived and seductively uncontrolled areas.

In this country, where public agencies such as local authorities intervened in the housing market, the same concentration tended to be found – even between council housing estates of generally similar quality (though, again, it was the least desirable, lowest-rent ones that had the highest delinquency rates). The English studies, however (Gill, 1977) suggested other factors are at work, such as deliberate policies by housing authorities of concentrating the most economically deprived and the effects of 'stigmatisation' once they are there (a point to which we shall return later).

Although such studies as these seemed to establish fairly well a relation between socio-economic deprivation and concentration into the relatively worst housing – the exact mechanism of the relationship with delinquency did not seem to be very well described by the idea of 'social disorganisation'. However, out of such findings, two of the most famous general theories of crime were generated – differential association and anomie.

3 Differential association

This was an ambitious general theory intended to account for all crime, first propounded by Edwin Sutherland and later developed by Donald Cressey (Sutherland & Cressey, 1970). It starts by pointing out that we all grow up in environments where we receive, from our associates, definitions both favourable and unfavourable to the acquisition of the motives for and techniques to commit crime. The theory simply states that if we receive an excess of definitions favourable over those unfavourable, then we will commit crime (this was assumed to apply, for example, to those growing up in the kinds of criminal area described by the Chicago School).

Differential association, then, was stated at a very general level – so general, some claimed, as to say no more than that 'crime is learned'. It certainly proved extremely difficult to clarify and test. What counted as 'definitions favourable'? How could they be measured? Cressey himself concluded that it was probably untestable.

Worse, there were attempts at takeover by behaviourist psychologists (e.g. Burgess and Akers) whose highly mechanistic version of the learning process was totally alien to the original spirit in which the theory was framed, allowing as it seemed to, for human cognition and motives. The problem was that its extreme generality did leave it vulnerable to such attempts at appropriation.

These problems severely restricted the influence of differential association. It is now mainly of interest as a brave attempt at some kind of general theory. The fundamental point, however, that learning plays a part in the development of criminal careers, was to live on to play a part in later developments.

4 Anomie

Another of the limitations of differential association was that while it addressed itself to the question of how criminal motives and behaviour patterns are transmitted to new recruits, it failed to account for where such motives and behaviour patterns came from in the first place. This was to be provided, though from a different source, in the version of 'anomie' theory propounded by Robert Merton.

It was Emile Durkheim (1964), however, who first introduced the idea of 'anomie'. It very roughly translates as 'normlessness' – a situation where the rules governing social life have become unclear, people being no longer sure 'what goes' and what does not. One of the causes suggested by Durkheim was that rapid social change can create a situation where there is an imbalance between people's goals (what they expect to achieve in their lives) and the available opportunities to achieve them.

Merton (1957) borrowed this idea, and related it specifically to crime and deviance in contemporary Western, capitalist society (especially America). Western capitalism is dependent on constant economic growth and consequently requires high levels of economic aspiration among its members. In America, he suggested, this has given rise to the 'log cabin to the White House' dream – the view that lofty goals are available to everyone. At the same time, the goals are in fact only available to those who succeed via education and career and there are structural barriers to this route (determined by class and race). There is thus a conflict between cultural goals (the American dream, available to all) and the social structural means of achieving them (class and racial barriers to educational and occupational achievement).

One solution to this conflict, especially for the lower social class groups where the pressure is greatest, is to use alternative (deviant) means of achieving success goals. Transcribed to the 'criminal areas' described by the Chicago school, the inhabitants aspire to the same ambitions of wealth and status as everyone else, in a setting which effectively prevents them from achieving them. For this reason they turn to crime. Note again, that individually, criminals are seen as entirely 'normal' – indeed identical to their conforming counterparts living in more privileged settings. If there is any 'pathology' involved, it is in the social structure (as with the 'social disorganisation' described by the Chicago school).

Anomie has undoubtedly been the most complete, widely quoted sociological explanation of crime, yet it encountered severe difficulties and criticisms from the start. It seemed to predict far too much crime – far more people were subject to 'anomie' than became criminal. It depended on crime being predominantly, if not entirely, lower-class. Empirical research repeatedly failed to find criminals having a greater 'gap' between their aspirations and expectations than non-criminals. It did not seem to account for an important feature of recorded crime – that it was most concentrated among young adolescents. In this last respect, however, new ideas came temporarily to the rescue, in the form of the 'delinquent subculture' theorists.

5 Delinquent subcultures

The most well known of the subcultural theorists (Cohen, 1955; Cloward and Ohlin, 1960) used versions of anomie theory but related it directly to the experience of lower-class adolescent boys growing up in a class-stratified society. Cohen introduced the idea of delinquent sub-cultures to refer to the culture shared by the adolescent gangs found in most Western cities. The content of the 'subculture' shared by these gangs consisted of a commitment to delinquency. Starting out wishing to achieve conventional status, lower-class boys found themselves disadvantaged by middle-class dominated institutions such as the school. Consequent failure and frustration led to them creating their own, alternative status system. For Cloward and Ohlin, the delinquency stemmed from the fact that it was the available alternative means of achieving conventional goals. For Cohen, however, it also had a more symbolic meaning; it was a deliberate negation of middle-class values – to get back at the source of frustration. Thus vandalism, which was difficult to explain in terms of the conventional version of anomie used by Cloward and Ohlin was, for Cohen, a deliberate negation of the middle-class esteem for property.

Delinquent subculture theory seemed to neatly tie together existing theories: anomie proved the initiating impetus for the formation of groups which could then 'transmit' delinquent values via differential association. But it, again, had its problems. Yablonsky (1962) showed that 'gangs' in the sense of structured groups with a continuing identity and membership were extremely hard to come by. Bordua (1961) objected to the idea that delinquents were 'frustrated' and 'venting their spleen on conventional values' (he put Cohen's view down to middle-class paranoia). Rather, delinquency was fun in its own right – always a strong competitor to convention.

But most important was the central idea of delinquent subcultures – that the members had to be committed to delinquency to belong. Empirical research both in the US and this country failed to find groups requiring such commitment (Short and Strodtbeck, 1965; Downes, 1966). Partly for this reason, sociological interest in lower-class youth culture drifted away from a particular concern with delinquency into a more general interest in its style, differentiation and social and political meaning (Hall and Jefferson, 1976).

One of the severest critics of delinquent subcultural theory's dependence on the idea of commitment to delinquency, was David Matza (1964). But his criticism went much further. He saw the root of the problem as lying with the whole tradition of positivist criminology and its assumptions from Lombroso to Cohen.

Neo-classical criminology

In 1964, exactly 200 years after Beccaria had published 'On Crimes and Punishments', Matza wrote 'Delinquency and Drift' in which, in addition to a criticism of delinquent subculture theory, he proposed a 'neo-classical' revolution. One of his criticisms of delinquent subculture theory was that it was absurd to suggest that adolescents could sustain a separate 'commitment' to crime in an environment dominated by adult conventions and agencies. Instead, he suggested a return to a less deterministic conception of the delinquent, more in line with classical criminology, of being committed to neither delinquency nor convention but being in a position of 'drift' somewhere between the two (though he was later to suggest a more complete break with determinism, 1969).

Matza also forged a second link with classical criminology: a return to an interest in 'crime' rather than just 'the criminal'. He pointed out that the definition and application of the legal rules that define 'crime' were a crucial feature of the environment of the delinquent, yet their significance had been almost completely ignored by positivist criminologists (their implicit 'absolutist' conception of crime being mainly responsible).

These two themes – a return to indeterminism and a new interest in the implications of the operation of the criminal justice system – were also features of the 'interactionist' school (such as Becker, 1964; and Lemert, 1967) writing at the same time as Matza. Between them, these writers created a significant break with the traditions of positivist criminology.

1 Symbolic interactionism and labelling theory

The 1960s and early 1970s was the period of the 'hippie counter-culture': the experimentation with alternative life styles, freer attitudes towards drug use and sexuality, the revolt against the fruits of science and technology in the form of industrial pollution, the threat of nuclear weapons and the actual use of weapons in the Vietnam War. Students and intellectuals protesting or in revolt found themselves being defined as 'criminals', while the perpetrators of war and pollution and intolerant repression were not.

Traditional, 'corrective' criminology, with the view of the criminal as having committed acts that could be taken for granted as being wrong, and who were consequently in need of correction by scientific methods, was clearly out of tune with these events.

A new image was needed – the criminal as victim, or hero even. This involved a relativist conception of crime and (since they were to be seen as fighting against oppression) a less deterministic conception of criminals.

This was the background to the resurgence of the 'interactionist perspective' – a perspective which was to prove, in the end, a little too shaky to bear all these radical demands. It was based on the ideas propounded, much earlier, by G. H. Mead in his theory of 'symbolic interactionism'. Human beings are seen as constructing their social action in a process of interaction with others. The interaction is via symbols (e.g. language), hence the name. We are not merely passive recipients in these interaction processes, we bring our own, autonomous motives and meanings to bear on them, i.e. we are at least partially 'free'. One important feature of these interactions, which was to play a major part in the new interactionism, was that we use stereotypical 'labels' to make 'sense' of other people based on cues or knowledge that we have of them. One such important label is that of 'criminal' or 'deviant'. The main thesis of the new interactionists was that the 'official' application of these particular labels (via agencies such as schoolteachers, police etc.) had profound consequences for the persons so labelled, and for the way we perceive and understand crime and deviance.

The first consequence, already implied in the last paragraph, was a change in perception of the subject matter – from 'crime' to the wider category of 'deviance'. This followed naturally from the new, relativist conception of crime: that it was not defined by intrinsic features of the criminal acts themselves (almost *anything* could be, and probably has been a crime at some time or other) but by the way it is responded to – the way it is labelled. The defining feature of crimes is that they are defined unfavourably – but in that respect they are similar to many other categories of acts, i.e. all 'deviant' acts. In practice, however, it is probably fair to say that, with a few exceptions, the new perspective did not incorporate many acts other than crimes, the major exception being the inclusion of mental illness.

A second consequence was a new view of data on crime and deviance – in particular the criminal statistics. Traditional criminology, while acknowledging certain deficiencies, generally accepted criminal statistics as an objective measure of the nature of criminals and extent of crime (against which it tested its theories). The new view emphasised the point that they represented the successful application of labels to acts – on a highly selective basis, reflecting who agents of control such as the police regard as likely suspects, or people dangerous enough to warrant official action. Thus, for example, if police believe 'real' delinquents come from broken homes (thanks to psychological theories of delinquency) then they will be more likely to take action against offenders from broken homes, and hence a subsequent analysis of 'delinquents' confirms the theory! Interactionists also stressed how the self-fulfilling-prophecy effect could produce what they called 'deviancy amplification': if the public (informed of rises in criminal statistics by the media) believe crime is on the increase and more of a 'problem' they will be more sensitive to it, report more to the police who will record more and produce a further rise, which is then fed back to the public by the media, and so on.

Lemert (1967) proposed a second 'amplifying' effect. A consequence of being officially labelled 'deviant' or 'criminal' is that people come to see you differently, as a different kind of person. This cuts off access to conventional settings and identities. In time, Lemert suggested, this leads to 'deviants' acquiring a different conception of themselves, and they live up to the new identity. He called this 'secondary deviation'.

A third consequence of the new perspective was that it prescribed a different aim for the sociology of deviance, via different methods. It was no longer appropriate to look for 'causes' of crime via clinical, statistical, 'scientific' methods. Instead, Matza (1969) proposed that the job of the sociologist was 'appreciation' – entering into the world of the deviant and appreciating the motives, meanings and understandings that constitute it.

Interactionism and labelling theory had a profound, debunking effect on traditional criminology. But it too soon came under fire – though mainly for not going far enough. Despite its commitment to indeterminism, labelling theory, particularly Lemert's concept of 'secondary deviation', had a peculiarly deterministic ring to it: it seemed as if once you had a label slapped on you, that was it, you had no choice but to live up to it! As we shall see, it was its failure to take the implications of indeterminism and relativism far enough that was the basis of the attack from phenomenological sociology.

Perhaps less justifiable, but equally significant, was the attack on its political inadequacies. Although it came to terms with political power (it was the powerful who were seen as the labellers, the powerless as the labelled) it was attacked, mainly by Marxists, for getting stuck at the 'lower' level of street interactions between deviants and 'low level functionaries', such as the police. This is obviously true, since 'interaction' was its focus of attention! But Marxists wanted things to go further – to look at whose rules they were, whose interests were served (though, of course, they already knew the answer).

2 Control theory

Although Matza laid claim to a neo-classical revolution, the end product of his own work and that of the interactionists bore little resemblance to that of the original classical school. Strangely, a theory put forward by contemporary writers usually associated with traditional 'corrective' criminology bore a much closer resemblance (partly because, as was suggested earlier, there were closer links between classical and 'corrective' criminology than Matza allowed). This was 'control theory', particularly in the version put forward by Hirschi (1969).

Hirschi started by criticising most sociological theories of crime (especially anomie and subculture theory) for what he called their 'strain' assumption; that is, they assume human beings to be 'naturally' conforming. Hence some 'strain' (such as thwarted conventional ambitions) is needed to 'push' them into crime. Hirschi proposed the opposite starting assumption: that human motives are naturally diverse, often self-seeking and hence likely to favour violation of whatever rules there are defining 'crimes'. For 'control theory' the problem thus becomes 'what causes people to conform?'.

Note the similarity between the starting point and that of classical criminology. An important difference is that control theory does not take the diversity of human motives as constituting 'free will' in the way classical criminology did. However, in taking them as 'given' (i.e. beyond current capabilities of causal explanation) it *in practice* turns out very much the same.

Another similarity is in the general answer that control theory gives to the question 'why do we conform?' It answers – because it is (usually) in our interests to do so. If it is not, then we will not. This again echoes the classical, utilitarian, 'rational self-seeking' view of human beings. But the similarity ends there – there is no return to the vague, mystical idea of a 'social contract'. Hirschi treats the question of what 'bonds' individuals to conformity as an empirical problem. He proposes four bonds; attachment (the extent to which individuals have close emotional ties to other people), commitment (the extent to which they see conventional behaviour, e.g. at school, as offering immediate or long-term rewards), involvement (the extent to which their time is taken up with conventional activities) and belief (the extent to which their beliefs coincide with conventional ones). He subjects these bonds to rigorous empirical testing – using the standard techniques (survey, statistical analysis) of positivist criminology.

In many ways the less ambitious, less deterministic formulation of control theory seemed to offer the most promising framework for the objectives of traditional corrective criminology. Unfortunately, it appeared at a time when these objectives themselves were under attack. Its subsequent unfashionability has to some extent restricted its development.

Post neo-classicism

The main tenets of the neo-classical revolution have had a continuing influence, even though interactionism and labelling theory have gone into decline, and control theory out of fashion. Positivism is now generally on the run in sociology.

Ironically, the further development of the themes of indeterminism and relativism, and the switch of interest from the defined to the definers has had the effect of making a specific, substantive 'sociology of crime' less and less tenable. The currently dominant phenomenological and Marxist perspectives in sociology have a tendency to 'lose' a specific interest in crime in their own central theoretical concerns.

1 Phenomenological sociology

The various strands of phenomenologically inspired 'interpretive' sociology have taken indeterminism and anti-positivism to their logical extremes. They insist that human action can only be understood in terms of the meanings that humans attach to actions and situations, and are highly critical of traditional sociology's (including interactionism's) use of concepts such as crime, deviance, anomie and so on. They point out that sociologists' use of such terms bears an unknown relation to the meanings and understandings of the people they purport to describe: delinquents have never heard of anomie, they either do not refer to themselves as 'delinquents', 'deviants' or 'criminals', or, if they do, there is no way of knowing whether their understanding of such terms are the same as sociologists. Consequently, phenomenological sociologists do not accept what has counted previously as 'sociological knowledge'.

Their work has concentrated on much more basic levels of meaning construction by social actors (opening and closing telephone conversations, for example). Although they sometimes use examples from crime and deviance, they are not usually concerned with contributing to a sociology of that substantive area, but are simply using them as settings for examining these more fundamental problems.

2 Marxist criminology

The criticisms of the political inadequacies of interactionism and labelling theory developed into a 'new' Marxist criminology. Taylor, Walton and Young (1973) appeared to promise a new formulation, taking into account both Marxist theory and a less deterministic conception of human beings. In the event, this failed to appear and the 'new' criminology contented itself with Marxist critique. Part of the reason for this was the assumption that crime (or 'the need to criminalise' as Taylor, Walton and Young put it) was the product of the dehumanising features of the capitalist mode of production. This ruled out doing anything about crime within the existing system (it was considered as worthless, liberal 'tinkering'). The only 'solution' was the transition to socialism – hence any particular interest in crime was incorporated, and lost, in the central concern of Marxism.

Instead, Marxist writers have tended to focus their attention on the criminal law and penal system. Much recent work has been concerned with the historical changes in these institutions as they have adapted to the emerging needs of the capitalist class. This can still be seen as having some links with the earlier focus of inter-actionism on the 'definers' of crime rather than criminals them-selves. But Marxist writers have seen themselves as going further than the 'street level interaction' analysis of interactionism, into the wider, social structural level.

Interactionism's emphasis on the 'selectivity' in the definition and application of legal rules has also been taken up by Marxists and other writers – particularly the social class implications. They have argued that formal definitions of 'crime' are biased towards lower-class misdeeds. Analogous activity of the powerful (often much more socially injurious) have either not been defined as crimes or, when they have been, the criminal law has been rarely used. This was not a new idea. Sutherland had made similar points much earlier in his work on what he called 'white collar crime'. However, there has undoubtedly been a considerable resurgence of interest and work in this field.

Generally, the focus of Marxist criminology has shifted away from the 'criminal' and on to criminal law. In this respect, though for different reasons and with quite different conclusions, it too has returned to the earlier concerns of classical criminology. And, again, like classical criminology, this has meant that their contri-bution has been much more towards the traditional concerns of the sociology of law rather than to those of criminology.

3 Feminist criminology

A conspicuous omission from almost all previous criminology – classical, positivist, neo-classical and Marxist – has been a concern with women's crime. This is perhaps least surprising with respect to positivist criminology. Their slavish acceptance of the crime pattern given in the criminal statistics and their commitment to causal-corrective objectives automatically ruled out any interest in women: according to the statistics, women simply were not a

causal-corrective problem. Though even there, one might have
thought that the apparent lack of women's crime was an interesting
comparative phenomenon, well worth some attention.

For recent feminist writers, this lack of interest is seen as yet
another example of sexist attitudes in yet another male-dominated
area (academic criminology): women, even when they are in trouble
with the law, are seen as less important and interesting than men.
There is a slight problem with this argument. The one area of
women's crime or deviance that *has* received a lot of attention has
been prostitution. Yet feminists have also criticized what they have
seen as over-attention given to the female prostitutes, at the
expense of any consideration of their equally deviant male clients.
It seems that male sexism is manifested in both an under and over
concern with women's deviance. But perhaps this illustrates the
point that it is only when women are involved in sexual 'deviation'
that they are deemed worthy of male attention (and control).

Certainly, recent feminist writers have corrected this omission.
Initially, their main concern was with drawing attention to the
omission, or criticising the inadequacies of the limited attempts
that have been made to incorporate women's crime in male
perspectives. Subsequently they have dealt with issues such as to
what extent the low statistical crime rate for women is 'real' or the
result of male (sexist) 'chivalry', the relation between female crime
patterns and women's social position, what kind of effect female
'liberation' might be expected to have on women's crime, and the
extent to which the apparent leniency of the criminal justice system
conceals areas of oppression.

Partly because the contributors have often come from outside of
sociology, feminist writings have sometimes been inconsistent in their
position on the problems of starting assumptions, methods and so
on that we have considered here. Yet they have, also, been responsible for keeping alive some of the issues of traditional criminology.

Conclusion

The history of sociology's involvement with crime and deviance is
a good illustration of the problematic history of sociology as a
whole. External social, political and technological factors,

combined with changing philosophical and ideological fashions have been major factors in its development. As we have seen, because of traditional taken-for-granted assumptions about crime, the pressures for a 'problem solving' approach have been particularly influential in this area. Yet, where sociology has taken on this responsibility, its 'findings' have been almost entirely negative or debunking and have emphasised that the 'problem' of crime is too intimately tied up with wider social, economic and political issues to be solvable simply by changes in the penal system. This has meant that the sociology of crime and deviance has had little influence outside of purely academic circles.

Recent developments have seen sociology more self-consciously disengaging itself from the problem-solving role. This has undoubtedly extended its academic freedom and opened up neglected issues. But it has also had the effect of leaving the problem-solving arena even more open to the endless rehashing of old, long-discredited ideas and programmes.

Suggestions for further reading

For a critical overview of the development of criminology

Jeffery, C. R. (1960), 'The historical development of criminology', in H. Mannheim (ed.), *Pioneers in Criminology*, (London: Stevens) pp. 364–394 is brief and useful.

On classical criminology

Monachesi, E. (1960), 'Cesare Beccaria', in H. Mannheim (ed.), *Pioneers in Criminology*, (London: Stevens) pp. 36–50 for an assessment of Beccaria's contribution.

Vold, G. (1958), *Theoretical Criminology*, (New York: OUP). Chapter 2 provides an introduction.

On the founders of positivist criminology and their legacy

Ellis, L. (1982), 'Genetics and criminal behaviour', *Criminology*, vol. 20, no. 1, pp. 43–66, on genetic theories.

Hall Williams, J. E. (1982), *Criminology and Criminal Justice*, (London: Butterworths) Chapters 1–5.

On the main sociological theories and perspectives

Downes, D. and Rock, P. (1982), *Understanding Deviance*, (Oxford: Clarendon Press) provides an excellent introduction, including chapters on interactionism, phenomenology and Marxist (radical) criminology.

On Marxist criminology

Taylor, I., Walton, P. and Young, J. (1975) (eds.), *Critical Criminology*, (London: Routledge and Kegan Paul).

On feminist criminology

Campbell, A. (1981), *Girl Delinquents*, (Oxford: Blackwell) helps redress the balance.

Heidensohn, F. (1985), *Women and Crime*, (London: Macmillan) provides a discussion of the current position on research into women's crime.

Resources

New Society regularly contains articles, findings etc. relating to crime and deviance.

The main academic journal covering the field in this country is the *British Journal of Criminology*, published quarterly.

Criminal Statistics, published annually by HMSO contain data on crime, criminals and crime trends. However, it should be remembered that they reflect changes in reporting and recording crime as much as they reflect changes in actual criminal activity.

Questions for discussion

1 Describe and assess the differences between sociological approaches to studying crime and deviance and the approaches of other disciplines.

2 What advantages, if any, follow from viewing conformity as being more problematic and in need of explanation than deviance?

3 What consequences follow from regarding 'crime' as a status *conferred* on acts (by 'labellers') rather than a particular *quality* of acts?

4 Why do you think women's crime has been neglected so much by all 'schools' of criminology? Are their theories and perspectives applicable to women, or is a separate 'feminist criminology' required?

Chapter 10

After sixteen: what choice?

Helen Roberts

This chapter, like the one which follows it, deals with a particular research project and some of the problems involved in the research process. By focusing on a research project concerning the choices which young people make when they reach the minimum school leaving age I intend to describe something of the way in which sociologists work in practice.

What are sociologists' data, and how do they go about studying them?

A choice with which sociologists, in common with other professionals (and particularly those in the so-called liberal professions) are faced is the choice concerning the general direction their work should take. For sociologists, this choice is a wide one, and many factors will influence what particular sociologists find themselves examining, as Stacey (Chapter 7) and Burgess (Chapter 11) point out. Not all the considerations will be purely intellectual. Among those factors affecting choice may be the sociologist's theoretical orientation, the availability of funding for certain sorts of research, personal commitment and personal experiences as well as concerns such as the 'usefulness' of the work in practical and in disciplinary terms.

In the research described below, all of these considerations played some part. Towards the end of 1979, I became involved in a rather minor way in a study called *After Sixteen* which was being undertaken in the Bradford Metropolitan District. This study was designed to monitor the educational and career aspirations and achievements of a sample of 16-year-olds in the district for a period of 18 months beginning in March 1980. As one of four representatives of local colleges who formed a steering group for the project, my involvement in the research in the early stages was peripheral. It was only as the extent and the quality of the data became evident that I became more deeply involved in one aspect of the study, as I shall describe below.

The Main Study

The group of young people who were to be the respondents in the research on the aims and aspirations of young people reached their sixteenth birthdays between 1 September 1979 and 31 August 1980. From approximately 8,000 16-year-olds attending either state or private schools in Bradford during the spring term 1980 and whose homes were within the Bradford Metropolitan District, a sample of 760 was drawn up on the basis of dates of birth. A postal questionnaire was used to obtain information from this group on three occasions:

a) March 1980 (before leaving school, taking examinations or continuing full time education);

b) November 1980 (when examination results were known and after two or three months at work, college, school or unemployed);

c) June 1981 (after one year when fresh career or educational decisions might have been made).

The original sample size of 760 (approximately 10 per cent of 16-year-olds in the district at the time) drew an extremely high response rate of 87 per cent. Postal questionnaires normally have rather low rates of response, and it is possible that the high response rate says something not only about the research design, but also about the concern of the young people being researched with the topic of the research – their own futures. Over the course of the survey, the response rate fell, although not dramatically. 535 young people responded to the second questionnaire in November

1980 (70 per cent response) and 450 (59 per cent) responded to the third and final postal questionnaire in July 1981, a year after they had reached minimum school leaving age.

If someone did not reply to the questionnaire within three weeks, he or she was sent a reminder letter. If this failed to produce a response within two weeks, a second copy of the questionnaire was sent. Replies to the questionnaire were coded and were entered into computer held files. These files were supplemented with information from other sources, for instance examination results from the Department of Education and Science (DES), and information on the postal districts of the respondents to see what the spread of response was like across the district.

As indicated above, the response was high. Over the course of the three surveys which took place in under a year, there were over 1,600 responses. As a rule, research is not particularly generously funded in the non-university sector of higher education, and there was only one research fellow working on these data.[1] Although he eventually had a secretary and some clerical assistance it was impossible for even the most energetic researcher to make the fullest use of the large amount of data generated in the time available to him. (Like many researchers, he was working on a short term contract.) It was therefore decided that he and I would apply for funding from another source to facilitate more work on the data.

The girls

For some time, I had been doing work on sexual divisions in society and I was particularly interested in looking at what was happening to the girls in the district. Did equal opportunities legislation mean that girls were now being offered – and taking up – the same opportunities as boys? Were they employed or unemployed in similar numbers? Were they going on to Youth Opportunities Programme (YOP) schemes, (the predecessors of Youth Training Schemes (YTS)), and were the schemes they went on different from the schemes offered to or chosen by the boys? In order to look more closely at these questions, we made an application to the Equal Opportunities Commission (EOC) for a research assistant to work on the data with us for six months. The sorts of theories I was most interested in as a sociologst were those which attempted to explain inequalities in society, and the data showed clear inequalities across the district. It seemed likely, given what we know about the sorts of work that boys go into and the sorts of jobs that girls go into (and the differences in pay and prospects), that there would also be inequalities between the sexes that would require explanation.

As a feminist, I was concerned by the fact that far from things getting better for women over the past few years (as is frequently popularly supposed), things are getting worse in many respects, for instance, the earnings gap between men and women is growing. As a feminist, I wanted to know what things were like for girls in the district where I was living and working. I knew that there was a source of research funding for this type of work from the Equal Opportunities Commission which, in common with other research funding bodies, is increasingly concerned with the 'relevance' of the work it funds. Since this piece of research would or could have policy implications for, for instance, careers guidance, it seemed to me likely that we would be funded. We were. Our commitment to the EOC was firstly, to look specifically at the statistical data on girls, including any comments they may have returned with their questionnaires, and secondly, to interview a sample of the girls in depth.

On reaching minimum school leaving age at 16, five possibilities were available to the young people in the survey. These were:

a) to remain at school;
b) to go to a college of further education (or continue full time education in some other institution);
c) to start work;
d) to become unemployed;
e) to enter a youth opportunities scheme (this of course involved being unemployed, since it was only available to those young people registered as unemployed).

For the girls, there was another possibility, and this was the 'choice' to opt for full time domestic labour. The availability of this option for women in itself tells us something about the sexual division of labour in our society, and the way in which gender affects the choices we make (see Stacey, Chapter 7; and Finch, Chapter 8).

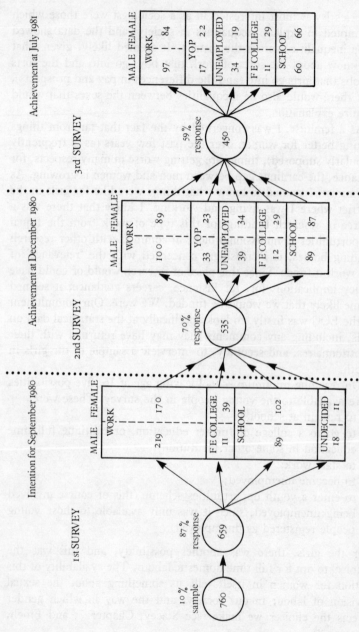

Figure 10.1 16-year-olds in Bradford Metropolitan District, 1980: Their work intention and achievement.

The statistical evidence from the surveys is summarised in Figure 10.1, and the first part of our research involved looking again at these data, breaking them down by sex (as they appear here) and examining in more detail the computer held data from the questionnaires. The statistical data give us a broad overview, but statistics are by no means the whole story. As the American sociologist Pauline Bart points out, everything is data but data isn't everything. We can see from Figure 10.1 that similar proportions of boys and girls seeking work, for instance, find it, but that leaves a lot of questions unanswered. What sort of work are they doing? Are they taking the jobs they hoped to get while they were still at school? Are all the boys brain surgeons and all the girls shop assistants or vice versa? What patterns emerge when we look at the data more closely, and how do the young people experience their situations?

The second part of our commitment to the Equal Opportunities Commission – the interviews – were intended to illuminate the reality of the girls' situation, and to switch the emphasis from what 'happens' to the young people to how they perceive their lives. Needless to say, the perspective of the girls is probably very different from the perspectives of teachers, careers officers or parents. Like the statistics, the interviews need to be interpreted and analysed, but the interviews do give a picture of the world as seen by the girls to set alongside other data.

The sociological perspective

If the perspective of the girls in the interviews was different from careers officers, teachers or parents, in what ways did our sociological perspective differ from the approach of, for instance, a social worker, a journalist or just a plain nosey parker? This comes back to some of the questions asked by other contributors to this volume, and particularly Janet Finch who writes about the difference between sociology and common sense. One of the differences lies in the sort of methods we used to go about our research. Like much empirical research (see Burgess, Chapter 11) we used not one method but several. These included:

a) Familiarising ourselves with relevant sociological and non-soci-
   ological literature on the subject we were studying. There is
   quite a substantial body of sociological literature on the transition from school to work, and we also looked at official statistics and reports, magazines from the National Association of
   Youth Clubs and newspaper reports on, for instance, youth
   unemployment.
b) Familiarising ourselves with the local situation and factors
   concerning Bradford which might make it similar to, or
   different from, the situation in other areas. The decline in the
   textile industry in Bradford has had a marked effect on the local
   economy for instance, and we also needed to be aware of the
   fact that in Bradford there had been both a long tradition of
   women working outside the home and a long tradition of
   working-class radicalism.
c) Examining and analysing the statistical data which had been
   collected, often described as quantitative research or 'hard' data.
d) Understanding the interviews, in other words doing the sort of
   qualitative research which is often characterised as 'soft' data.

Unlike social workers, our primary aim was not to 'help' the young
people in any direct way although we hoped that ultimately our
research would be helpful rather than not. Unlike the careers officer,
we were not there to counsel or give careers advice. Unlike the
journalist, we were not going in looking for a particular 'line' or
story. We were collecting data systematically, placing it in its
social, economic and political context, and attempting to theorise
about, in other words make sense of, what we found.

Problems in research

There is clearly more than one way of making sense of the same
data. What follows describes some of our problems in doing the
research and something of what we found. Several recent books
(Platt, 1976; Bell and Newby, 1977; Roberts, 1981a; Bell and
Roberts, 1984; Burgess, 1984a) have made clear that research is not
always the simple linear process it would appear to be from some
research monographs. It is not just a matter of getting the research

grant, appointing the personnel, sailing through the research and publishing the results.

Just three of the problems that can, and in our case did, appear *en route* can be described here. The first is a problem quite common in research and described by Jennifer Platt in her book *The Realities of Social Research* (1976). This is the problem of the research 'team'. Our team comprised four people, the research fellow working on the broader research project, myself, the research assistant who was appointed to work under our direction and a part-time secretary. Ensuring that a research report reached the Equal Opportunities Commission at the end of the project was ultimately my responsibility.

The 'team' was top heavy with two chiefs and one assistant. (The secretary was really in a team of her own.) Hanmer and Leonard (1980) have graphically described the exploitative way in which research assistants (often female) are treated by research principals (often male) and while our research assistant was not, I hope, badly treated, there can be no doubt that the division of labour was not ideal. Of the thirty interviews completed, she did the great majority. On the other hand, when we came to the end of the project, she moved back to the teaching post from which she had been seconded and we were faced with the problem either of my writing up the data entirely, or the research assistant taking on large amounts of writing at the same time as a taxing teaching load. In fact we were in a better position than many researchers in this respect, since once the project was over, we were still working in the same institution, and therefore able to discuss the final report. In many cases, researchers appointed on short term projects move on to their next job before the writing up is complete – which means that either they, or worse still, the data become inaccessible.

A second problem we faced was that of arranging interviews with our young women. We wrote to the girls asking to interview them, and four replies received the same morning may give some impression of the diversity of our respondents. A first wrote on a scrap torn from a notebook:

. . . Thanks for the letter. Of course you may come on
Tuesday but couldn't you make it for 6 o'clock, also I'm sorry
to say that I didn't receive the third questionnaire.
Bye for now

A second sent a beautifully handwritten letter on good quality notepaper:

> . . . Thank you for your letter dated 29th June. I'm sorry but I shall not be available on Monday 6th of July. I shall be going on holiday . . . for $2\frac{1}{2}$ months on 4th July.
> I apologise for any inconvenience I may have caused and wish every success with your survey . . .

A third wrote a letter which amply illustrates some of the problems which may face girls in this age group; problems touched on by Janet Finch's discussion in Chapter 8 on the care of the frail elderly:

> . . . I received my third questionnaire and I have returned it. I have also received your letter, but I'm afraid that Wednesday 8th July would not be convenient, as my grandma at the moment is ill and will have to go into hospital so we are looking after my backward aunt at my grandma's house so until it is all sorted out it would be very difficult with other problems as well to talk to you on that day however I will be glad to arrange it for another day later on . . .

The fourth response in the post on that particular morning was the tersest and most worrying. Asked for an interview at eight o'clock one evening, a girl had replied:

> . . . No. My dad's always drunk by then.

This last letter raises an issue which is seldom seriously discussed. What do researchers do about the problems of human relations between researcher and respondent? What does the researcher do when the person being researched turns the tables and starts to ask questions – whether these questions are personal ones ('Have you got any children?) or 'advice' questions ('What would you do?'). Ann Oakley (1981b) provides a useful discussion of this problem, and makes clear the responsibility that researchers have to respondents.

Those who wrote back refusing interviews were left alone, because although they may have been an interesting group, we felt we could not invade their privacy. But even among those who accepted, there was the problem that few of those we were interviewing seemed to lead the sort of lives which required them to keep a diary. This meant that they were not always around when the interviewer called. This in turn had implications for the research time-table. Since arranging the interviews took longer than planned, analysis and writing the research up were in turn pushed back, with the repercussions outlined above in terms of the research process.

A third and rather serious problem which occasionally confronts researchers appeared after the research was completed and written up. This problem concerned the way the research was reported in the local press. As one of the people who wrote the report, I was surprised to read a headline on the local women's page one evening saying: **Bradford girls lack drive – report says**. As it happens, far from thinking (or reporting) that the girls we interviewed lacked drive, we were frequently impressed by what they did manage to achieve in the face of all sorts of difficulties. But once this kind of newspaper report has appeared it is very difficult to do anything to change the impression given. Although few – possibly none – of the girls we interviewed will read our research report or anything we write on the research, quite large numbers of them – or their parents, read the local evening paper. Will they give their time to be researched again? One way of partially overcoming this sort of problem is to write one's own press releases. Journalists are busy, and will frequently adopt the 'line' taken in a press release. But if one wants to make the results of one's research public (and who wants their research to sit in a filing cabinet and have no impact?) the problem remains. These are some of the difficulties we came across in the research process. In what follows, something of the way we went about our research is described.

The interviews

The interviews were semi-structured. We had no set questionnaire, but we had a checklist of questions we covered in each interview. Within the constraints of ensuring this checklist was covered, we tried to encourage the girls we interviewed to talk as freely as possible, and to raise other areas which they thought important. Every interview was tape-recorded, and large parts of the interview were subsequently transcribed verbatim. Each interview began with a brief description of the purpose of the interview, namely to look at work and career experiences and aspirations from the final year of compulsory schooling, through the year just completed, and, hopefully, on to intentions and aspirations for the future.

In almost every case it seemed appropriate to ask the respondent to begin on relatively straightforward and factual ground, with a description of the course followed in the fifth-form (the final year of compulsory schooling). This included an account of subjects studied and qualifications achieved. The other area of particular enquiry here was the respondent's thinking about careers: how far subject choices were made with careers in mind; to what extent she could see any development in her thinking about careers; how far careers guidance seemed relevant to her needs and aspirations. We asked about decisions taken at the end of the fifth-year, or as a consequence of exam results, and the impact of transition to the first period offering major life choices to the young adult. Since all the interviews took place in June and July 1981, all the young people had twelve months since the end of compulsory schooling to look back on. Finally the interview was an opportunity to look forward – to 19, to 21, to 25 and perhaps beyond? Are any career and life intentions formulated for the future? How does the young woman of 17 perceive the future? Are there in any sense plans? These are the sorts of questions we wanted answered. What of the context in which the research took place?

The local context

Bradford is a city of nearly half a million people and has the fastest growing population of any Metropolitan District in the country. The dole queue had nearly doubled from 13,000 in 1980 to over 24,000 in 1981 and by June 1984 was nearly 30,000. There is a slump in house building, and according to the local policy unit's report, the traditional fabric which has supported the city, the economy, transport, houses – even drains – is decaying. The textile industry is in decline. Many schools are in a poor state of repair. The maintained sector of higher education (that is, the colleges) has experienced severe cuts, and of all universities in the UK, the local one was one of the worst cut. All of these mean not just less education, but less money circulating in the district. The area is not as deprived as some (Northern Ireland, for instance) but in looking at our findings, it was important to bear in mind that we were looking at a very disadvantaged community. Many of the young people in our survey were not only unemployed themselves; they also had mothers, fathers, brothers, sisters, boyfriends and neighbours who were unemployed. It is in this context that we need to set the research.

What we found

I described at the beginning of the chapter how we interviewed girls in and out of work, girls on YOP schemes, girls at school and girls at college. What follows describes something of what we found about the girls who were in work at the time they were interviewed.

The relatively powerless appear frequently, perhaps predominantly in social research. It is easier in educational research to gain access to school children than to teachers, to teachers than to heads, to heads than to under secretaries and ministers. Similarly with other topics covered in this book. In research on the sociology of work, it is easier to gain access to shop floor workers than to top management, and in the sociology of health and illness, patients are more accessible for interview than consultants, or the Minister of State for Health. The logical result of research on the powerless one might think, is that the powerless who are being researched might be given a voice in what is actually written about them.

One does not have to go far to see that that is not normally the case. Researchers tend to feel, perhaps with some justification, that if, as experts, they are commissioned to do research, then it is important to put an expert's gloss – an expert's analysis and interpretation – on to the findings. Such analysis is undoubtedly necessary. Facts do not speak for themselves. But if facts do not speak for themselves, people often may not, or cannot, speak for themselves, or at least do not do so in the contexts where what they say might have some influence.

We were therefore careful to report in some detail what the girls told us. What were their experiences?

Figure 10.2 Work in Bradford

At the first survey: total response 659	170 girls and 219 boys intended to be in work by September 1980
At the second survey: total response 535	89 girls and 100 boys actually were in work in December 1980
At the third survey: total response 450	84 girls and 97 boys were in work in July 1981

Some of the experiences of girls in Bradford were highlighted for us in one interview by a girl we will call Patsy. Patsy has had four jobs and five months of unemployment in the year since leaving school. In some ways it has been a bad year, moving from one job to another, but in the end 'can't complain' is her summing up. School – sometimes tolerated, sometimes enjoyed – was seen as a prelude to work; there was never any question of staying on beyond the fifth-year, and it was Patsy's choice not to take any examinations.

Patsy had a job to go to when she left school.
'I had a letter on Friday to say I started on a Monday. Me auntie used to work there and she put me name down, and I went down to see't supervisor, and she said, 'We'll get in contact with you.' I was scared stiff of leaving school because of no jobs.
The job Patsy got was making shoulder pads for a chain of men's outfitters.
'A lad used to cut the pattern out and we used to make 'em . . . The first morning they sat me on a table, showed me how to do it and I carried on all through the day. Then the next day, I went on the machines. They just learn you. I learned the whole job in a week.'

After four months, Patsy faced redundancy for the first time. First the part-timers went, and then Patsy because she was the youngest. Now the firm has closed down. Then a neighbour told Patsy about a job that involved sorting birthday cards into packs. She rang up, and went for an interview the same day. 'It's a bit hard ringing up, because you don't know who to ask for. No, they hadn't told us at school'. The job was hers, but when she arrived for work she found it was only temporary for four weeks.

After a gap of two months, job three was at a fisheries, taking eyes out of potatoes.

Me mum's mate told me. So I went there and they said, 'Right, you start tomorrow', so I went. I had to sign a form for't dole place, and they said 'What were your job?' and I didn't know what to say so I said, 'Picking eyes out of potatoes' [laugh]. I got finished from there. One morning I fell down't steps and I did something to me shoulder and I couldn't move, so they finished me there and then. But me mum said I should have took them to tribunal. And I got . . . me lowest wage were £15 and I worked 5 days a week. And one day I came out wi' £10. They used to finish awkward times – sometimes at 11, we started at 8, sometimes at half 7, sometimes we used to work on a Sunday. Me mum says it's slave labour.

When I'm unemployed, sometimes I help me mum. Most of time, I'm in town looking for a job. I go round all big stores like Marks and Spencers and just ask supervisor if there's any vacancies. I used to go in job centre which that didn't help very much because I wasn't old enough. They used to give me appointments card at Careers Office, but there wasn't much on offer . . . I went to Careers Office and I said 'I'm not walking out of here until I've got a job'. Anyway, they had one full time vacancy. And there were twenty of us who went, and he picked me. It were sewing carpets.

You just sit down and tack round carpet. Kept sticking needle into me thumb. Now I'm on to binding. It's getting easier and easier as I go on. I'm only a trainer. Another three months to go then I've done six months. Everybody says I'm catching up to them, and they've been there nearly 13 years.

. . . Me boyfriend's just been made redundant, so I don't think we'll have our own home . . . we're getting married in October. Not this one, next year. We've fixed a date. Can't go back now. We've told everybody. He got redundancy just after his 21st birthday. He's a fridge engineer. He's been with that firm since he left school. Anyway, he's going for an interview tomorrow so we'll just keep us fingers crossed . . . We've just managed to save to get engaged and go on us holiday next week, then we'll start saving.

Spare time? . . . Take dog for a walk. I like swimming and ice skating. But I've given them up. Couldn't afford them when I lost me first job.

Patsy had four jobs since leaving school. She has been unemployed for five months, and her boyfriend has been made redundant. Nevertheless her case raised issues echoed elsewhere. Firstly, just as the literature on boys and work points to a 'lads of dads' pattern in finding work (see Lee and Wrench, 1981; Bell, Chapter 3 in this volume), Patsy, like many of the other girls in the survey, got her job through personal networks. The first job, through 'me auntie', the second through a neighbour, the third through 'me mum's mate'. It was only her fourth job that she got through careers.

By and large, those we interviewed were satisfied. A year after leaving school, what was important was to have a job rather than to have a particular job. Far from indicating the 'lack of drive' indicated in the newspaper, this is probably a realistic view given what the options are. On a November day in 1981 for instance, the Careers Office had only eleven vacancies in the district for young people, apart from a number of training posts in nursing coming up in 1982.

How typical was Patsy in the type of work she went into? At the time of the second survey, the largest proportion of girls responding were in sales jobs (41 per cent). The next largest group was clerical work with 26 per cent and then textiles with 10 per cent. Smaller proportions were in hairdressing and packaging. Only one girl in the survey had no traditional aspirations. She had wanted to be a lorry driver. What became of her?

I am a care attendant taking care of old people in a private nursing home. I found the job through my relative. I am doing this job because I would rather be in a job than on the dole.

Since May 1980 I took my exams, did my fair share of job hunting (and still do). I like the job, but I would rather be driving a long distance lorry. When I am 18, I might go in for SEN nursing, and then do geriatric nursing . . . But I still like the idea of long distance lorry driving. It's the only way to see the world.

The above gives an indication of some of the interview material. What did we find out about work from the surveys?

The third survey indicated that many more boys are expecting (and getting) work with training. Asked what they thought they would be doing at 18, ninety-three boys and sixty-seven girls mentioned work with training. Thirty-three boys and fifty-two girls mentioned work without training. Job satisfaction, according to the results of the third survey, appeared to be higher among boys than girls, with four boys and eight girls saying they were not very satisfied. Particularly revealing in the third survey were attitudes towards promotion. Seventy-seven boys and sixty-three girls were interested in promotion. Two boys and twenty-two girls were not.

Making sense of the data

Although it is not possible within the space of this chapter to make full sense of these data, it is possible to indicate how sociology can help us theorise about our findings. In C. Wright Mills (1970) terms, the sociological imagination can help us distinguish between 'the personal troubles of milieu' and 'the public issues of social structure'. If Patsy were the only girl in Bradford experiencing work problems, the only girl with an unemployed boyfriend, or in a job with little or no training, the only girl earning a low wage, we might feel it useful to look more closely at Patsy as a person for the source of these problems. Since we can see that she is not alone, but forms part of a wider pattern, we need to explain both why young people in general have the sorts of futures they do in the 1980s, and why girls in particular, when they get jobs at all, are going into traditional low paid girls' jobs with little training and little chance of promotion.

Paul Willis (1977) remarks at the beginning of his book *Learning to Labour*:

The difficult thing to explain about how middle class kids get middle class jobs is why others let them. The difficult thing to explain about how working class kids get working class jobs is why they let themselves.

Willis, 1977, p. 1.

The same goes for these girls. Why are they not in jobs with training? Why do they not feel a sense of injustice about their position in relation to boys? The final question is relevant since a factor which clearly emerged from our interviews was that for the girls themselves, equality between men and women was not a burning issue. From this, it should be said, we conclude not that there is no problem, but that any lack of equality is only one problem among many for most of these girls. It is not near the top of their agendas. They do not, on the whole, seem to feel a sense of injustice about their lot. The girls' limited ambitions are perhaps particularly worrying in the light of analysis such as that of Roberts (1977). He suggests that the transition to work is best understood not as an 'occupational choice' but rather as an 'opportunity structure'. In other words, it is not ambitions which lead to particular jobs at 16, but some jobs may lead to ambitions. The opportunity to go into these sorts of jobs is therefore crucial. According to Roberts, young people going to work at 16 do not typically 'choose' occupations in any meaningful sense: they simple take what is available. This seemed to be more than ever true in 1981, and of the girls in our sample. Patsy has been willing to take whatever work came her way. For her there is no obvious pattern of developing skills.

In the survey as a whole, the differences between boys and girls in terms of training were:
a) Forty-two girls and twenty-two boys have a job which provides no training;
b) One girl and sixteen boys have block release for training;
c) Twenty-one girls and twenty-nine boys have day release for training;
d) One girl and eight boys have a college training of between 6 and 12 months;

e) Seventeen girls and ten boys have some other kind of training (for example, on the job);

f) Eight girls and forty-nine boys have training which lasts between 3 and 5 years.

The notion of a 'career' is probably not an appropriate one for most of the girls going into employment at 16. The name of the game is getting a job, getting a wage, keeping off the dole.

Some of the interview material above bears out Ashton and Maguire's (1980) observation that 'young people at school are all too well aware of the rules governing educational selection, but are largely ignorant of the rules governing selection in the labour market' (p. 157). While it was clear that for the high achievers, opportunity led to greater opportunity, for those girls who did less well, their worlds tended to shrink. What we know of sociological theories of socialisation and social control might lead us to think that we can explain patterns of female employment, but such theories would be inadequate. They might explain why things remain as they are, but not why they are as they are.

Sociological theories which are not informed by a feminist perspective might lead us, if we were conservative, to say, that is the way things are; this is one of the ways in which society maintains stability; women doing one sort of job and men doing another is functional. If we were more radical, theories of socialisation and social control might lead us to say that nothing can be changed until everything is changed.

Neither of these positions is very helpful to the young women who are now unemployed, in poorly paid jobs, or not getting any training. But sociological theorising on the nature of social change indicates that changes can and do take place. While the sociology of social change cannot be fully discussed here, it is clear that strutures of attitude and structures of opportunity reinforce each other. Changes in either can lead to changes in the other. Any changes in the employment and opportunity patterns of girls – through, for instance, innovative YOP schemes or Youth Training Schemes or imaginative counselling from careers officers – will involve changes in the examples that are set before young women, and changes in the young women's conceptions of what is natural, normal and desirable. The consequences of small scale reforms are seldom therefore limited to the immediate benefits which they secure. If one form of discrimination can reinforce another, so can opportunity lead to more opportunity.

Note

1 The research fellow on the main *After Sixteen* study was Ivan Maxted, Research and Information Officer, Directorate of Education, Administrative Division, Provincial House, Bradford 1. Copies of the *Users Guide* to the data included in the full survey are available from him, price £2.00. Copies of the full report, H. Roberts and M. Sharp (1982), *After Sixteen: What Happens to the Girls* (Bradford: Bradford Metropolitan District) are also available from him, price £2.50. I am grateful to Ivan Maxted for permission to use the data from the main survey, to Mabeth Sharp who worked with us on the girls study, to the Equal Opportunities Commission for funding the survey, and to Rodney Barker, Bob Burgess, Janet Finch, Hilary Graham, Robert Moore for comments, and to Sue Sinclair and Shirley Middlemiss for technical assistance.

Suggestions for further reading

On the research process

Bell, C. and Newby, H. (1977) (eds.), *Doing Sociological Research*, (London: Allen and Unwin). A collection of essays on how research gets done. The contributors give their versions of what it was like doing particular research projects. Includes an article by Robert Moore (1977) on the background to the influential *Race Community and Conflict*, (Rex and Moore, 1967).

Bell, C. and Roberts, H. (1984), *Social Researching: Politics, Problems and Practice*, (London: Routledge and Kegan Paul). A collection of essays on various aspects of doing research including interviewing and participant observation.

Platt, J. (1976), *The Realities of Social Research*, (London: Chatto and Windus for University of Sussex Press). An excellent discussion of the research process, including an examination of how research gets funded and how research gets completed.

Roberts, H. (1981) (ed.), *Doing Feminist Research*, (London: Routledge and Kegan Paul). A collection of essays on how a feminist perspective has altered both the content and the process of research in sociology.

On being a sociologist and doing sociology

Becker, H. S. (1970), *Sociological Work*, (Chicago: Aldine) contains selections from the author's own methodological and substantive writing. It includes a discussion of the ethical and political decisions that researchers have to make.

Hanmer J. and Leonard D. (1980), 'Men and Culture: the sociological intelligentsia and the maintenance of male domination or superman meets the invisible woman'. This paper was presented to a British Sociological Association conference.

Mills, C. Wright (1970), *The Sociological Imagination*, (Harmondsworth: Penguin) provides an inspiring discussion of sociology both for the beginner and for the more experienced scholar. The appendix of this book 'On Intellectual Craftsmanship' is particularly useful for starting to think about doing research.

On the transition from school to work

Brelsford, P.; Smith, G. and Rix, A. (1982), *Give us a Break*, (Manpower Services Commission Research and Development Series No. 11). This clearly written research report was the result of a one year action research study sponsored by the MSC into opportunities for girls on the Youth Opportunities Programme. In September 1983, the Youth Opportunities Programme was replaced by the Youth Training Scheme, and the report, which is subtitled: *Widening Opportunities for Women within YOP/YTS* gives some suggestions of ways in which the current situation could be improved. The report can be obtained from the Manpower Services Commission Training Division, Moorfoot, Sheffield S1 4PQ.

Clarke, L. (1980), *The Transition from School to Work: A Critical Review of Research in the UK* (London: HMSO), provides an excellent discussion and guide to the literature.

Willis, P. (1977), *Learning to Labour*, (Farnborough: Saxon House), looks at the passage of a group of working-class boys from school to work. It provides an extremely interesting insight into and interpretation of a certain sort of working-class culture, although the discerning reader may find the boys' extreme sexism rather hard to take.

On sexual divisions in society, and particularly on girls

Barker, D. L. and Allen, S. (1976) (eds.), *Dependence and Exploitation in Work and Marriage*, (London: Longman), and Barker, D. L. and Allen, S. (1976) (eds.), *Sexual Divisions and Society: Process and Change*, (London: Tavistock), are two important collections of essays from a British Sociological Association conference on sexual divisions in society.

Spender, D. and Sarah, E. (1981), *Learning to Lose*, (London: The Women's Press). A useful collection of essays on girls and schooling.

Stacey, M. (1981), 'The division of labour revisited or overcoming the two Adams' in Abrams, P.; Deem, R.; Finch, J. and Rock; P. (eds.), *Practice and Progress: British Sociology 1950–1980*; (London: Allen and Unwin); pp. 172–90; provides a most important theoretical discussion of the sexual division of labour.

Resources

The Equal Opportunities Commission, Overseas House, Quay Street, Manchester produce useful documents and pamphlets on girls, and women, some of them free. They have a library and helpful information officers.

The Feminist Library and Information Centre (formerly the Women's Research and Resources Centre) has a library with a wide range of feminist publications and keeps an index of work/projects/research in progress. Free library use to all; income related membership fee for borrowing. Their address is: Hungerford House, Victoria Embankment, London WCZN 6PA, Tel: 01 930 0715.

The Department of Education and Science has various free pamphlets, although the weightier publications are sold through the HMSO bookshop in High Holborn, London WC2.

Questions for discussion

1 How far is it possible for research to be objective? Can someone who has a political commitment (a member of the Conservative, Labour or Liberal/SDP Parties for instance) do reliable research? Can you think of a sociological study which you believe to be objective? What is involved in being objective?

2 In what ways might the approach of a sociologist and the approach of a journalist differ in writing about the problem of young people leaving work and looking for a job? How would you prepare a press release on the research described in this chapter which would both describe the work sociologically, and capture the imagination of the newspaper reader?

3 What sort of sociological theories could help you look at some of the issues outlined in this chapter? Give at least two examples of ways of making sense of:
   a) the sexual division of labour, that is, the fact that on the whole, men do 'men's jobs' and women do 'women's jobs';
   b) the apparent lack of ambition on the part of the girls.
   In what ways do these sociological ways of making sense of the data differ from 'common sense' explanations?

Chapter 11

The practice of sociological research: some issues in school ethnography

Robert G. Burgess

A popular television panel game invites members of the public to mime an action or activity that is involved in their day to day work so that the panelists can guess their occupations. I have often wondered what activity might be performed by a sociologist who is doing empirical research. Some people may consider this to be a relatively simple task as they might argue that sociologists engaged in empirical research are instantly identifiable by the clip boards and interview schedules that they carry. An action such as completing an interview schedule might, therefore, be considered to be part of the normal daily routine of the sociologist. However, such an action signifies a very narrow conception of doing sociological research. Firstly, it treats the social survey as if it were the only form of sociological research. Secondly, it suggests that sociological research practice only involves techniques. Thirdly, it assumes that research can be equated with the collection of data.

A brief glance at a number of general methodology text books reveals further assumptions about the conduct of social research. Sociological research is discussed as if research activities were governed by a set of rules. Methods of social research are not examined in relation to theoretical perspectives and there is little discussion of the *actual* processes and problems that confront the sociologist while doing research.

In part, these omissions can be attributed to the model of social investigation that is presented in many of the text-books where discussions of social research begin with an account of scientific method. In a simplified form it is argued that scientific method follows a series of stages. First, we start with a body of theory from which hypotheses are deduced. The main concepts that are used in the hypotheses are operationalised in an experiment and the hypotheses are tested. If our hypotheses are proved, confidence in the theory is increased, whereas if they are disproved the theory is modified and the process is continued. Such an account is no more than an idealised version of what occurs in the natural sciences as reports by scientists, such as Watson (1968) writing about the discovery of DNA, indicate that scientific research involves a social process that cannot be reduced to a series of steps or stages. It is, therefore, not surprising that there are problems when attempts are made to apply the principles of scientific method to sociological activities. First, it assumes that sociologists do nothing more than test theories whilst studies demonstrate that many sociologists are concerned with generating as well as testing theories. Secondly, it assumes that researchers work with inanimate objects who can be questioned, observed and manipulated as they have little influence over the collection, analysis and interpretation of data. The result is that the process of social research is hidden from view.

In recent years, some sociologists have tried to demystify research activities by discussing the problems, processes and procedures involved in sociological research. The result is that attention has been focused on such problems as: gaining entry to a research site, negotiating access to documents, handling relationships with informants and resolving the social, ethical and political problems involved in research. For as Bechhofer suggests 'research is not a clear-cut sequence of procedures following a neat pattern but a messy interaction between the conceptual and the empirical world' (Bechhofer, 1974, p. 73). However, if this 'messy interaction' is to be understood it is vital to examine the conduct of research within a specific area of sociology where problems, theories and methods intertwine with one another and where data collection and data analysis take place alongside each other. We turn, therefore, to the field of education and to the ethnographic study of schools.

Sociological research in schools

The sociologist of education is concerned with the world of educational systems, schools and classrooms. However, these settings can be studied from a number of different perspectives using a range of methodological tools depending on the problems posed. Many sociological studies in education have been preoccupied with attempts to examine the relationship between social class on the one hand and educational achievement on the other. In these circumstances, sociologists have considered that the most effective way of collecting data was by conducting social surveys among parents, teachers and children. While this provides data on success and failure in education, it overlooks what actually happens in the school and classroom and the patterns of social interaction and social relations between teachers and pupils. Sociologists who have wanted to focus on these activities have, therefore, gone into schools and classrooms to work alongside teachers and pupils. Their accounts have not been based upon the logic of experimental design, nor upon the collection and analysis of survey data. Instead, a range of research strategies have been used to focus on the patterns of social interaction and social relationships among teachers and pupils in a variety of school settings. But what strategies are available to the social researcher? How are strategies selected? How can different strategies be used in an investigation? What social processes and problems are involved in using these strategies to collect and analyse data?

Four main research strategies have been identified by Martin Bulmer (1984) in the conduct of sociological investigation: social survey research, unobtrusive measures, historical sources and interpretative procedures. He points out that these different styles of research are ideal types which are often used together in a research project. Indeed, the kind of methods that are used in an investigation do not depend upon the superiority of one method over another but upon the research problem that is posed by the investigator, for as Trow remarks:

> Let us be done with the arguments of participant observation *versus* interviewing – as we have largely dispensed with the arguments for psychology *versus* sociology – and get on with

the business of attacking our problems with the widest array of conceptual and methodological tools that we possess and they demand.

Trow, 1957, p. 35.

Sociologists, therefore, need to consider the different ways in which they can combine research strategies in a sociological investigation: an approach that is commonly known as 'triangulation' (Denzin, 1978).

In studying schools and classrooms many sociologists have worked from an interactionist perspective and utilised interpretative procedures (ethnographic methods) involving participant observation, structured and unstructured interviews and documentary sources. The result has been a range of school studies based upon a variety of research interests and methodologies. (For a review of this material see Hammersley, 1982). However, if we merely focus upon the strategies and techniques involved in a sociological investigation we shall fail to understand the relationships between problems, theories and methods in the research process. To examine some of these issues we now turn to an analysis of elements of the research process, drawing upon illustrative material from an ethnographic study that I conducted in a purpose built, co-educational Roman Catholic comprehensive school that I called Bishop McGregor (Burgess, 1983)[1].

The research process

1 Starting research

The starting point of many sociological studies can be traced to earlier themes and questions in other sociological work. The early British studies of schools by Hargreaves (1967) and by Lacey (1970) were linked to debates on the relationship of social class and educational achievement but in relation to schools. Subsequent studies of secondary schools (by Woods (1979) of a secondary modern school and by Ball (1981) of a comprehensive school) built upon this earlier work and increased our knowledge of the processes involved in schooling by working within the symbolic interactionist tradition[2]. Alongside these accounts, were studies of pupil perspectives of schooling by Willis (1977) and Corrigan (1979) working within a Marxist framework and by Woods and his colleagues working from an interactionist perspective (Woods, 1980).

These research projects appear to have been based upon socio-logical concerns alone, as Corrigan remarks:

> Sociologists seem to claim that they became interested in topics because they read the work of other sociologists. It is true that other people's work has an effect upon the way in which they choose a research problem; but the main set of reasons for choice is to be found in the biography of the researcher.
>
> Corrigan, 1979, p. 4.

Indeed, if we turn to the work of Hargreaves and Lacey we find that the research roles that they adopted were based on their former teacher status. Furthermore, the roots of Corrigan's study can be traced not merely to his sociological interests but also to his experiences of schools and schooling as a pupil. In my own study I was interested in utilising my former teacher status in addressing certain sociological questions about the way in which situations were defined and redefined by teachers and pupils in a compre-hensive school. My study was conducted from an interactionist perspective utilising a range of ethnographic methods. Here, I was able to bring together my personal experience as a school-teacher with my sociological knowledge of schools and schooling. Indeed, it was my intention to extend the work of Hargreaves and Lacey by taking a teacher role in a purpose built, co-educational compre-hensive school[3] where I could examine questions concerning the definition of the situation from a teacher's point of veiw. However, having decided what to investigate a researcher has to locate a research site. Here, the first task is to gain entry, but how is this brought about?

2 Gaining entry

Researchers are often advised that gaining entry to a research site can be easily achieved by going to the most powerful person in a social setting who, it is argued, will sponsor the researcher in that setting. However, this is not as simple as it may seem. If you want to study the teachers and pupils in a comprehensive school, from whom do you seek permission? Do you gain entry through the Director of Education? Through the chairperson of the school governors or through the headteacher? Or through all of these individuals? In addressing these questions it is important to consider the influence that your choice of person will have upon the relations that you can establish with the individuals involved in your study. If you gain entry through the Director of Education it may mean that the headteacher and teachers will be suspicious of your motives. Meanwhile, if you gain entry through the head-teacher will this incur the suspicion of the teachers and the pupils?

However, the problems do not end there. While it may appear that entry is gained through a powerful individual on the research site, in practice the researcher has to negotiate and renegotiate entry to different social situations. Indeed, once the research is under way it is often found that what appeared to be *carte blanche* permission involves further negotiation. I was given permission to do research in Bishop McGregor Comprehensive School by the headmaster. However, access to particular classrooms had to be negotiated with individual teachers. Furthermore, I had to ask individual pupils for their permission for me to tape-record inter-views with them. Entry to situations and access to teachers and pupils was not automatic.

As far as collecting documents was concerned I was given permission by the headmaster to collect the circulars that were regularly issued to teachers. In addition, he gave me permission to consult the notes, circulars, letters and plans relating to school administration that were located in the school office. However, when I went to the office to obtain these documents I found that access had to be renegotiated with the school secretary who wanted some assurance about what I was going to do with the materials as she said, 'There will be bloody hell to pay if the staff found out that you knew all about their salary scales'. She was acting as the self-appointed guardian of this material and I had, therefore, to tell her what my research was about and the way in which I intended using the documents before she would give me permission to examine the material. Furthermore, access to 'confidential docu-ments' on pupils was subject to further negotiation with the senior staff who were responsible for pastoral care as the headmaster indicated that he had to seek permission from these teachers if he wanted to consult a pupil's file.

Gaining entry to situations, to individuals and to documentary evidence is, therefore, not restricted to one person or to one period of time but involves numerous negotiations taking place throughout the research project. Indeed, the requirements for access to situations may change as the research project is developed. As new themes emerge it will be important to develop new contacts and gain access to new situations and new sources of data. The researcher cannot, therefore, be the dogged follower of a set of rules and procedures but needs to be flexible in modifying the research design and applying the principles of social research. Once the researcher has gained entry to a situation a decision has to be taken about what to study and who to study. In survey research this is usually resolved by selecting a sample of the population to be studied, while in ethnographic work the researcher needs to decide what to study, when to study it, where to study it, and who to study. The ethnographer is, therefore, involved in questions of selection which are partly resolved by developing relationships with particular individuals who are known as key informants.

3 Working with informants

At Bishop McGregor School I was involved in observing teachers drawn from different sections of the school and representative of different status levels. Of the senior staff (head, deputy head and senior mistress) it was the headmaster who I selected as a key informant in order to learn about the aims and objectives that he had for establishing a new school. A major division among the teachers was between those who were engaged in pastoral care and worked in houses and those who taught in departments. I needed to get to know a range of these teachers. There were six teachers (three men and three women) who were responsible for pastoral care. While all of these teachers were included in the study, one man and one woman and their relationships with other teachers and with pupils were studied in some depth. Meanwhile, if I was to understand the way the school worked from a teacher's point of view, I also needed to establish a group of teacher informants from academic, practical, subject and non-subject departments. Furthermore, I also needed to work with teachers who represented different status levels in the departments. It was, therefore, important to get established in the school and to develop relationships with different groups of teachers, but how do you find informants? How do you explain your work? How do you establish relationships with informants?

When you begin research in a social situation you are often a stranger. In these terms, you need to develop relationships with individuals who can sponsor you into a variety of social settings. However, it is important to select individuals who will assist rather than close off situations. In these terms, informants need to be selected for the perspective they can provide, for their knowledge of a social setting and for their abilities to guide and teach the researcher the customs that are relevant in the situation being studied.

As I focused my observations on the Newsom department[4] at Bishop McGregor School I had a range of teacher and pupil informants in the department who I knew with different degrees of intensity. Among the teachers, I particularly got to know Sylvia Robinson, who was the self-styled head of the department and Tony Davis, who took up a new appointment in the department. On the basis of my work with these two teachers, I was able to examine the processes by which a qualified school-teacher has to learn how to become a Newsom teacher. These teachers, together with their colleagues and the pupils, taught me how different work norms were established in Newsom classes as teachers and pupils defined and redefined the curriculum. Among the numerous examples of this phenomena that I recorded in my notebook was the situation whereby teachers wanted to reward pupils for hard work by allowing them to make cups of coffee in the classroom. However, the situation was renegotiated by the pupils so that they would only work if they were first allowed to make coffee. Similarly, while pupils were forbidden to swear and smoke in other parts of the school, teachers in the Newsom department allowed their pupils to smoke in stock cupboards and to swear in conversation in order that they could survive in the classroom. In these terms, my informants taught me the essential elements involved in being a Newsom teacher which were cross-checked in the course of collecting and analysing data on other aspects of the school.

4 Collecting and analysing data

Ethnographers use a range of research methods. In my study participant observation, unstructured interviews, documents and diaries were all used. But how are these methods *actually* used to collect data? How are these methods used alongside one another to cross-check data? It is to these questions that we now turn by looking at the way in which I collected data on punishment in the school; a topic that gave rise to further themes on which data were collected.

One of the first documents that I read in the school concerned 'sanctions'. Here, the headmaster outlined a variety of punishments that could be used among which was corporal punishment. In the course of conversation, teachers told me about pupils they had caned, and pupils told me about punishments they had received. In addition, I observed situations in which pupils were physically punished by teachers.

During a series of unstructured interviews with pupils I was told about their experience of punishment in the school. One example was provided by John Slattery and David Jones:

R.B.   Have you ever been caned?

John   Oh yes.

R.B.   What have you been caned for then?

John   Burning a girl's tights, helping Pete Vincent in a fight.

R.B.   Who caned you for that?

John   Hippo, yes it must have been Mr. Murray, I also got the cane for chucking a snowball down Mrs. Dickinson's back. I got two across me backside for that from Goddard (the headmaster) didn't I.

R.B.   Throwing a snowball down Mrs. Dickinson's back, I see.

John   I can't remember them all, if I could I'd tell you.

R.B.   What did you think about being caned?

John   It's all right. It's better than getting a letter sent home isn't it?

David	They sent a letter home to my house anyway when I was caned. On a Monday I was caned for truanting. On a Tuesday of the same week I was caned for truanting. On the Wednesday Miss Rolls came round to me house. Just as she was going me Mam said, 'Say goodbye to Miss Rolls', and I said, 'I ain't saying goodbye to that bitch' and I got caned for that, and two kids were saying something about me Dad and I hit them behind the gym and Mr. Horne saw me and took me and caned me and that was at ten past one on the Tuesday of that week.
John	His Dad's very ill.
David	And on the Friday I truanted again and in that week I think I had 21 or 22 lashes of the old stick.
R.B.	What do you think about that?
David	Don't know.
R.B.	You think it's fair do you?
David	It's over in a couple of minutes ain't it and it just pains for ten minutes. There have been people who have been truanting from here for about six months. When they come back they ain't gonna get suspended, they're gonna get caned. Whack, ten minutes that's it. To have six months for ten minutes, it's worth it isn't it?[5]

This extract from a tape-recorded interview supported several observations I had already made on the basis of my conversations with teachers. Firstly, Maggie Rolls always caned pupils for truancy. Secondly, when she wanted pupils caned she always got Peter Horne to do it. Thirdly, pupils saw corporal punishment as one of the 'occupational hazards' of truancy. However, this account also raised several problems: had the boys been caned for the offences they indicated? Had David Jones been caned the number of occasions that he maintained? Had he been caned for truancy and for the way he spoke to Miss Rolls?

To check David Jones' story I talked to his teachers in the Newsom department who could tell me about his truancy and could recall that he had been in trouble with Maggie Rolls and Peter Horne. Secondly, I turned to documentary evidence. To begin with I looked at David's personal file where I found letters between his house head and his parents, notes about his misdemeanours in school and visits to his home. At the end of a long note concerning a weekend visit to David Jones' parents to discuss his truancy and the theft of a bicycle, I found the following instruction from Maggie Rolls to Peter Horne:

Re DAVID JONES
David will receive:
2 strokes on one hand for his TRUANCY
1 stroke on the other hand for taking the bike
I don't mind when you cane him but I'd like him to admit he thoroughly deserves the cane on both counts. I did not like the way he answered me back on Saturday . . .[6]

These data were checked out with the school punishment book and by talking with Maggie Rolls and Peter Horne. Both the documentary evidence and my conversations confirmed that David Jones had been caned on a number of occasions during the week in question for his truancy and for theft. Indeed, Maggie Rolls and Peter Horne indicated that they disliked this boy and were constantly involved in checking his behaviour which often resulted in corporal punishment. By obtaining these different accounts I was able to confirm aspects of the original discussions I had with David Jones and his Newsom teachers about corporal punishment. However, it also gave me scope to work on two further themes: the relationship between Newsom pupils and teachers who were responsible for pastoral care, and 'bullshitting among pupils'; that is the way in which pupils tell 'tall stories' in order to ensure that they are always on the side which suffers grave injustice from teachers who they consider are unfair to them. But how were these themes followed up? How were notes made? How was the analysis developed?

The themes that I extracted from the interviews were followed up by asking similar questions of other pupils in subsequent group interviews. This led me to ask pupils about their relationships with teachers who were responsible for pastoral care, to observe the way in which pastoral staff related to pupils and in turn to talk to pastoral staff about the ways in which they perceived their relationships with pupils. However, all these data had to be recorded and analysed.

Although the final research report is constructed out of field notes, interviews and conversations, documents, and diaries, it is rare to find these available to the reader or to find discussions of how this material was produced. Yet this is an important dimension of the research process as the data that are recorded by the sociologist provides an essential link between data collection and data analysis. The data that are obtained on the basis of participant observation are originally produced in the form of field notes but how are these notes assembled? It is usual for ethnographers to record their notes away from the field of study unless the situation that is being observed is one in which individuals usually take notes. But how does an ethnographer remember the people, events and situations, that are observed?

I found that it was easiest to begin making notes based on the sequence in which events and conversations occurred. Each set of notes was therefore organised around phases of the school day: before school began, early morning meetings, school assembly, lessons, break, lessons, lunchtime and so on. Usually I found some time while in the school to note down key words and phrases that would then form the basis of more extensive notes that were written up each evening. These notes were then tape-recorded as this provided me with a duplicate set of materials; a precaution against loss or damage of the original set. These tape-recordings also gave me an opportunity to extend my accounts, to provide further details of the situations I had observed and an opportunity to begin to think about concepts and categories that were beginning to emerge from the data and which could be used to organise the collection of further materials.

It is essential to identify gaps in the research material if questions, concepts and categories are to be followed up in subsequent data collection. In my research many hours were, therefore, devoted to writing up field notes, listening to tapes and analysing data. Already I have indicated how work with key informants (both pupils and teachers) helped me to develop themes relating to punishment in the school. Further work on this theme through tape-recorded interviews, conversations and documentary evidence helped me to build up accounts on specific relations between teachers and pupils. By talking to pupils about punishment I began to learn about ways they avoided being punished by negotiating with teachers and entering into bargains with them. In short, my initial observations and interview materials could be used to focus on the *strategies* that pupils deployed in classrooms. The focus of my study (Burgess, 1983) was, therefore, upon social processes which could be examined through case studies as the strength of this approach is in the depth and detail of the analysis rather than generalisation.

Analysis did not just occur at the end of my fieldwork but was ongoing and developmental. Field notes were constantly read and re-read, categorised and indexed; this being an early stage of data analysis. Secondly, tape-recorded interviews were replayed and carefully transcribed; a task which is notoriously slow, difficult and time-consuming. Thirdly, the documents that I collected had to be read to see what links (if any) could be made between my observational work, data from unstructured interviews and the documentary evidence.

It was these materials that were used to present an account of the social world of the participants. Yet from the field notes, tape-recordings and documents only a selection of material was subsequently used. The sociologist is, therefore, once again involved in the business of selection. As Woods (1981) indicates, it is important to consider what should be included in the report on the basis of four criteria: validity, typicality, relevance and clarity. In many research reports the researcher makes use of extensive quotations from interviews, documents and field notes so that the informants are allowed to speak for themselves (see Roberts in this volume). The themes and categories that emerge, therefore, belong to the participants, but it is the sociologist's task to present a selection of this material for analysis.

A variety of approaches have been suggested for analysing data. Gluckman (1967) has argued that in analysing ethnographic data, situations should be examined involving the same persons or groups over a period of time in order to illuminate the way in which participants operate within a social setting. Meanwhile, other writers suggest that the research report can be constructed out of the concepts that emerge from the data and the way in which the research material is organised (Glaser and Strauss, 1967). Here, it is essential to have available the questions posed and the data that were collected in order that readers may evaluate the report and consider alternative interpretations of the data on the basis of the available evidence. Yet researchers are aware that in reporting their findings and in making sociological evidence available some consideration has to be given to ethical issues.

5 Some ethical problems

Ethical concerns are involved throughout the research process from the time a research site is selected to the time when research findings are reported. Sponsorship is essential for the conduct of social research. However, we might ask: what does the sponsor expect in return for assistance? Will sponsors influence what is studied and who is studied? Does the researcher have a duty to report exactly what is observed? In what form should research findings be published? Under what conditions? What can be done to minimise harm to those individuals who are studied?

Such issues are often debated by social scientists. However, there are no 'solutions' to these problems as much will depend upon the researcher, those who are researched and the context in which the work is being done. Nevertheless, in an attempt to offer some protection to informants, groups such as the American Anthropological Association (1973) and the British Sociological Association (1973) have drawn up statements of ethical principles which provide a framework within which it is suggested researchers can work. These statements are not 'codes' of ethics as no set of rules can be enforced where individuals are working in social situations. The conduct of sociological research is, therefore, subject to compromise between the researcher and the researched. One way in which ethnographers attempt to resolve some of the ethical problems is by allowing informants to comment on their final manuscript prior to publication. Indeed, in my own research I discussed my observations with the teachers on a formal and informal basis and the report of my research was read in draft form by the headmaster. While this does not provide a 'solution' to the problems that arise in the research process, it does go some way to avoiding misrepresentation of the informants and major errors in the research report.

6 The reception of a research report

Nevertheless, researchers are unable to protect the institutions and individuals that they study from adverse criticism. In the preface to my study of Bishop McGregor School I commented 'I trust that the pseudonyms I have used and the changes I have made will cause no offence and will prevent individuals who were so generous with their time from being harmed in any way' (Burgess, 1983, p. x). However, reviews that have appeared have not only been concerned with the way in which I conducted the study but have also focused attention on the school and the headmaster. Indeed, while some reviewers have considered the head to be a wily, competent individual who ran a good school, others have seen McGregor as a 'rather conservative school' with a head who was 'woefully inadequate'. Remarks such as these have not gone unnoticed by those who were part of the original study. While they see that some of these criticisms are deserved, others are seen as unfair, unwelcome and uncalled for. Perhaps we should consider whether those people who are researched should be given the right of reply in which they could enter into dialogue and debate with researchers and reviewers.

Conclusion

The conduct of sociological research involves a knowledge of substantive problems, sociological theory and research methodology. Indeed, sociological research does not merely involve the application of principles and procedures to a particular social setting. Research involves creativity, imagination, precision and theoretical flair alongside substantive and methodological knowledge. If we are to understand what constitutes 'doing' sociological research it is vital to look at the links between problems, theories and methods, and between data collection and data analysis. Furthermore, it is essential to consider the personal experience of the social investigator (see Stacey and Roberts in this volume).

The purpose of this account has been to examine some of the major issues involved in the research process, drawing on examples from my own experience of conducting ethnographic research in a comprehensive school. Sociological research, it would seem, cannot be neatly reduced to a set of steps or stages that can be applied to any situation. Instead, sociologists need to constantly monitor the research process as they take decisions about the collection and analysis of data. In these terms, sociological researchers are active decision-makers.

Equally, the reader of the research report is also a decision-maker as decisions have to be made regarding the value of the research report. But how can we begin to evaluate a research report? The following questions might be used to start evaluating the methodology in a sociological account:

How did the research begin?

What basic questions were asked?

How did the questions relate to the theoretical perspective employed in the study?

How did the researcher select an area of study?

How was access achieved in this setting?

What kinds of people, groups, or events were studied?

How were they selected?

What was the sampling strategy involved?

How effective were the strategies used?

What methods of social investigation were used?

How did these methods relate to the questions posed and the theoretical perspective used?

What was the pattern of collecting and analysing data?

What problems did the researcher encounter?

How were these problems resolved?

What kinds of research questions remain unanswered and how might these be used in subsequent studies?

These questions focus upon what researchers do and how they go about doing it; both of which are essential to an understanding of the processes and problems involved in doing sociological research.

Notes

1 This research was funded by the SSRC (now the ESRC). All the names of institutions, places and people that are used in this study are pseudonyms in order to maintain confidentiality.

2 This is in the tradition of the work of Mead (1934), Blumer (1969), Goffman (1969) and Becker (1970).

3 At the time this research was conducted (1973–74) there were no studies of co-educational schools or of comprehensive schools.
4 The Newsom department provided courses for pupils for whom the maximum expectation of success in public examinations seemed likely to be three CSE Grade 5's or less.
5 Extract from a transcript of a tape-recorded interview with John Slattery and David Jones.
6 Extract from a copy of an internal (hand written) note from Maggie Rolls to Peter Horne in David Jones' personal file. This refers to the same event that David reports took place on Wednesday.

Suggestions for further reading

On research methods

Bulmer, M. (1984) (ed.), *Sociological Research Methods*, (2nd edn.), (London: Macmillan) provides a discussion of the relationship between problems, theories and methods by looking at four major approaches to sociological research: the social survey, unobtrusive measures, historical sources, and interpretative procedures.

Burgess, R. G. (1982) (ed.), *Field Research: a Sourcebook and Field Manual*, (London: Allen and Unwin) deals predominantly with the ethnographic style of research. Social scientists discuss the use of a range of methods (participant observation, interviewing and documentary sources) and there is a consideration of the processes and problems involved in sociological research.

Burgess, R. G. (1984), *In the Field: An Introduction to Field Research*, (London: Allen and Unwin) discusses the use of methods in field projects. There are numerous illustrations from the author's research.

Stacey, M. (1969), *Methods of Social Research*, (Oxford: Pergamon) a basic textbook which covers a range of methods of social investigation. Here, there is a discussion of the way in which methods of investigation have actually been used in a variety of research projects.

Stacey, M. and Burgess, R. G. (1979), 'The research process',

(Oxford: Sussex Publications) is a tape-recorded discussion of some of the main problems involved in research in the study of localities, hospitals and schools.

On Research Experience

A series of edited volumes in which researchers have provided accounts of informal processes involved in their research and the way in which they have handled research problems. In addition to all the books listed by Roberts in this volume, you should also consult:

Burgess, R. G. (1984) (ed.), *The Research Process in Educational Settings: Ten Case Studies*, (Lewes: Falmer Press) provides reflections on educational research projects concerned with schools, classrooms and curricula.

Hammond, P. (1964) (ed.), *Sociologists at Work*, (New York: Basic Books). A useful set of essays that focus on the formal and informal processes of doing research (see especially the essay by Geer, 1964).

Spindler, G. (1982) (ed.), *Doing the Ethnography of Schooling*, (New York: Holt, Rinehart and Winston). An advanced text – useful for teachers. The essay by Wolcott (1982) is worth reading.

Empirical studies

For studies of empirical research in schools and classrooms, see:

Ball, S. (1981), *Beachside Comprehensive: a Case Study of Mixed Ability Teaching*, (Cambridge: CUP).

Burgess, R. G. (1983), *Experiencing Comprehensive Education: A Study of Bishop McGregor School*, (London: Methuen).

Corrigan, P. (1979), *Schooling the Smash Street Kids*, (London: Macmillan).

Hargreaves, D. H. (1967), *Social Relations in a Secondary School*, (London: Routledge and Kegan Paul).

Lacey, C. (1970), *Hightown Grammar: the School as a Social System*, (Manchester: Manchester University Press).

Stanworth, M. (1983), *Gender and Schooling*, (London: Hutchinson).

For a 'taste' of research in schools and classrooms see the papers in:

Delamont, S. (1984) (ed.), *Readings in Classroom Interaction*, (London: Methuen).

Hammersley, M. and Woods, P. (1984) (eds.), *Life in School: The Sociology of Pupil Culture*, (Milton Keynes: Open University Press).

Hargreaves, A. and Woods, P. (1984) (eds.), *Classrooms and Staffrooms: The Sociology of Teachers and Teaching*, (Milton Keynes: Open University Press).

Resources

For papers on the way in which large scale research is conducted in Britain, write to:

The Office of Population, Censuses and Surveys (OPCS), St Catherine's House, 10 Kingsway, London WC2B 6JP.

For copies of statements of ethical principles, write to:

The British Sociological Association, 10 Portugal Street, London WC2A 2HU.

The American Anthropological Association, 1703 New Hampshire Avenue, N.W., Washington D.C. 20009, USA.

For information and reviews of research on education and on schools, write to:

Department of Education and Science, Elizabeth House, York Road, London SE1 7PH.

National Foundation for Educational Research, The Mere, Upton Park, Slough, Berks SL1 2DQ.

National Union of Teachers, Hamilton House, Mabledon Place, London WC1H 9BD.

Two useful sources for teachers:

Bulmer, J. (1977), *Guide to the Teaching of Anthropology in Schools and Colleges*, (London: School of Oriental and African Studies) contains numerous cross-cultural references on fieldwork.

Bulmer, M. and Burgess, R. G. (1981) (eds.), *The Teaching of Research Methodology*, special issue of *Sociology*, vol. 15, no. 4.

Questions for discussion

1 What do you think are the main problems involved in doing sociological research? How can the problems be overcome?

2 Examine the problems involved in conducting a sociological study in:
a) your school or college;
b) a village or section of a town or city.

3 Select *one* of the following studies:
S. J. Ball, *Beachside Comprehensive*, (CUP);
R. G. Burgess, *Experiencing Comprehensive Education*, (Methuen);
M. Stanworth, *Gender and Schooling*, (Hutchinson);
and examine the way in which the research was conducted. Among the topics you will need to consider are:
a) the theoretical perspectives used;
b) the questions asked;
c) the people selected for study;
d) the methods of social research;
e) the problems involved in using different methods;
f) the social, ethical and political problems involved in conducting the research.

4 Conduct a series of interviews with local newspaper reporters about the ways in which they research their articles. Compare and contrast their research procedures with the ways in which sociologists work.

Glossary

Editor's note: The contributors have provided brief entries on some of the key terms used in this book. Some important terms have been omitted because they are already discussed in the context of particular chapters. The entries have deliberately been kept brief and so in many cases suggestions are given concerning other texts and articles where more detailed information can be obtained. Further material on sociological terms is provided in:

Mann, M. (1983) (ed.), *The Macmillan Student Encyclopedia of Sociology*, (London: Macmillan).

Mitchell, G. D. (1979) (ed.), *A New Dictionary of Sociology*, (London: Routledge and Kegan Paul).

Sills, D. (1968) (ed.), *International Encylopedia of the Social Sciences*, (New York: Macmillan and The Free Press).

Weeks, D. R. (1972), *A Glossary of Sociological Concepts*, (Milton Keynes: The Open University Press).

alienation: a concept introduced into sociology by Marx who utilised it in his model of capitalism. Alienation was generally seen by Marx as a condition whereby 'men' were unable to realise the extent to which external processes or situations were determined by their own actions; the cause of this condition being within capitalism. For further details, see, for example, Bottomore and Rubel (1963), Lee and Newby (1983).

anomie: a concept introduced into sociology by Durkheim. It refers to a situation where social norms are absent, unclear, conflicting or unintegrated. For further details see Durkheim (1897) and Merton (1968).

bio-medicine: contemporary Western medicine based upon a scientific study of human beings as bio-chemical organisms. To be contrasted with cosmologies which explain illness and other disasters supernaturally and with other sophisticated healing systems, such as the Ayurvedic of the Indian sub-continent.

bourgeoisie: a term used by Marx to refer to one of two great classes (the bourgeoisie and the proletariat). Marx claimed that 'Society as a whole is more and more splitting up into two great hostile camps, into two great classes directly facing each other – bourgeoisie and proletariat' (Bottomore and Rubel, 1963, p. 207). For further discussion see Lee and Newby (1983).

clinical medicine: the practice of medicine applied to healing or alleviating disease conditions in individuals.

community: an ambiguous term used to refer to a group inhabiting the same locality where individuals carry out their daily activities. For a review of the concept see Bell and Newby (1971) and for criticisms see Stacey (1969b).

concept: an idea about a class of objects or a general notion. It is a classification. Concepts are part of the basic language of sociology.

conflict: a form of interaction that involves a struggle over resources, status and power. See, for example, Cuff and Payne (1979), Rex (1961).

definition of the situation: a concept that is useful in understanding social action. W. I. Thomas maintained 'If men define situations as real, they are real in their consequences' (Thomas, 1928, p. 584). This concept focuses upon meaning in social action.

documentary evidence: commonly taken to refer to written materials but this term has been broadened to include the use of written *and* oral sources in social research. See, for example, Burgess (1982), Plummer (1983).

empiricist: this term refers to those who base their knowledge and action on knowledge gained from observation and experiment without the benefit of theory.

empiricist healers or empiric: one who heals using knowledge gained from observation, trial and error and passed down informally (as opposed to a theoretically based healing system, such as bio-medicine, which has a theoretical basis and formal training). Sometimes equated stereotypically with quacks.

epidemiology: a branch of medicine which concentrates on the distribution of diseases in the population in contrast to clinical medicine.

ethnography: traditionally this has been an approach used by social anthropologists who study culture by direct observation in particular societies. The approach involves fieldwork or field research and has been used by sociologists to study factories, schools, hospitals, prisons, street gangs, drug takers, and numerous other social settings within industrial societies. For a discussion see, for example, Burgess (1982), Burgess (1984b). For empirical studies see, for example, Ditton (1977), Burgess (1983).

Fabians: British socialists of the late nineteenth century and early twentieth century whose organisation and activities continue; distinguished by their conviction that socialism can be achieved by gradual change and using democratic means; a strong belief in the power of reason and ordered evidence to persuade.

family: relationships established through marriage (or relationships treated as being equivalent to marriage) and parenthood (including all forms of adoptive parenthood). The *nuclear family* is the unit of father, mother and children; *extended family* relationships are those ties beyond the nuclear family, including grandparents or grandchildren, brothers and sisters in so far as they are involved in separate nuclear families and aunts and uncles. To be distinguished from *household*. See Harris (1983).

feminist: feminists come in a number of varieties, as to their analyses and their prescription for action, but all agree that women continue to be disadvantaged as compared with men in all their life chances.

feminist sociology: a critical approach which examines sex and gender as principles of social organisation and division. One result of this has been the increased visibility of women and men as groups in sociological work. See, for example, Roberts (1981a; 1981b), Spender (1981) and Stacey (1981).

gender: differences between men and women in so far as these are differences which are recognised as important in society and have important social consequencs. Conventionally, gender is distinguished from *sex*, which refers to the biological differences between men and women although in practice it is probably more useful to see the biological and the social aspects as being closely related to each other. Simply, gender may be seen as the social patterning of sex differences. See Oakley (1972) and Morgan (1984).

historical sources: includes a range of quantitative and qualitative materials. It includes census materials, wills, registers and inventories as well as personal documents: diaries, letters, autobiographies, oral histories and life histories. For a discussion of these sources see, for example, Plummer (1983).

household: persons living under one roof and sharing facilities, usually meals, together. While households conventionally consist of family members they need not necessarily do so; similarly members of the same family will live in different households. See Harris (1983).

ideology: a general term that refers to the influence that ideas have on social organisation. Ideology was used in Marx's analysis of capitalist society. See, for example, Bottomore and Rubel (1963), Lee and Newby (1983).

interpretative procedures: a range of methods of investigation that are used to look at social situations from the informant's point of view. This style of research is also referred to as field research, fieldwork or ethnography. For a discussion of this approach see, for example, Burgess (1982, 1984b).

interviews: a method of social research which is based upon conversations that are conducted for a specific purpose. Social scientists use a range of different interviews including: structured (formal) interviews, unstructured interviews and group interviews. For further details on structured interviews see Moser and Kalton (1971) and on unstructured interviews see Burgess (1982; 1984b). For a good discussion on interviewing see Oakley (1981b).

key informant: individuals who are befriended by, or who befriend participant observers and who help to acquaint the researcher with the social setting under study. A classic example is 'Doc' in Whyte (1981). For further discussion see Burgess (1984b).

methodology: a term used to refer to the systematic and logical study of the general principles that guide social inquiry. See Bulmer (1984) and Burgess and Bulmer (1981).

moral panic: a situation where a social activity or group of persons becomes defined as a threat to common values or interests. Their activities become the focus of media coverage and political debate, and are often presented in a stereotyped form. In the process, the prevalence of the activity or group gets inflated. Often associated with young people or youth culture. For the seminal discussion, see Cohen (1972).

neo-Marxists: those who follow the basic analysis as to the nature of the economy and the society first enunciated by Karl Marx, but who have revised and developed the theory in the light of social and economic change and of further learning.

participant observation: a process of gathering data by taking roles in social situations. Participants observers need to observe situations, to listen to conversations and to record data. For a discussion see, for example, Burgess (1982, 1984b), Filstead (1970) and McCall and Simmons (1969).

patriarchy: the system of social relations through which men dominate women.

positivism: an approach to sociological explanation which emphasises that the social sciences should be like the natural sciences, by identifying facts in the social world, and causes of social phenomena through objective, scientific study. For discussion of its philosophical basis, see, for example, Benton (1977), Keat and Urry (1975).

private (or domestic) domain: the area of society covered by the household and the family, the women's domain, but a domain which has never been exclusively women's and which is increasingly shared with (invaded by?) men and under State surveillance. For further details see Smith (1973), Stacey (1981).

proletariat: a term used by Marx to refer to workers who owned no capital other than their labour. Marx considered that the proletariat were in conflict with the bourgeoisie. For further discussion, see Bottomore and Rubel (1963), Lee and Newby (1983).

public domain: that area of society in which are to be found industry, the state and the market place; a domain exclusively inhabited by men in the nineteenth century and still, despite the vote, the sex discrimination and the equal opportunities legislation, heavily dominated by men. The domain wherein sociological theories originated. For further details, see Smith (1973), Stacey (1981).

quacks: those who practise medicine without benefit of formal training and who may be charlatans or may be traditional healers including empirics.

qualitative research: a style of social investigation that includes such methods as participant observation, unstructured interviews and documentary evidence. For further discussion see Burgess (1982, 1984b).

quantitative research: as its name suggests, this is a term which denotes research with a statistical basis. This is sometimes referred to as 'hard data' just as qualitative research is sometimes referred to as 'soft data'. As the American sociologist Pauline Bart has observed, this distinction is based on a male sexual metaphor. She replaced these terms with the terms 'wet' and 'dry' data. For further discussion, see Moser and Kalton (1971).

questionnaires: these are an important means of collecting data. Postal questionnaires are relatively cheap (since interviewers do not need to be employed), and they can reach people who might not otherwise be available to be interviewed. See Moser and Kalton (1971) for a full discussion of the advantages and disadvantages of various methods of data collection.

research role: a role is the pattern of behaviour that is expected of a person occupying a particular status. Participant observers take or play social roles by following particular patterns of behaviour. See, for example, Burgess (1982, 1984b) and McCall and Simmons (1969).

research technique: a term used to refer to a fact-finding operation used to obtain social data. See Bulmer (1984) and Burgess and Bulmer (1981).

respondent: a person who answers a written questionnaire or who takes part in a structured (formal) interview. See, for example, Moser and Kalton (1971).

sampling: the selection of units for study and sources of data. For a discussion in these terms, see Sjoberg and Nett (1968). For a discussion of statistical sampling see, for example, Moser and Kalton (1971). For a discussion of sampling in ethnographic work see, for example, Burgess (1982, 1984b).

sex: see gender.

sexual division of labour: the different jobs performed by men and women within the home, within the economy outside the home and as between the home and work. See Stacey (1981).

social administration: one of the social science disciplines which takes welfare and social policy as its topic of study. Sometimes called social policy. There is some dispute among practitioners about whether it constitutes a discipline in its own right, or simply an area of study to which other social science disciplines contribute. For discussion, see, for example, Titmuss (1974).

social class: a concept that is used to refer to categories of individuals based on income, power, relationship to the means of production, and wealth. Extensively discussed by Weber and Marx and used in numerous sociological studies where it is important to clarify the exact way in which the concept is used. For further details see, for example, Bottomore (1965), Parkin (1973), Westergaard and Resler (1976).

social institution: a term that is used to refer to the basic framework within which individuals live. Social institutions include: the family, economic and political institutions and so on. For a further discussion, see, for example, Bottomore (1962).

socialisation: sociologists have often discussed socialisation in relation to childhood but it is a life-long process of social learning. For further discussion see Danziger (1971) and for the use of the concept in relation to adults see Lacey (1977).

social norm: a standard of behaviour shared by members of a group to which individuals are expected to conform. See, for example, Aubert (1968), Berger and Luckmann (1971) and Lee and Newby (1983).

social stratification: a system of institutional social inequality. This may include stratification based around class, gender, ethnicity, status. See, for example, Béteille (1969).

social survey: the most widely used approach to social research and often mistakenly equated with sociological research. It involves the use of questionnaire and interview schedules. Commonly used in large scale investigations especially when quantitative data are required. For further discussion see, for example, Moser and Kalton (1971).

structural functionalism: a theoretical perspective developed in the work of Comte, Spencer and Durkheim in sociology and Radcliffe-Brown in social anthropology. This perspective was used by Talcott Parsons and is committed to the idea of stability, consensus and integration in society. See, for example, Cuff and Payne (1979), Rex (1961).

symbolic interactionism: a theoretical perspective in sociology that is based on the work of Mead, Blumer and Becker. It is concerned with the meanings that participants attribute to social situations in the course of defining their own social reality. For a discussion of this approach see, for example, Cuff and Payne (1979) and for its use in an investigation see Woods (1979).

triangulation: a term used to refer to the use of different methods, investigators, data and theories in a sociological investigation. This approach, it is argued, overcomes the problems of the single method, single investigator, single theory study. The term has been used by Denzin (1978). A similar approach is combined operations (Stacey, 1969a), mixed strategies (Douglas, 1976), and multiple strategies (Burgess, 1982, 1984b). However, each writer gives a different emphasis.

unobtrusive measures: may include data that are collected for other purposes and can include archival material, physical traces and official statistics. For a discussion of the range of materials see, for example, Bulmer (1984), Webb *et al.* (1966).

References

Abel-Smith, B. (1964), *The Hospitals 1800–1948: a Study in Social Administration in England and Wales*, (London: Heinemann).

Abercrombie, N. and Urry, J. (1983), *Capital, Labour and the Middle Classes*, (London: Allen and Unwin).

Abrams, P. (1977), 'Community care: some research problems and priorities' in Department of Health and Social Security/Centre for Studies in Social Policy, *Social Care Research*, (London: Bedford Square Press), pp. 78–99.

Abrams, P. and Brown, R. K. (1984) (eds.), *U.K. Society: Work, Urbanism and Inequality*, (2nd edn.) (London: Weidenfeld and Nicolson).

Acheson, R. M. and Aird, L. (1976) (eds.), *Seminars in Community Medicine, Volume I: Sociology*, (London: OUP).

Adams, A. (1982), 'Senegal River Valley: What Kind of Change? in H. Johnson and H. Bernstein (eds.), *Third World Lives of Struggle*, (London: Heinemann/Open University), pp. 67–90.

Alavi, H. and Shanin, T. (1982) *Introduction to the Sociology of 'Developing Societies'*, (London: Macmillan).

American Anthropological Association (1973), *Professional Ethics: Statements and Procedures of the American Anthropological Association*, (Washington: American Anthropological Association).

Anderson, M. (1980) (ed.), *Sociology of the Family*, (Harmondsworth: Penguin).

Armstrong, D. (1983), *The Political Anatomy of the Body*, (Cambridge: CUP).

Ashton, D. N. and Maguire, M. J. (1980), 'The function of academic and non academic criteria in employers' selection strategies', *British Journal of Guidance and Counselling*, vol. 8, no. 2, pp. 146–57.

Aubert, V. (1968), *Elements of Sociology*, (London: Heinemann).

Bachrach, P. and Baratz, M. (1970), *Power and Poverty: Theory and Practice*, (New York: OUP).

Backett, K. C.(1982), *Mothers and Fathers*, (London: Macmillan).

Ball, S. J. (1981), *Beachside Comprehensive: a Case Study of Mixed Ability Teaching*, (Cambridge: CUP).

Banton, M. (1984), 'Keeping the Force in Check', *Times Higher Educational Supplement*, 13th March.

Barker, D. L. and Allen, S. (1976a) (eds.), *Dependence and Exploitation in Work and Marriage*, (London: Longman).

Barker, D. L. and Allen, S. (1976b) (eds.), *Sexual Divisions and Society: Process and Change*, (London: Tavistock).

Barker, M. and Beezer, A. (1984), 'The Language of Racism – an examination of Lord Scarman's Report on the Brixton Riots', *International Socialism*, vol. 2, no. 18.

Barrington Moore (1966), *Social Origins of Dictatorship and Democracy*, (Harmondsworth: Penguin).

Beccaria, C. (1963), *On Crimes and Punishments*, (Indianapolis: Bobbs Merrill).

Bechhofer F. (1974), 'Current approaches to empirical research: some central ideas' in J. Rex (ed.), *Approaches to Sociology: an Introduction to Major Trends in British Sociology*, (London: Routledge and Kegan Paul), pp. 70–91.

Becker, H. S (1963), *Outsiders: Studies in the Sociology of Deviance*, (New York: The Free Press).

Becker, H. S. (1964) (ed.), *The Other Side: Perspectives on Deviance*, (New York: Free Press).

Becker, H. S. (1970), *Sociological Work*, (Chicago: Aldine).

Beechey, V. (1982), 'The sexual division of labour and the labour process: a critical assessment of Braverman' in S. Wood (ed.), *The Degradation of Work? Skill, deskilling and the labour process*, (London: Hutchinson).

Bell, C. and Newby, H. (1971), *Community Studies*, (London: Allen and Unwin).

Bell, C. and Newby, H. (1977) (eds.), *Doing Sociological Research*, (London: Allen and Unwin).

Bell, C. *et al.* (1984), *Fathers, Childbirth and Work*, (Manchester: Equal Opportunities Commission).

Bell, C. and Roberts, H. (1984) (eds.), *Social Researching: Politics, Problems and Practice*, (London: Routledge and Kegan Paul).

Benton, T. (1977), *The Philosophical Foundation of the Three Sociologies*, (London: Routledge and Kegan Paul).

Berger, P. and Luckmann, T. (1971), *The Social Construction of Reality*, (Harmondsworth: Penguin).

Béteille,A. (1969) (ed.), *Social Inequality*, (Harmondsworth: Penguin).

Beynon, H. (1984), *Working for Ford*, (2nd edn.) (Harmondsworth: Penguin).

Blauner, R. (1964), *Alienation and Freedom: the factory worker and his industry*, (Chicago: Chicago University Press).

Blumer, H. (1969), *Symbolic Interactionism*, (Englewood Cliffs, N. J.: Prentice Hall).

Bordua, D. (1961), 'Delinquent sub-cultures: sociological interpretations of gang delinquency', *The Annals of the American Academy of Political and Social Science*, vol. cccxxxviii, November, pp. 120–136.

Bottomore, T. B. (1962), *Sociology: a Guide to Problems and Literature*, (London: Allen and Unwin).

Bottomore, T. B. (1965), *Classes in Modern Society*, (London: Allen and Unwin).

Bottomore, T. B. and Rubel, M. (1963) (eds.), *Karl Marx: Selected Writings in Sociology and Social Philosophy*, (Harmondsworth: Penguin).

Boulton, M. G. (1983), *On Being a Mother*, (London: Tavistock).

Braverman, H. (1974), *Labor and Monopoly Capital*, (New York and London: Monthly Review Press).

Brelsford, P., Smith, G. and Rix, A. (1982), *Give Us a Break: Widening Opportunities for Women within YOP/YTS*, MSC Research and Development Series no. 11.

British Sociological Association (1973), 'Statement of ethical principles and their application to sociological practice' (memo with amendments in 1982).

Britten, N. and Heath, A. (1983), 'Women, men and social class' in E. Gamarnikow, D. Morgan, J. Purvis and D. Taylorson (eds.), *Gender, Class and Work*, (London: Heinemann), pp. 46–60.

Brown, R. (1984), 'Work' in Abrams, P. and Brown, R. K. (eds.), *UK. Society: Work, Urbanism and Inequality*, (2nd edn.) (London: Weidenfeld and Nicolson), pp. 129–197.

Bruce, M. (1968), *The Coming of the Welfare State*, (London: Batsford.

Bulmer, J. (1977), *Guide to the Teaching of Anthropology in Schools and Colleges*, (London: School of Oriental and African Studies).

Bulmer, M. (1984) (ed.), *Sociological Research Methods*, (2nd edn.), (London: Macmillan).

Bulmer, M. and Burgess, R. G. (1981) (eds.), *The Teaching of Research Methodology*, special issue of *Sociology*, vol. 15, no. 4.

Burgess, R. G. (1982) (ed.), *Field Research: a Sourcebook and Field Manual*, (London: Allen and Unwin).

Burgess, R. G. (1983), *Experiencing Comprehensive Education: A Study of Bishop McGregor School*, (London: Methuen).

Burgess, R. G. (1984a) (ed.), *The Research Process in Educational Settings: Ten Case Studies*, (Lewes: Falmer Press).

Burgess, R. G. (1984b), *In the Field: An Introduction to Field Research*, (London: Allen and Unwin).

Burgess, R. G. (1985), *Education, Schools and Schooling*, (London: Macmillan).

Burgess, R. G. and Bulmer, M. (1981), 'Research methodology teaching: trends and developments', *Sociology*, vol. 15, no. 4, pp. 477–489.

Burnett, J. (1974), *Useful Toil: Autobiographies of working people from the 1820s to the 1920s*, (London: Allen Lane).

Burns, T. (1967), 'Sociological explanation', *British Journal of Sociology*, vol. 18, no. 4, pp. 353–69, reprinted in D. Emmet and A. Macintyre (1970) (eds.), *Sociological Theory and Philosophical Analysis*, (London: Macmillan), pp. 55–75.

Butterworth, E. and Holman, R. (1975) (eds.), *Social Welfare in Modern Britain: an Introductory Reader*, (London: Fontana).

Cambridge Women's Studies Group (1981), *Women in Society*, (London: Virago).

Campaign Against Racism and Fascism/Southall Rights (1981), *Southall: the Birth of a Black Community*, (London: Institute of Race Relations).

Campbell, A. (1981), *Girl Delinquents*, (Oxford: Blackwell).

Cartwright, A. (1964), *Human Relations and Hospital Care*, (London: Routledge and Kegan Paul).

Cartwright, A. (1979), *The Dignity of Labour?* (London: Tavistock)

Cartwright, A. (1983), *Health Surveys in Practice and in Potential: A Critical Review of their Scope and Methods*, (London: King Edward's Hospital Fund for London).

Cartwright, A. and Anderson, R. (1981), *General Practice Revisited:*

a Second Study of Patients and their Doctors, (London: Tavistock).

Castles, F. and Kosack, G. (1973), *Immigrant Workers and Class Strucure in Western Europe*, (London: OUP for the Institute of Race Relations).

Central Statistical Office (1984), *Social Trends*, (London: HMSO).

Charlesworth, A., Wilkin, D. and Durie, A. (1984), *Carers and Services*, (Manchester: Manchester University Press).

Clarke, L. (1980), *The Transition from School to Work: a Critical Review of Research in the UK*, (London: HMSO).

Claus, L. M. (1983), 'The development of medical sociology in Europe', *Social Science and Medicine*, vol. 17, pp. 1591–1597.

Cloward, R. and Ohlin, L. (1960), *Delinquency and Opportunity: a Theory of Delinquent Gangs*, (Chicago: Free Press).

Cockburn, C. (1982), *Brothers*, (London: Pluto Press).

Cohen, A. K. (1955), *Delinquent Boys: the Culture of the Gang*, (Chicago: Free Press).

Cohen, R. (1980), 'Migration, late capitalism and development', Address to the Plenary Session of the Annual Conference of the Development Studies Association, University College, Swansea.

Cohen, S. (1972), *Folk Devils and Moral Panics*, (London: MacGibbon and Kee) (reprinted with a new introduction by Martin Robertson in 1980).

Collins, R. (1985), '"Horses for Courses": Ideology and the division of domestic labour' in P. Close and R. Collins (eds.), *Family and Economy in Modern Society*, (London: Macmillan).

Community Development Project (1977), *The Cost of Industrial Change*, (London: CDP).

Conference of Socialist Economists (1980), *Microelectronics: Capitalist Technology and the Working Class*, (London: CSE Books).

Cokerham, W. C. (1983), 'The state of medical sociology in the United States, Great Britain, West Germany and Austria: Applied vs. pure theory', *Social Science and Medicine*, vol. 17, pp. 1513–1527.

Corrigan, P. (1979), *Schooling the Smash Street Kids*, (London: Macmillan).

Council for Science and Society (1981), *New Technology: Society, Employment and Skill*, (London: CSS).

Counter Information Services (1979), *The New Technology*, (Anti-Report no. 23) (London: CIS).

Coulson, A. (1979), *African Socialism in Practice: the Tanzanian Experience*, (Nottingham: Spokesman).

Crompton, R. and Jones, G. (1984), *White Collar Proletariat: deskilling and gender in clerical work*, (London: Macmillan).

Cuff, E. C. and Payne, G. C. F. (1979) (eds.), *Perspectives in Sociology*, (London: Allen and Unwin).

Cunningham-Burley, S. (1984), '"We don't talk about it . . ." Issues of gender and method in the portrayal of grandfatherhood', *Sociology*, vol. 18, no. 3, pp. 325–338.

Dahrendorf, R. (1959), *Class and Class Conflict in Industrial Society*, (London: Routledge and Kegan Paul).

Daniel, W. W. (1981), *The Unemployed Flow*, (London: PSI).

Danziger, K. (1971), *Socialization*, (Harmondsworth: Penguin).

Davis, A. and Horobin, G. (1977) (eds.), *Medical Encounters: the Experience of Illness and Treatment*, (London: Croom Helm).

Deakin, N. (1970), *Colour, Citizenship and British Society*, (London: Panther).

Delamont, S. (1984) (ed.), *Readings in Classroom Interaction*, (London: Methuen).

Delphy, C. (1984), *Close to Home*, (London: Hutchinson).

Denzin, N. K. (1978), *The Research Act*, (2nd edn.) (London: McGraw Hill).

Department of Health and Social Security (1970), *Domiciliary Midwifery and Maternity Bed Needs*, Report of the sub-committee (Peel Report) The Standing Maternity and Midwifery Advisory Committee (London: HMSO).

Department of Health and Social Security (1980), *Inequalities in Health*, Report of a Research Working Group (The Black Report) (London: HMSO).

Department of Health and Social Security (1984), *Report of the Committee of Enquiry into Human Fertilisation and Embryology*, (The Warnock Report) Cmnd 9314 (London: HMSO).

Dingwall, R., Heath, C., Reid, M. and Stacey, M. (1977) (eds.), *Health Care and Health Knowledge*, (London: Croom Helm).

Dionne, E. (1982), 'Race, community and equality: a study of public opinion in Britain and the United States', unpublished DPhil (Oxford: University of Oxford).

Ditton, J. (1977), *Part-Time Crime: an Ethnography of Fiddling and Pilferage*, (London: Macmillan).

Donnelly, L. (1969) (ed.), *Justice First*, (London: Sheed and Ward).

Douglas, J. D. (1976), *Investigative Social Research*, (Beverley Hills, California: Sage).

Downes, D. (1966), *The Delinquent Solution*, (London: Routledge and Kegan Paul).

Downes, D. and Rock, P. (1982), *Understanding Deviance*, (Oxford: Clarendon Press).

Doyal, L. with Pennell, I. (1979), *The Political Economy of Health*, (London: Pluto Press).

Dunnell, K. and Cartwright, A. (1972), *Medicine Takers, Prescribers and Hoarders*, (London: Routledge and Kegan Paul).

Durkheim, E. (1897), *Le Suicide: Étude de Sociologie*, (Paris: Alcan). Published in English as: Durkheim, E. (1951), *Suicide*, (New York: Free Press).

Durkheim, E. (1964), *The Division of Labour in Society*, (New York: Free Press).

Ehrenreich, B. (1978) (ed.), *The Cultural Crisis of Modern Medicine*, (New York and London: Monthly Review Press).

Ehrenreich, B. and English, D. (1974), *Complaints and Disorders: the Sexual Politics of Sickness*, Glass Mountain Pamphlets no. 2 (New York: The Feminist Press).

Ehrenreich, B. and English, D. (1979), *For Her Own Good*, (London: Pluto Press).

Eldridge, J. (1980), *Recent British Sociology*, (London: Macmillan).

Elger, A. (1979), 'Valorisation and deskilling – a critique of Braverman', *Capital and Class*, no. 7, Spring, pp. 58–99.

Elling, R. H. and Sokolowska, M. (1978) (eds.), *Medical Sociologists at Work*, (Rutgers, New Jersey: Transaction Books).

Ellis, L. (1982), 'Genetics and Criminal Behaviour', *Criminology*, vol. 20, no. 1, pp. 43–66.

Elston, M. A. (1977), 'Women in the medical profession: whose problem?' in M. Stacey, M. Reid, C. Heath and R. Dingwall (eds.), *Health and the Division of Labour*, (London: Croom Helm), pp. 115–38.

Equal Opportunities Commission (1982a), *Caring for the Elderly and Handicapped*, (Manchester: EOC).

Equal Opportunities Commission (1982b), *Who Cares for the Carers?*, (Manchester: Manchester University Press).

Evans, M. and Ungerson, C. (1983) (eds.), *Sexual Divisions: Patterns and Processes*, (London: Tavistock).

Eysenck, H. (1970), *Crime and Personality*, (London: Paladin).

Fagin, L. and Little, M. (1984), *The Forsaken Families*, (Harmondsworth: Penguin).

Family Policy Studies Centre (1984), *The Forgotten Army: Family Care and Elderly People*, (London: FPSC).

Feierman, S. (1979), 'Change in African therapeutic systems', *Social Science and Medicine*, vol. 13B, no. 4, pp. 277–84.

Filstead, W. J. (1970) (ed.), *Qualitative Methodology: Firsthand Involvement with the Social World*, (Chicago: Markham).

Finch, J. (1983), *Married to the Job*, (London: Allen and Unwin).

Finch, J. (1984), 'Community care: developing non-sexist alternatives', *Critical Social Policy*, no. 9, pp. 6–18.

Finch, J. and Groves, D. (1980), 'Community care and the family: a case for equal opportunities?', *Journal of Social Policy*, vol. 9, no. 4, pp. 487–511.

Finch, J. and Groves, D. (1983) (eds.), *A Labour of Love: Women, Work and Caring*, (London: Routledge and Kegan Paul).

Foucault, M. (1967), *Madness and Civilization: a History of Insanity in the Age of Reason*, (London: Tavistock).

Fraser, R. (1968) (ed.), *Work: Twenty Personal Accounts*, (Harmondsworth: Penguin).

Fraser, R. (1969) (ed.), *Work 2: Twenty Personal Accounts*, (Harmondsworth: Penguin).

Freidson, E. (1970), *The Profession of Medicine*, (New York: Dodd Mead).

Friedmann, A. (1977), 'Responsible autonomy versus direct control over the labour process', *Capital and Class*, no. 1, pp. 43–57.

Freud, S. (1930), *Civilization and its Discontents* (reprinted in volume XXI of the Standard Edition of the Complete Psychological Works of Sigmund Freud (1961)), (translated by J. Strachey), (London: The Hogarth Press and the Institute of Psycho-Analysis), pp. 59–243.

Fröbel, F., Heinrichs, J. and Kreye, O. (1980), *The New International Division of Labour*, (Cambridge: CUP).

Gamarnikow, E. (1978), 'Sexual division of labour: the case of nursing' in A. Kuhn and M. Wolpe (eds.), *Feminism and Materialism: Women and Modes of Production*, (London: Routledge and Kegan Paul), pp. 96–123.

Geer, B. (1964), 'First days in the field' in P. Hammond (ed.),

Sociologists at Work, (New York: Basic Books), pp. 322–44.

Gershuny, J. E. and Pahl, R. E. (1980), 'Britain in the decade of the three economies', *New Society*, vol. 51, no. 900, pp. 7–9.

Giddens, A. (1982), *Sociology: A brief but critical introduction*, (London: Macmillan).

Gill, O. (1977), *Luke Street: Housing Policy, Conflict and the Creation of the Delinquency Area*, (London: Macmillan).

Glaser, B G. and Strauss, A. L. (1967), *The Discovery of Grounded Theory: Strategies for Qualitative Research*, (Chicago: Aldine).

Gluckman, M. (1967), 'Introduction', in A. L. Epstein (ed.), *The Craft of Social Anthropology*, (London: Tavistock), pp. xi–xx.

Glueck, S. and Glueck, E. (1956) *Physique and Delinquency*, (New York: Harper and Row).

Goffman, E. (1969), *The Presentation of Self in Everyday Life*, (New York: Doubleday Anchor).

Goldthorpe, J. (1978), 'The current inflation: towards a sociological account' in Hirsh, F. and Goldthorpe, J. (eds.), *The Political Economy of Inflation*, (Oxford: Martin Robertson).

Goldthorpe, J. (1983), 'Women and class analysis: in defence of the conventional view', *Sociology*, vol. 17, pp. 465–488.

Goldthorpe, J. H., Lockwood, D., Bechhofer, F. and Platt, J. (1968a), *The Affluent Worker: Industrial Attitudes and Behaviour*, (Cambridge: CUP).

Goldthorpe, J. H., Lockwood, D., Bechhofer, F. and Platt, J. (1968b), *The Affluent Worker: Political Attitudes and Behaviour*, (Cambridge: CUP).

Goldthorpe, J. H., Lockwood, D., Bechhofer, F. and Platt, J. (1969), *The Affluent Worker in the Class Structure*, (Cambridge: CUP).

Goldthorpe, J. H. with Llewellyn, C. and Payne, C. (1980), *Social Mobility and Class Structure in Modern Britain*, (Oxford: Clarendon Press).

Gough, I. (1979), *The Political Economy of the Welfare State*, (London: Macmillan).

Gouldner, A. (1969), 'The unemployed self' in R. Fraser (ed.), *Work 2: Twenty Personal Accounts*, (Harmondsworth: Penguin), pp. 346–65.

Graham, H. (1984), *Women, Health and the Family*, (Brighton: Wheatsheaf).

Graham, H (1985), *Health and Welfare*, (London: Macmillan).

Hadley, R. and Hatch, S. (1981), *Social Welfare and the Failure of the State*, (London: Allen and Unwin).

Hall, D. and Stacey, M. (1979) (eds.), *Beyond Separation: Further Studies of Children in Hospital*, (London: Routledge and Kegan Paul).

Hall, S., Critcher, C., Jefferson, T., Clarke J. and Roberts, B. (1978), *Policing the Crisis: Mugging, the State and Law and Order*, (London: Macmillan).

Hall, S. and Jefferson, T. (1976) (eds.), *Resistance Through Rituals*, (London: Hutchinson)

Hall Williams, J. E. (1982), *Criminology and Criminal Justice*, (London: Butterworth).

Hammersley, M. (1982), 'The sociology of classrooms' in A. Hartnett (ed.), *The Social Sciences in Educational Studies*, (London: Heinemann), pp. 227–242.

Hammersley, M. and Woods, P. (1984) (eds.), *Life in School: The Sociology of Pupil Culture*, (Milton Keynes: Open University Press).

Hammond, P. (1964) (ed.), *Sociologists at Work*, (New York: Basic Books).

Hanmer, J. and Leonard, D. (1980), 'Men and culture: the sociological intelligentsia and the maintenance of male domination: or superman meets the invisible woman'. Paper presented at British Sociological Association Annual Conference.

Hargreaves, A. and Woods, P. (1984) (eds.), *Classrooms and Staffrooms: the Sociology of Teachers and Teaching*, (Milton Keynes: Open University Press).

Hargreaves, D. H. (1967), *Social Relations in a Secondary School*, (London: Routledge and Kegan Paul).

Harris, C. C. (1983), *The Family and Industrial Society*, (London: Allen and Unwin).

Heath, A. (1981), *Social Mobility*, (London: Fontana).

Heidensohn, F. (1985), *Women and Crime*, (London: Macmillan)

Hill, M. (1983) (ed.), *Understanding Social Policy*, (2nd edn.) (Oxford: Basil Blackwell).

Hiro, D. (1971), *Black British, White British*, (London: Eyre and Spottiswoode).

Hirschi, T. (1969), *Causes of Delinquency*, (Berkeley: University of California Press).

Homans, H. (1980), 'Pregnant in Britain: a sociological approach to Asian and British women's experiences', unpublished PhD thesis (Coventry: University of Warwick).

Houte, H. van and Melgert, W. (1972), *Foreigners in Our Community: a New European Problem to be Solved*, (Amsterdam: Keesing).

Humphry, D. (1972), *Police Power and Black People*, (London: Panther).

Humphry, D. and John, A. (1971), *Because They're Black*, (Harmondsworth: Penguin).

Hunt, P. (1980), *Gender and Class Consciousness*, (London: Macmillan).

Husband, C. (1982) (ed.), *'Race' in Britain*, (London: Hutchinson).

Illsley, R. (1980), *Professional or Public Health? Sociology in Health and Medicine*, (London: The Nuffield Provincial Hospitals Trust).

Institute of Race Relations (1979), *Police Against Black People*, (evidence submitted to the Royal Commission on Criminal Procedure) (London: Institute of Race Relations).

Jeffery, C. R. (1960), 'The historical development of criminology' in H. Mannheim (ed.), *Pioneers in Criminology*, (London: Stevens) pp. 364–394.

Jeffereys, M. and Sachs, H. (1983), *Rethinking General Practice*, (London: Tavistock).

Jewson; N. D. (1974), 'Medical knowledge and the patronage system in eighteenth century England', *Sociology*, vol. 8, no. 3, pp. 369–85.

Jewson, N. D. (1976), 'The disappearance of the sick man from the medical cosmology', *Sociology*, vol. 10, no. 2, pp. 225–44.

Johnson, H. and Bernstein, H. (1982), *Third World Lives of Struggle*, (London: Heinemann/Open University).

Jones, K., Brown, J. and Bradshaw, J. (1978), *Issues in Social Policy*, (London: Routledge and Kegan Paul).

Joshua, H. and Wallace, C. (1984), *To Ride the Storm*, (London: Heinemann).

Keat, R. and Urry, J. (1975), *Social Theory as Science*, (London: Routledge and Kegan Paul).

Lacey, C. (1970), *Hightown Grammar: the School as a Social System*, (Manchester: Manchester University Press).

Lacey, C. (1977), *The Socialization of Teachers*, (London: Methuen).

Lambeth (1981), *Final Report of the Working Party into Community Police Relations in Lambeth*, (London: London Borough of Lambeth).

Lee, D. and Newby, H. (1983), *The Problem of Sociology*, (London: Hutchinson).

Lee, G. and Wrench, J. (1981), 'Inequality in the skilled labour market: the case of black youths in Birmingham'. Paper presented at British Sociological Association Annual Conference.

Leeson, J. and Gray, J. (1978), *Women and Medicine*, (London: Tavistock).

Lemert, E. M. (1967), *Human Deviance, Social Problems and Social Control*, (New York: Prentice Hall).

Lewis, G (1976), 'A view of sickness in New Guinea' in J. B. Loudon (ed.), *Social Anthropology and Medicine*, (London: Academic Press), pp. 49–103.

Lockwood, D. (1958), *The Blackcoated Worker: A Study in Class Consciousness*, (London: Allen and Unwin).

London Borough of Lambeth (1981), *First Report of the Working Party into Community Relations in Lambeth*, (London: London Borough of Lambeth).

Macintyre, S. (1977), 'Old age as a social problem' in R. Dingwall, C. Heath, M. Reid, and M. Stacey (eds.), *Health Care and Health Knowledge*, (London: Croom Helm), pp. 39–63.

MacManus, J. (1978), 'Graveyard for white elephants', *Guardian Third World Review*, 6 March.

McCall, G. J. and Simmons, J. L. (1969) (eds.), *Issues in Participant Observation: A Text and Reader*, (Reading, Massachusetts: Addison-Wesley).

McKee, L. and O'Brien, M. (1982) (eds.), *The Father Figure*, (London: Tavistock).

McKeown, T. (1971a), 'A sociological approach to the history of medicine' in G. McLachlan and T. McKeown (eds.), *Medical History and Medical Care*, (London: OUP for the Nuffield Provincial Hospitals Trust), pp. 1–26.

McKeown, T. (1971b), 'A historical appraisal of the medical task' in G. McLachlan and T. McKeown (eds.), *Medical History and Medical Care*, (London: OUP for the Nuffield Provincial Hospitals Trust), pp. 27–55.

Madan, R. (1979), *Coloured Minorities in Great Britain: a Compre-*

hensive Bibliography 1970–77, (London: Aldwych).

Mann, M. (1983) (ed.), *The Macmillan Student Encyclopedia of Sociology*, (London: Macmillan).

Manning, M. (1985) (ed.), *Social Problems and Welfare Ideology*, (Aldershot: Gower).

Marsh, D. C. (1979) (ed.), *Introducing Social Policy*, (London: Routledge and Kegan Paul).

Marshall, A. (1973), *The Import of Labour: the Case of the Netherlands*, (Rotterdam: Rotterdam University Press).

Marx K. (1967), *The Communist Manifesto*, (Harmondsworth: Penguin).

Mascarenhas, O. and Mbilinyi, M. (1983), *Women in Tanzania*, (Scandinavian Institute of African Studies: Uppsala, Sweden).

Matza, D. (1964), *Delinquency and Drift*, (New York: Wiley).

Matza, D. (1969), *Becoming Deviant*, (Englewood Cliffs: Prentice Hall).

Mead, G. H. (1934), *Mind, Self and Society*, (Chicago: University of Chicago Press).

Merton, R. K (1957), *Social Theory and Social Structure*, (New York: Free Press).

Merton, R. K. (1968), *Social Theory and Social Structure*, (3rd edn.) (New York: Free Press).

Merton, R. K. and Nisbet, R. (1966) (eds.), *Contemporary Social Problems*, (2nd edn.) (New York: Harcourt Brace and World Inc.).

Mills, C. Wright (1970), *The Sociological Imagination*, (Harmondsworth: Penguin) (originally published in 1959).

Ministry of Health (1959a), *Report of the Maternity Services Committee*, (Cranbrook Report) (London: HMSO).

Ministry of Health (1959b), *The Welfare of Children in Hospital*, (Platt Report) (London: HMSO).

Mishra, R. (1977), *Society and Social Policy: Theoretical Perspectives on Welfare*, (London: Macmillan).

Mitchell, G. D. (1979) (ed.), *A New Dictionary of Sociology*, (London: Routledge and Kegan Paul).

Monachesi, E. (1960), 'Cesare Beccaria' in H. Mannheim (ed.), *Pioneers in Criminology*, (London: Stevens), pp. 36–50.

Moore, R. (1975), *Racism and Black Resistance in Britain*, (London: Pluto Press).

Moore, R. (1977), 'Becoming a sociologist in Sparkbrook', in C. Bell and H. Newby (eds.), *Doing Sociological Research*, (London: Allen and Unwin), pp. 87–107.

Moore, R. and Wallace, T. (1975), *Slamming the Door: the Administration of Immigration Control*, (Oxford: Martin Robertson).

Moore, R. and Wallace, T. (1981), 'Evidence submitted to Lord Scarman's enquiry'.

Morgan, D. H. J. (1984), *Gender*, (Teaching Papers in Sociology) (London: Longman).

Morris, A. and Gelsthorpe, L. (1981), *Women and Crime: Papers Presented to the Cropwood Round Table Conference December 1980*, (Cambridge: Institute of Criminology).

Morris, P. (1969), *Put Away: A Sociological Study of Institutions for the Mentally Retarded*, (London: Routledge and Kegan Paul).

Moser, C. and Kalton, G. (1971), *Survey Methods in Social Investigation*, (2nd edn.) (London: Heinemann).

National Council for Civil Liberties (1980a), *Southall, 23rd April 1979*, (London: NCCL).

National Council for Civil Liberties (1980b), *The Death of Blair Peach*, (London: NCCL).

Nichols, T. (1980) (ed.), *Capital and Labour*, (London: Fontana).

Nisbet, R. (1966), 'Introduction: the study of social problems' in R. K. Merton and R. Nisbet (eds.), *Contemporary Social Problems*, (2nd edn.) (New York: Harcourt, Brace and World, Inc.), pp. 3–18.

Nissel, M. and Bonnerjea, L. (1982), *Family Care of the Handicapped Elderly: Who Pays?*, (London: Policy Studies Institute).

Nwabughugu, A. I. (1982), 'Oil mill riots in Eastern Nigeria 1948–51: A study in indigenous reaction to technological innovation' in *Africa Development*, vol. VII, no. 4, Dakar, Senegal, pp. 66–84.

O'Brien, M. (1981), *The Politics of Reproduction*, (London: Routledge and Kegan Paul).

Oakley, A. (1972), *Sex, Gender and Society*, (London: Temple Smith).

Oakley, A. (1974), *The Sociology of Housework*, (Oxford: Martin Robertson).

Oakley, A. (1981a), *From Here to Maternity*, (Harmondsworth: Penguin).

Oakley, A. (1981b), 'Interviewing women: a contradiction in terms?' in H. Roberts (ed.), *Doing Feminist Research*, (London: Routledge and Kegan Paul), pp. 30–61.

Oakley, A. (1981c), *Subject Women*, (Oxford: Martin Robertson).

Office of Population, Censuses and Surveys (1978), *Demographic Review 1977*, Series DR, no. 1 (London: HMSO).

Oyono, F.(1966), *Houseboy*, (London: Heinemann).

Pahl, R. E. (1980), 'Employment, work and the domestic division of labour', *International Journal of Urban and Regional Research*, vol. 4, no. 1, pp. 1–20.

Pahl, R. E. (1984), *Divisions of Labour*, (Oxford: Basil Blackwell).

Paine, S. (1974), *Exporting Workers: the Turkish Case*, (Cambridge: CUP).

Parkin, F. (1973), *Class Inequality and Political Order*, (London: Paladin).

Parkin, F. (1979), *Marxism and Class Theory: a Bourgeois Critique*, (London: Tavistock).

Parsons, T. (1951), *The Social System*, (Glencoe, Illinois: Free Press).

Peach, C. (1968), *West Indian Migration to Britain*, (London: OUP for the Institute of Race Relations).

Pearson, G. (1975), *The Deviant Imagination: Psychiatry, Social Work and Social Change*, (London: Macmillan).

Phizacklea, A. and Miles, R. (1980), *Labour and Racism*, (London: Routledge and Kegan Paul).

Pierce, G. (1982), 'Unleashing an uncritical press', the *Guardian*, 15th March, p. 10.

Platt, J. (1976), *Realities of Social Research*, (London: Chatto and Windus for Sussex University Press).

Platt, J. (1984), 'The *Affluent Worker* revisited' in C. Bell and H. Roberts (eds.), *Social Researching: Politics, Problems and Practice*, (London: Routledge and Kegan Paul), pp. 179–198.

Plummer, K. (1983), *Documents of Life*, (London: Allen and Unwin).

Poulantzas, N. (1973), *Political Power and Social Class*, (London: New Left Books).

Ramsay, M. (1982), 'Mugging: fears and facts', *New Society*, vol. 59, no. 1010, pp. 467–9.

Randall, V. (1982), *Women and Politics*, (London: Macmillan).

Rapoport, R. *et al.* (1982) (eds.), *Families in Britain*, (London: Routledge and Kegan Paul).

Review of African Political Economy (1979), Special issue on Nigeria, No. 13.

Rex, J. (1961), *Key Problems of Sociological Theory*, (London: Routledge and Kegan Paul).

Rex, J. (1970), 'The concept of race in sociological theory' in S. Zubaida (ed.), *Race and Racialism*, (London: Tavistock), pp. 35–55.

Rex, J. and Moore, R. (1967), *Race, Community and Conflict*, (London: OUP for the Institute of Race Relations).

Roberts, H. (1981a) (ed.), *Doing Feminist Research*, (London: Routledge and Kegan Paul).

Roberts, H. (1981b), 'Some of the boys won't play any more: the impact of feminism on sociology' in D. Spender (ed.), *Men's Studies Modified: the Impact of Feminism on the Academic Disciplines*, (Oxford: Pergamon Press), pp. 73–81.

Roberts, H. (1981c) (ed.), *Women, Health and Reproduction*, (London: Routledge and Kegan Paul).

Roberts, H. and Sharp, M. (1982), *After Sixteen: What Happens to the Girls*, (Bradford: Bradford Metropolitan District).

Roberts, K. (1977), 'The social conditions, consequences and limitations of careers guidance', *British Journal of Guidance and Counselling*, vol. 5, no. 1, pp. 1–9.

Rodney, W. (1972), *How Europe Underdeveloped Africa*, London, Bogle L'Ouverture.

Room, G. (1979), *The Sociology of Welfare: Social Policy, Stratification and the Political Order*, (Oxford: Blackwell/Martin Robertson).

Rose, E. J. B. *et al.* (1969), *Colour and Citizenship: a report on British Race Relations*, (London: OUP for the Institute of Race Relations).

Roth, J. A. (1963), *Timetables: Structuring the Passage of Time in Hospital Treatment and Other Careers*, (New York: Bobbs-Merrill Company Inc.).

Roxborough, I. (1979), *Theories of Underdevelopment* (London: Macmillan).

Ruzek, S. B. (1978), *The Women's Health Movement: Feminist Alternatives to Medical Control*, (New York: Praeger).

Ryan, W. (1971), *Blaming the Victim*, (London: Orbach and Chambers).

Scully, D. and Bart, P. (1972–73), 'A funny thing happened on the way to the orifice: women in gynaecological textbooks', *American Journal of Sociology*, vol. 78, no. 4, pp. 1045–50.

Shaw, C. R. and McKay, H. D. (1942), *Juvenile Delinquency and Urban Areas*, (Chicago: Chicago University Press).

Shivji, I. (1976), *Class Struggles in Tanzania*, (London: Heinemann).

Short, J. F. Jr. and Strodtbeck, F. L. (1965), *Group Process and Gang Delinquency*, (Chicago: Chicago University Press).

Showler, B. and Sinfield, A. (1981) (eds.), *The Workless State*, (Oxford: Martin Robertson).

Sills, D. (1968) (ed.), *International Encyclopaedia of the Social Sciences*, (New York: Macmillan and Free Press).

Sinfield, A. (1981), *What Unemployment Means*, (Oxford: Martin Robertson).

Sivanandan, A. (1979), 'Imperialism and disorganic development in the silicon age', *Race and Class*, vol. xxi, no. 2, pp. 111–26.

Sjoberg, G. and Nett, R. (1968), *A Methodology for Social Research*, (New York: Harper and Row).

Smith, D. (1973), 'Women, the family and corporate capitalism' in M. Stephenson (ed.), *Women in Canada*, (Toronto: New Press) pp. 2–35.

Smith, D. J. *et al.* (1983), *Police and People in London*, 4 volumes.

Spender, D. (1981) (ed.), *Men's Studies Modified: the Impact of Feminism on the Academic Disciplines*, (Oxford: Pergamon Press).

Spender, D. and Sarah, E. (1981) (eds.), *Learning to Lose*, (London: The Women's Press).

Spindler, G. (1982) (ed.), *Doing the Ethnography of Schooling*, (New York: Holt, Rinehart and Winston).

Stacey, M. (1969a), *Methods of Social Research*, (Oxford: Pergamon).

Stacey, M. (1969b), 'The myth of community studies', *British Journal of Sociology*, vol. 20, no. 2, pp. 134–47.

Stacey, M. (1981), 'The division of labour revisited or overcoming the two Adams' in P. Abrams, R. Deem, J. Finch, and P. Rock (eds.), *Practice and Progress: British Sociology 1950–1980*,

(London: Allen and Unwin), pp. 172–90.

Stacey, M. (1984), 'Who are the health workers? Patients and other unpaid workers in health care', *Economic and Industrial Democracy*, vol. 5, pp. 157–184.

Stacey, M. and Burgess, R. G. (1979), 'The research process', (Oxford: Sussex Publications). Taped discussion.

Stacey, M., Dearden, R., Pill, R. and Robinson, D. (1970), *Hospitals, Children and their Families*, (London: Routledge and Kegan Paul).

Stacey, M., Reid, M., Heath, C. and Dingwall, R. (1977) (eds.), *Health and the Division of Labour*, (London: Croom Helm).

Stacey, M. with Homans, H. (1978), 'The sociology of health and illness: its present state, future prospects, and potential for health research', *Sociology*, vol. 12, no. 2, pp. 281–307.

Stanworth, M. (1983), *Gender and Schooling*, (London: Hutchinson).

Stanworth, M. (1984), 'Women and class analysis: a reply to John Goldthorpe', *Sociology*, vol. 18, no. 2, pp. 159–170.

Stewart, A., Prandy, K. and Blackburn, R. M. (1980), *Social Stratification and Occupations*, (London: Macmillan).

Street-Porter, R. (1978), *Race, Children and Cities*, (Milton Keynes: Open University Press).

Sutherland, E. and Cressey, D. (1970), *Principles of Criminology*, (Philadelphia: Lippincott).

Taylor, I., Walton, P. and Young, J. (1973), *The New Criminology*, (London: Routledge and Kegan Paul).

Taylor, I., Walton, P. and Young, J. (1975) (eds.), *Critical Criminology*, (London: Routledge and Kegan Paul).

Terkel, S. (1972), *Working*, (New York: Random House).

Thomas, W. I. (1928), *The Child in America*, (New York: Knopf).

Thompson, E. P. (1967), 'Time, work-discipline and industrial capitalism', *Past and Present*, no. 38, pp. 56–97.

Thorne, B. and Yallom, M. (1982) (eds.), *Rethinking the Family*, (London: Longman).

Tinker, A. (1981), *The Elderly in Modern Society*, (London: Longman).

Titmuss, R. M. (1974), *Social Policy*, (London: Allen and Unwin).

Titmuss, R. M. (1976), *Essays on the Welfare State*, (3rd edn.) (London: Allen and Unwin).

Tolson, A. (1977), *The Limits of Masculinity*, (London: Tavistock).

Townsend, P. (1962), *The Last Refuge*, (London: Routledge and Kegan Paul).

Townsend, P. and Davidson, N. (1982) (eds.), *Inequalities in Health: the Black Report*, (Harmondsworth: Penguin).

Trow, M. (1957), 'Comment on "participant observation and interviewing: a comparison"', *Human Organization*, vol. 16, no. 3, pp. 33–5; reprinted in G. J. McCall and J. L. Simmons (eds.), *Issues in Participant Observation: a Text and Reader*, (Reading, Massachusetts: Addison Wesley) pp. 332–8.

Ungerson, C. (1985) (ed.), *Women and Social Policy: A Reader*, (London: Macmillan).

UNESCO (1969), *Four Statements on the Race Question*.

Vold, G. (1958), *Theoretical Criminology*, (New York: OUP).

Walby, S. (1983), 'Patriarchal structures: the case of unemployment' in E. Gamarnikow, D. Morgan, J. Purvis and D. Taylorson (eds.), *Gender, Class and Work*, (London: Heinemann) pp. 149–166.

Walby, S. (1985), *Patriarchy at Work*, (Oxford: Polity Press).

Walker, A. (1982) (ed.), *Community Care: the Family, the State and Social Policy*, (Oxford: Basil Blackwell).

Walters, H. (1976), 'Guide to the literature on race relations in Britain, 1970–1975', *Sage Race Relations Abstracts*, vol. 1, no. 2, pp. 97–105.

Watson, J. (1979) (ed.), *Between Two Cultures*, (Oxford: Basil Blackwell).

Watson, J. D. (1968), *The Double Helix*, (Harmondsworth: Penguin).

Webb, E. J., Campbell, D. T., Schwartz, R. D. and Sechrest, L. (1966), *Unobtrusive Measures: Non-reactive Research in the Social Sciences*, (Chicago: Rand McNally).

Weeks, D. R. (1972), *A Glossary of Sociological Concepts*, (Milton Keynes: The Open University Press).

Westergaard, J. and Resler, H. (1976), *Class in a Capitalist Society: a Study of Contemporary Britain*, (Harmondsworth: Penguin).

White, R. (1980), *Absent With Cause: Lessons of Truancy*, (London: Routledge and Kegan Paul).

Whitelegg, E. *et al.* (1982) (eds.), *The Changing Experience of Women*, (Oxford: Martin Robertson/Open University).

Whyte, W. F. (1981), *Street Corner Society*, (3rd edn.) (Chicago: University of Chicago Press).

Williams, G. (1980), *State and Society in Nigeria*, Afrografika.

Williams, R. (1968), 'The meanings of work' in R. Fraser (ed.), *Work: Twenty Personal Accounts*, (Harmondsworth: Penguin) pp. 280–98.

Williams, R. (1976), *Keywords: a Vocabulary of Culture and Society*, (London: Fontana).

Willis, P. E. (1977), *Learning to Labour*, (Farnborough: Saxon House).

Wilson, A. (1978), *Finding a Voice*, (London: Virago).

Wilson, E. (1977), *Women and the Welfare State*, (London: Tavistock).

Wolcott, H. F. (1982), 'Mirrors, models and monitors: educator adaptations of the ethnographic innovation' in G. Spindler (ed.), *Doing the Ethnography of Schooling*, (New York: Holt, Rinehart & Winston) pp. 68–95.

Wolfgang, M. (1960), 'Cesare Lombroso' in H. Mannheim (ed.), *Pioneers in Criminology*, (London: Stevens) pp. 168–227.

Woods, P. (1979), *The Divided School*, (London: Routledge and Kegan Paul).

Woods, P. (1980) (ed.), *Pupil Strategies: Explorations in the Sociology of the School*, (London: Croom Helm).

Woods, P. (1981), 'Understanding through talk' in C. Adelman (ed.), *Uttering, Muttering: Collecting, Using and Reporting Talk for Social and Educational Research*, (London: Grant McIntyre) pp. 13–26.

World Bank (1981), *World Development Report*, Washington DC.

Worsley, P. (1972) (ed.), *Problems of Modern Society*, (Harmondsworth: Penguin).

Yablonsky, L. (1962), *The Violent Gang*, (New York: Macmillan).

Young, J. (1972), *The Drugtakers*, (London: Paladin).

Index